Rereading Isaiah 40–55 as the Project Launcher for the Books of the Law and the Prophets

A Redactional Critical Reading of the Law and the Prophets

Rereading Isaiah 40–55 as the Project Launcher for the Books of the Law and the Prophets

A Redactional Critical Reading of the Law and the Prophets

Iskandar Abou-Chaar

OCABS PRESS
ST PAUL, MINNESOTA 55124
2021

Rereading Isaiah 40–55 as the Project Launcher for the Books of the Law and the Prophets

A Redactional Critical Reading of the Law and the Prophets

Copyright © 2021 by Iskandar Abou-Chaar

All rights reserved.

ISBN 1-60191-054-7

Cover art: Panoramic view of the Samaria region.

Published by OCABS Press, St. Paul, Minnesota.

Printed in the United States of America.

Books are available through OCABS Press at special discounts for bulk purchases in the United States by academic institutions, churches, and other organizations. For more information please email OCABS Press at press@ocabs.org.

In Homage to the Pedagogical Work of

Paul Nadim Tarazi

In the Service of the Word of Scripture
Stretching now over more than half a century and continuing

And in Memory of

Jaber Bathiche

A true disciple of the Word in Service

Contents

Dedication	5
Contents	7
Foreword	11
Preface	15
A Note on Abbreviations and Transliteration	19
Chapter 1: Analytical Reading of Isaiah 40–55 as the Parable of Abraham and Sarah and its Reenactment in Genesis 32	**21**
1. Introductory Remarks on the Proposed Reading and Method	21
1.1 Remarks on Method	22
2. An Attempt at Deciphering the Redactional Framework of Isa 40–55	23
2.1 Terminological Matrices of Isa 40–55	23
2.2 Elements of the Redactional Scheme of Isa 40–55	27
2.2.1 Part One: Isaiah 40:1–49:26	28
2.2.2 Part Two: Isaiah 50:1–55:13	38
3. The Reenactment of the Lesson of Isa 40–55 in Gen 32	52
3.1 The Name Jacob	53
3.2 The Name Israel	54
3.3 Mahanaim	58
3.4 Genesis 32: Reenactment of Isa 40–55 and Reinterpretation of the Title Israel	59
4. Interim Conclusions	62
4.1 Postscript	63
Chapter 2: The Impact of Isa 40–55 on the Joseph Type and Its Transformation	**65**
Preamble	65
1. The Apparently Conflicting Use of the "Joseph" Type/Appellation in the OT	66
1.1 Conflicting Usages	67
1.2 The Name Ephraim	68
1.3 The Name Manasseh	69
1.4 The Question to Be Posed	71
2. An Attempt at Deciphering the Impact of Isa 40–55 on the Joseph Type	72
2.1 Joseph and the *tôlēdôt* of Jacob	73
2.1.1 The Name Benjamin as a Motif in the Jacob Story	75
2.1.2 The Name of Simeon as a Motif in the Storyline	78
2.2 Joseph the Dreamer and the Hidden Redactor/Servant of Isa 40–55	80
2.3 Analysis of the Dramatic Flow of the Joseph Story (Gen 37–50)	81
2.3.1 Chapter 37: Joseph is Jacob at the Outset of the Story	82
2.3.2 Chapter 38: Judah as Jacob	86
2.3.3 Chapter 39: Joseph and Isaac	88
2.3.4 Chapters 40–41: Crisis and False Denouement	93
2.3.5 Chapters 42–45 Inversion of Roles: Jacob as the Servant	97

2.3.6 Excursus: Joseph's silver cup in Gen 44:2–5	101
2.3.7 Chapters 46–47 Joseph as the *rahām* vs. Pharaoh as Joseph	103
2.3.8 The Redactional Use of the Words for Grain *br* and *šbr*	104
2.3.9 The Denouement (Gen 48:1–50:13): Jacob remains Jacob	107
2.3.10 The Servant-Joseph Comforts Jacob	115
2.3.11 Joseph and the *'ărôn*	116
2.4 Epilogue: The Blessing of Joseph by Moses in Deut 33:13–17	117
3. An Intermediate Summation: Retrospective and Prospective	119
3.1 Revisiting the Major Work of the God of the Servant in Isa 40–55	120
3.2 A prospective revisiting of "Joseph and the *'ărôn*"	123

Chapter 3: Joshua Son of Nun as the Continuation of the Transformed Joseph and Further Elements of the Redaction of the Books of the Law and the Prophets   125

Preamble	125
1. Joshua Son of Nun as the Continuation of the Transformed Joseph	125
1.1 The Name of Joshua Son of Nun	126
1.2 Joshua and the Tent of the Tabernacle	128
1.2.1 Joshua, Joseph, and the *'ărôn* (Ark)	130
1.2.2 Cyrus and the Tent of the Tabernacle	132
1.3 Joshua Takes on New Roles and Appellations in the Book of Numbers	133
1.4 Joshua and Moses in the Book of Deuteronomy	138
1.5 Summation re the Couple Joseph–Joshua	141
1.6 Revisiting the Blessings of Moses (Deut 33)	143
2. Further Elements of the Redaction of the Books of the Law and the Prophets	152
2.1 The Legislative Codes and the Structuring of the Pentateuch	152
2.2 Elements of Style that Span the Pentateuch and the Books of the Prophets	157
2.3 The Structural Framework of the Books of the Former and Latter Prophets	161
2.4 Redactional Elements Specific to Individual Books of the First Prophetic Tetrateuch, the Former Prophets	170
2.4.1 Redactional Methods in the Book of Joshua	170
2.4.2 The Redaction at Work in the Narratives of the Book of Judges	187
2.4.3 The Redaction at Work in the Narratives of the Book of Samuel	210
2.4.4 The Redaction at Work in the Narratives of the Book of Kings	216
2.5 Redactional Elements Specific to Individual Books of the Second Prophetic Tetrateuch, the Latter Prophets	219
2.5.1 Redactional Work in the Book of Isaiah	219
2.5.2 Redactional Work in the Book of Jeremiah	223
2.5.3 Redactional work with regard to the Book of Ezekiel	227
2.5.4 Redactional Work in the Book of the Twelve Prophets	229
2.6 Excursus: The Two Spellings of the Root and Name of Isaac	238

Chapter 4: The Third Part of the Canon and Epilogue   243

Prolegomena	243
1. The School of Isa 40–55 and the Third Part of the Canon	244

1.1 The Function and Framework of the Third Part of the Canon	244
1.2 A Brief Review of the Individual Books	248
1.2.1 The Book of Psalms	248
1.2.2 The Book of Job	257
1.2.3 The Book of Proverbs	260
1.2.4 The Book of Ruth	261
1.2.5 The Book of Canticles	263
1.2.6 The Book of Ecclesiastes	264
2. The Other Redactional Schools: Subsequent Additions and Editions	268
2.1 The Johanan School: A Derivative of the Maccabean Movement	268
2.2 The School of the Chronicler	274
3. Epilogue: Summation of the Thesis and Method	276
3.1 Some more exegetical pointers	279
3.1.1 Ethnicity has no place in Exegesis	280
3.1.2 Functionality and Artifice in Literature	282
3.1.3 Redactional framework and Exegesis	283
3.1.4 Names in Literature as Applied to Biblical Literature	283
3.2 In Conclusion: Resume of the Thesis	287
3.3 Postscript	291
Select Bibliography	**293**
About the Author	**297**

Foreword

The Law and the Prophets are traditionally regarded as two distinct parts of the Hebrew Bible. In advanced academic programs of theology, they are usually taught by different professors. At conferences (SBL, etc.), they are usually discussed in different program units. However, with the recent trend to date numerous texts of the Hebrew Bible, including those of the Pentateuch, to the Persian Period, the situation begins to change. We no longer think of the Pentateuchal texts as composed in some distant, premonarchic or monarchic past, much earlier than the texts of the great prophets of the period of the exile: Jeremiah, Ezekiel, and Deutero-Isaiah. This change of perspective naturally leads to the question of the relationship between the Law and the Prophets. It cannot be uncritically assumed that the Law precedes the Prophets simply because it is the foundational Israelite, and that the Prophets by definition merely comment upon it.

Iskandar Abou-Chaar approaches this issue from a particular point of view. He calls his approach "redactional critical", although he generally does not analyze hypothetical preliterary traditions or sources and their redactional use by the final composers of the biblical texts, as is usually done in redaction criticism of the Gospels. He rather traces literary relationships which can be observed or at least postulated between the texts that we know from the Law and from the Prophets.

His starting point is the great prophet of the exile, namely, the anonymous or pseudonymous prophet usually called by modern scholars Deutero-Isaiah. His anonymous character places him somehow in the shadow of the great prophets who preceded him in their activities: (Proto-)Isaiah, Jeremiah, and Ezekiel. He is most widely known from his four songs of the Servant of Yahweh and from his fierce polemic against other gods. According to Abou-Chaar, however, Deutero-Isaiah played a much greater role in the history of the religion of Israel.

In his opinion, the text of Isaiah 40–55 should be regarded not only as a prophetic call to return to Zion and restoration of the ruined Jerusalem, but as the literary-theological project launcher for the collection of the books of the Law and the Prophets.

Abou-Chaar first explains his idea in his analysis of Genesis 32 against the background of Isaiah 40–55. He sees linguistic and conceptual connections between these two texts. The linguistic connections which he detects are mainly based on the plays with the meanings of the key names within these texts: Jacob, Israel, Abraham, Sarah, etc. This interpretative approach is very insightful and in fact very desirable in modern biblical scholarship. Ancient writers were very sensitive to the meanings of proper names, and they delighted in constructing linguistic-conceptual connections with such names. Modern critical scholarship rather neglected this important phenomenon, which is widespread in both the Old and the New Testament. In fact, many biblical texts are not merely ornamented, but in fact organized around the various meanings of traditional and/or artificially constructed proper nouns. Therefore, Abou-Chaar's reconstructions of such plays, even if at times disputable, are certainly worth serious consideration in critical analyses of the Hebrew Bible.

What is also worth noting here is Abou-Chaar's inspiring use of his native Arabic language to elucidate the meaning of various Hebrew words. Such is the case, for example, with his comparison of the name Israel with that of Yasser. Following this line of thought, one could say that the Jewish state of Israel and the Palestinian president Yasser Arafat were in fact near of kin. In such intended or non-intended linguistic and extra-linguistic connections one can find, of course, bitter political irony but also, from a theological point of view, much spiritual hope.

The conceptual connections between the analyzed texts, which Abou-Chaar traces, are at times very loose, organized around such vague concepts as barrenness, darkness, testing, etc. In modern critical scholarship, such loose conceptual connections are usually disregarded, in line with Wittgenstein's positivist idea that "Whereof one cannot speak, thereof one must be silent." However, such epistemological positivism has been gradually overcome in more recent philosophical and literary studies.

For example, Genette's modern literary research on hypertextuality, a phenomenon that can be regarded as highly creative textual reworking, has opened the way to the study of the numerous loose conceptual connections whose existence cannot be proved in a typical literary way, that is, by means of pointing to the presence of explicit or implicit citations, etc.

Against this methodological background, Abou-Chaar's pursuit of loose conceptual connections in the Hebrew Bible can be very insightful. In fact, biblical authors seem to have been very sensitive to such loose conceptual connections, imaginative associations, etc. If the Genesis flood myth can illustrate the Deuteronomic idea of military conquest, in line with the widespread use of the motif of inundating waters in such connections, why could the Genesis idea of the nighttime testing of Jacob in Genesis 32 not correspond to the Deutero-Isaianic idea of the painful hiddenness of the servant's God? Of course, we must broaden our epistemological and hermeneutical horizons to detect such connections, but is such broadening of spiritual horizons not one of the most important aims of our study of the Bible?

The following chapters on the stories of Joseph and Joshua, analyzed against the background of Isaiah 40–55, generally display the same approach to the biblical texts. In fact, the chapter on Joshua evolves into a lengthy linguistic-conceptual analysis of two great parts of the Hebrew Bible, namely, the Former and the Latter Prophets. The reader can find here a kind of introduction to these important works, written from Abou-Chaar's particular perspective.

This interest in writing a kind of introduction to the books of the Hebrew Bible is further pursued in the final chapter, referring to the Writings, the third part of the Hebrew canon. Abou-Chaar does not limit his analyses to the Hebrew Bible, however. In pursuing various linguistic associations, he at times leaps to the world of the New Testament. The connections he discovers are often insightful. For example, he rightly connects the character of Zebedee in the Gospels with that of Zabdi in the book of Joshua. Likewise, he rightly notices that the Lukan story of Martha and Mary is in fact a story of Martha and Mariam. These examples may suffice to demonstrate that the endeavor of finding apparently loose linguistic and conceptual connections is really worth making, and that the work of Abou-Chaar can serve as a good guide in this kind of study of the entire Bible.

The work of Abou-Chaar builds upon the work of Professor Paul Nadim Tarazi. In fact, Abou-Chaar very often refers to the work of his great teacher, treating him on a par with but also in contrast to Gerhard von Rad, Martin Noth, and Claus Westermann, to name but a few. In this way, with the "founding" professor and his brilliant disciple, we can see the rise of a new Antiochene school of biblical exegesis and theology. May this school thrive and flourish!

Bartosz Adamczewski
Cardinal Stefan Wyszyński University in Warsaw

Preface

The style of this presentation is that of an exploratory journey. It joins the analytic style with the narrative style and thus is a discovery narrative. It is a study project, climactic and pedagogical. Thematic agglomeration was eschewed; motifs and some basic lines of argumentation function as part of the exploratory narrative and are introduced progressively and climactically. Arguments are built up through the analysis of texts, so that the texts and arguments reciprocally and climactically buttress one another. Narrative pedagogy allows the reader/listener to enter into the critical process at work in the argument, a challenging task for the student scholar, inviting engagement in the explorative process. The turns in the narrative prod the readers to change the direction of their thinking process, to widen the scope of their observation, to join in the exploratory field trip, to question and reacquire the ability to revise their views and have a change of mind.

This has to some extent resulted from following the sequence of the texts being studied and unwittingly conforming to their narrative pedagogical flow. In the process this has led the present writer to appreciate how much damage the thematic grouping in the Septuagint transmission has distorted the redactional intent for readers following this tradition of transmission, obliterating syntactical compositional elements that are essential for comprehension of the texts, placing them out of sight for the reader. The texts demand engagement not systematic organization. "Unevenness" sometimes functions like the "baroque," to propel to change; "unevenness" sometimes functions like some aspects of chaos to provoke creativity; but most of all, "unevenness" tends to function to create "free" space for others to exercise their freedom of thought and action.

Another reason for joining the analytical and the narrative in the exposition is that the present work is addressed to two types of readers: it is addressed on one hand to scholars of biblical literature who are versed both in biblical literature and critical exegetical scholarship; it is also addressed on the other hand to well-read educated readers with little knowledge of critical biblical scholarship. The narrative approach helps lighten the drudge of analytical passages for the latter by way of the climactic progression and repetition, again mimicking the method adopted by the texts themselves that are in question. The mix is a powerful means, whether in fictional or non-fictional literature, to draw the mind and engage it in what would otherwise be a tiresome analysis and description. (To cite just a few examples, one need only think of Heyerdahl's *Kon-Tiki*, Hardy's *The Return of the Native*, or Wilder's *The Bridge of San Luis Rey*, works that have left their mark on the mind of the present writer since junior high school.)

The third reason for this choice of style is the personal experience of the writer in teaching, and in being taught. As a beginning student in the study of biblical literature I was subjected to this method in the classroom and on the way to and back from the classroom by Nadim, that is, Paul Nadim Tarazi. The interweaving of analytical and narrative elements opened for me what would otherwise have been an inscrutable discipline and would always provoke me to try out different ways of thinking. His students, whether agreeing or disagreeing with him, would always remember his engaging and challenging/provocative style and would recognize in it their distinctive remembrance of his person. It is precisely in homage to his pedagogical work that this book was written. I should add, the comments in this preface are restricted to notes regarding the style of the presentation; notes on method and content are part and parcel of the main presentation.

This book is also in memory of Jaber Bathiche. On the eve of his graduation and engagement he sped ahead of his pedagogues ("pedagogues" in the sense of 1 Cor 4:15), who included Tarazi and myself, in the course of service to his colleagues. In spite of the proscription of Matt 23:8–10, I will always remember and treasure the endearing address "prof" that he awarded me and his pedagogues, reversing the roles. The impress of his discipleship to the word in service among his colleagues and community remains with all who knew him.

Iskandar Abou-Chaar
Beirut
Oct 31, 2021

A Note on Abbreviations and Transliteration

The abbreviations for the books of the Bible (as well as occasional other abbreviations) follow *The SBL Handbook of Style*, edited by Patrick H. Alexander, John F. Kutsko, James D. Ernest, Shirley Decker-Lucke, and David L. Petersen. Peabody, Mass.: Hendrickson, 1999.

The transliteration of Hebrew letters and vocalization follows the "academic style" as indicated in *The SLB Handbook*, 1999.

Chapter 1
Analytical Reading of Isaiah 40–55 as the Parable of Abraham and Sarah and its Reenactment in Genesis 32[1]

1. Introductory Remarks on the Proposed Reading and Method

Both traditional exegesis, including the modern fundamentalist, as well as critical study of the texts of the books of the Law and the Prophets share a common working premise/groundwork, approaching these texts as compositions disjunct in space and time and motivation. The traditionalist will see common ground in an extrapolated focal point designated as divine authorship. The critical scholar will, more often than not, decipher disjunct sources, traditions, texts and intentions. That the texts are transmitted as a corpus, most often held to be canonical by those transmitting the texts, is explained in terms of a sociological unifying factor. This factor is differently construed, depending on the ideology or sociopolitical premise of the scholar, but

---

[1] An edited version of this chapter was originally published in: Roddy, Nicolae, ed., *Festschrift in Honor of Professor Paul Nadim Tarazi: Volume 1: Studies in the Old Testament* (Bible in the Christian Orthodox Tradition: Volume 3; New York: Peter Lang Publishing, 2013). The editing introduced a considerable number of modifications to the original text which did not correctly represent the intention or argument of the author. The author did not see the edited form of the text before it was published. The text published here is the original text submitted by the author, with only minor corrections, mainly print copy corrections, introduced by the author. This version was first published in The Journal of the Orthodox Center for the Advancement of Biblical Studies (JOCABS) Vol. 6, No 1 (2013), pp. 23–46. As originally intended, it has been slightly adapted here for publication as chapter 1 of this monograph.

remains in practically all cases extraneous to the texts precisely as a unifying factor.

This study has benefited substantially from the previous work on the subject matter, but in the course of my own investigative efforts I have found that the basically assumed groundwork of the research in this field must be challenged.[2] My exploration of the various texts of the books of the Law and the Prophets has brought to the fore a pattern of organization of the material pointing more and more to redactional work recognizable as the redactional design and motivation behind chs. 40–55 of the book of Isaiah. These are commonly designated in critical literature as Deutero-Isaiah or Second Isaiah. The current study will argue that Isa 40–55 was written as a project launcher for what we have as the books of the Law and the Prophets. Consequently it will not be designated Second-Isaiah, but will be referred to as Isa 40–55. The first part of this study, presented here, is a rereading of Isa 40–55 based on the end point arrived at in my study of the relevant texts. The exegetical circle, commencing from this interim conclusion, will go on to display, illustrate and test this on several key and pivotal texts in the books under consideration. In this first part of the endeavor the thesis will be illustrated against the giving of a new name to Jacob in Gen 32.[3]

1.1 Remarks on Method

The basic method followed in this study is the redaction critical approach. This assumes that regardless of what traditions, sources and previous writings there may have been at the disposal of the redactor, the redactional effort is the paramount factor in the shape that a specific text takes. In this it is heavily indebted to the redaction critical work of Willi

---

[2] This work builds upon the work of Paul Nadim Tarazi in this respect. Cf. section 4.1 below.
[3] The originally announced study of the Joseph type and its transformation, which is a centerpiece of the argument, proved to be too long for the space limitation incumbent on the Festschrift. It is published here as chapter 2.

Marxsen.[4] The method is also a function critical and literary critical method. Motifs and appellations are seen to function as types, becoming, like arguments, determinative of the functional flow of a text. Names thus become a function of literary artifice and play a primary role in the argument of the storyline or lesson. They predispose the articulation in a given direction, and function as focal points, as attractors propelling forward the argument/action. Types are constructed and become determinative for the lesson, while the roles, in this sense, become secondary and may be subject to inversion and reversal.

2. An Attempt at Deciphering the Redactional Framework of Isa 40–55

The general parsing of the text adopted here is basically a two part division.[5] The first part is the Jacob part, Isa 40:1–49:26, while the second part is the Abraham part, Isa 50:1–55:13. Two different role models will be presented, the second being the solution offered to the problem posed by the first. The four servant songs function quasi as a Greek dramatic choir indicating how one should move out of the one role model and into the other—in other words, they indicate the lesson to be followed.

2.1 Terminological Matrices of Isa 40–55

Overlapping terminological matrices dominate Isa 40–55 and inform the flow of the text. They function as *dramatis personae*, or at least as accoutrement of ghost characters. It is incumbent to

---

4 Willi Marxsen, *Der Evangelist Markus: Studien zur Redaktionsgeschichte des Evangeliums* (2nd ed.; Göttingen; Vandenhoeck & Ruprecht, 1959).
5 For a review of recent proposals which seem to come close to the one being proposed here but diverge as regards the description of the second part, cf. Peter Höffgen, *Jesaya: Der Stand der Theologischen Diskussion* (Darmstadt: WBG, 2004), 101–105.

introduce these matrices before we embark on an analysis of the compositional structure.

The basic terminological matrix of Isa 40–55 seems to be dominated by the notions of barren land and power over the waters. The term Zion, as the epicenter of this matrix, spreads all across the work, and appears to be a construction conjured up by the writer for this text. It is extraordinary that we find it nowhere in the book of the prophet Ezekiel, considering that Ezekiel is an upper class priest stemming from Jerusalem and addressing basically Jerusalem, and through Jerusalem all the tribes. Nowhere is Zion used more repeatedly and centrally than in the book of Isaiah. Within the book of Isaiah, chapters 40–55 appear to have a very studied and deliberate use of the term, spread across all the work, Isa 52:8 being the last instance. What is the meaning of the term? The term ṣîyāh means parched land. It is used in Isa 41:18. It is a one-step literary construction to assimilate this term to ṣîdôn (Sidon), making it ṣîyôn (Zion). Jerusalem is for our author/redactor a barren and parched land. What speaks for the literary priority of our author is that the whole of the composition from 40:1 on is addressed from and to a parched wilderness. In the second part we have the barren Sarah coming to the fore in lieu of the parched land. Zion is a taunt and a call to attention to the words of the writer. The words of his Deity will water the parched Zion.[6] At the same time it stands in contrast to the fertile fields of Ephraim, attached to Joseph in the book of Genesis (Gen 41:52).[7]

A second linguistic matrix is adjoined to this basic one. It is that of victorious kingship. Yahweh is declared King of Israel (Isa 43:15). Consequently he is the Savior of Israel. Good tidings of victory are sent by him to Jerusalem, to Zion (cf. Isa 40:9; 41:27; 52:7 for the *pi'el* verbal form of *bśr*, to bring good tidings). The *hip'îl* verbal form of the root *yš'* (to save) is used profusely

---

[6] This is why the last instance of its use is in 52:8, just before the fourth servant song brings to the fore the resolution to the problem from the redactor's point of view.
[7] This is expanded upon below in chapter 2 on the Joseph story.

(cf. Isa 43:3, 11, 12; 45:15, 20, 21; 46:7; 47:13, 15; 49:25, 26) and exclusively in what is taken here to be the first part of Isa 40–55 to describe the action of the Deity. The noun *yšḥ* (salvation) is used at the end of the first part and in the second part to describe the result of the action of the deity (cf. Isa 49:6, 8; 51:6, 8; 52:7, 10). The "creator" deity with power over the waters is here described as also exercising the regal charge to provide victory/salvation, as happens in the psalms celebrating Yahweh as King. Indeed Isa 40–55 can be described as an extended kingly psalm.

A third linguistic matrix is adjoined to the two described above. It is that of kinship and its concomitant obligations. Yahweh is described as the *gōʾēl* (redeemer) of Israel across the whole of this work starting with Isa 41:14. Consequently he is also the one who comforts his people/family. The *piʿel* verbal form of *nḥm* (to comfort) is used to announce the work in 40:1 and used in 49:13; 51:3, 12, 19; 52:9; 54:11 (this last in the passive *puʿal*). Both noun forms and verbal forms derived from the root *rḥm* (from which come the nouns womb, Isa 46:3, and compassion, Isa 54:7, and the verb to have compassion/mercy, Isa 49:10, 13, 15; 54:8, 10; 55:7) are also used to describe the action of the deity.

We can conclude from this brief description of the linguistic matrices of this work that they describe an all-purpose deity: God over the waters, warrior king and family clansman!

One very important and characteristic verb of Isa 40–55 was left out. It can be construed as pertaining to all three matrices described. It is the verbal root *brʾ* (usually translated as "to create"). It is basically used in Isa 40–55 (40:26, 28; 41:20; 42:5; 43:1, 7, 15; 45:7 twice, 8, 12, 18 twice; 48:7; 54:16 twice) and the creation narrative in Genesis (Gen 1:1, 21, 27 thrice; 2:3, 4; 5:1, 2 twice; 6:7). Otherwise, its use is sporadic. Its characteristic use in these two compositions (together with the word *tōhû* "chaos, vanity" in Gen 1:2; Isa 40:17, 23; 41:29; 44:9; 45:18, 19; 49:4) is one of the reasons often taken to infer an influence of Isa 40–55 on the creation narrative in Genesis.[8] The meaning of the root in both Hebrew and Arabic appears diverse, but can be summed up as the taking something out of an obstructing shell/covering, free someone/something from dirt, sickness, guilt. As such it has a relation to the function of cleansing waters, to that of redemption, and to that of victorious/judicial acquittal. What issues out of the verb has the connotation of clean, out of the box, pristine, healthy, innocent, without any wart or shortcoming, free, filial. The closely related root *brr* (employed in Isa 49:2; 52:11, otherwise sporadically) shares practically the same domain of meaning. Among the related words from this domain, in this case from *brr*, is the Aramaic word for son, *br* (vocalized *bār*); (this is employed in Arabic also to denote an upright person, *bār*, and uprightness, *bir*). That the redactor of Isa 40–55 intentionally chose the root *br'* and made it characteristic of the weave of his composition is underscored by its amazing scarcity and casual use elsewhere in Scripture except for the creation narrative. The range of possible meanings corresponds, as we will see, to the function of the new action of God described in Isa 50–55 in terms of the "parable" of Abraham and Sarah and prepared for by the extensive use of this verb in Isa 40–49.

It is the contention of the basic thesis underlying this work that Isa 40–55 is the project launcher for the books of the Law and the Prophets, for Scripture. The use of *br'* in Isa 40–55 corresponds more aptly to the expected topic for this root than the stylized use in Gen 1:1. The creation narrative would seem to be dependent on Isa 40–55, announcing the new work of God, the five books of the Law, as in continuation of the initial action of God in creating the habitat of man.[9] This is how *br'* is

---

8 Cf. Paul Nadim Tarazi, *Genesis: A Commentary* (The Chrysostom Bible; St Paul, Minn.: OCABS Press, 2009), 27–33.
9 The functional connection between the use in Gen 1:1ff and in Isa 40–55 seems best reflected/given expression to in Isa 4:5, a pivotal verse in the introductory section of the book of Isaiah as a whole. The first five chapters of the book of Isaiah, which

employed in Isa 40–55, where it describes the modality of action of the deity hitherto in 40–49, on the basis of which the new action to be undertaken is announced in 50–55. Indeed in Isa 45:7-23 and 48:6-15 we have a programmatic announcement of such a projected endeavor. The address/words and intention of the deity will be brought forth out of the hiddenness of the deity, and will proclaim/are the new action of this deity. The root *br'* plays a pivotal role in both these passages. In analogy to the action of the deity who brings all things out into functional "ex-istence" and man/woman out of the womb, and in continuance thereof, the address/words of this deity, the "new" action, will be made clearly known, declared, "out-spoken" (cf. also 42:14).

2.2 Elements of the Redactional Scheme of Isa 40–55

The structuring of the work using these matrices seems to take the shape of problem description followed by delineation of the solution. The first part, the Jacob part, presents the problem track. The second part, the Abraham part, presents the solution. The foibles of Jacob are juxtaposed to the response of the deity. It is interesting that Jacob/Israel is used alternately with Jerusalem/Zion. The address is to Jerusalem/Zion, the perspective is Jacob/Israel (48:1). This runs parallel to what we have in the Pentateuch in general. Moreover, we seem to have in Isa 40–55 a work that runs in parallel to the book of Genesis, with two exceptions: The sequence Abraham to Jacob in the book of Genesis appears to be inverted to Jacob–Abraham, and the prospect of exodus in the Pentateuch is from Egypt, whereas

---

are probably the last part of the book of Isaiah to be redacted, are a summary of the whole book, and consequently introduce also Isa 40–55. The action of God as regards the reconstituted and cleansed remnant, Isa 4:2–6, is described as a creation event corresponding to the giving of the law on Sinai, and as a coming to the assembly where the reading of the law takes place: "Then the Lord will create (*br'*) over the whole site of Mount Zion and over its places of assembly (*miqrā'ehā*, assembly to hear a reading) a cloud by day and smoke and the shining of a flaming fire by night. Indeed over all the glory there will be a canopy." (Isa 4:5 NRSV).

in Isa 40–55 it is from Babylon. One major element though appears to be missing, the Joseph cycle/story. The question that poses itself is the following: do we have in Isa 40–55 a paraphrased reworking of the book of Genesis, or do we have a blueprint, technically speaking, of a project encompassing, at the very least, the book of Genesis?[10] To further explore this question an expansion on the compositional elements and the redactional scheme of Isa 40–55 is incumbent.

2.2.1 Part One: Isaiah 40:1–49:26

The first part is Isa 40:1–49:26. The appellation Jacob is used profusely and exclusively in this part. The problem is summed up in 40:27–31. God is willing and capable of bringing succor to Jacob. Jacob does not believe it.

The first major subsection, 40:1–41:29, introduces the problem. God declares that he is the creator God in a terminology that is practically identical with that of the creation account in the book of Genesis. He declares good tidings to Jacob. Jacob is not convinced. The last section of this subsection, 41:25–29, points in the direction of the following first song of the servant. God seeks to find someone up to the task, but no one is in sight! A cryptic announcement of God's new action is given in 41:25, which together with 42:14–16 brackets the first song of the servant.

The first song of the servant, 42:1–9, together with the commentary on it, 42:10–25, introduces the following central section (43:1–48:22) of the first part. The song introduces the problem from God's side. If Jacob bemoans lack of succor, God bemoans lack of Justice. The servant cannot speak; he is still in the womb as we will learn further on. God speaks about the servant in the third person. This will be paralleled by the last song in the second part. There the servant is no more, again

---

[10] It is precisely in a comparison with the apparently missing Joseph cycle that it will be possible to start giving an answer to this question. This will be discussed in chapter 2 of this work.

only God can speak. The second song (which comes at the end of the first part) and the third song (which comes at the beginning of the second part) have the servant speak in the first person: he is, at that point of the discourse/drama, onstage.

The first song (42:1-9) is in God's imaginary time. When the required servant is present, then he will administer justice. He will not blabber like an infant, nor break the broken in violence. The first part of the commentary on the song, vv. 10-17, is central to the flow. God announces that he will embark on a new venture. He has decided to release what he had kept held back like a pregnant woman for so long (v. 14). He is finally going to blurt out his guts. The second part of the commentary, vv. 18-25, is a bitterly acerbic contrasting of the wished for servant with Jacob. This lays the ground for the following indictment of Jacob.

The central subsection of part one, 43:1-48:22, contains the teaching incumbent upon the prospective servant. The first part in this subsection, 43:1-44:23, declares God's intention to bring salvation to the just. In ch. 43 there is a reiteration of God's will and capability to bring about salvation (vv. 1-7). There is no other God but He. His past actions, to which the people are witness, are brought forward in proof (vv. 8-13). God's new salvific action is about to unfold (43:14-20). There is one big snag though, Jacob stands contra expectation. He has "enslaved" God to the servicing of his iniquity. God had decided in consequence to blot out Jacob (43:22-28). Chapter 44 introduces the notion of conditional covenant. The promise of salvation applies to the upright (vv. 1-5). We have in v. 2 a new qualification requisite of Jacob for the promise to be applicable. He is called *yšrn* (Jeshurun). This epithet is used only here and in Deut 32:15; 33:5, 26, in a passage very similar to the one here. In Deuteronomy it brackets the condemnation of Jacob in the song of Moses and the pronouncement of the blessings of Moses, making the blessings hinge on Yahweh reigning as king in the midst of an upright Jacob. The epithet

Jeshurun, from the root *yšr* (to be upright), can be parsed as a conditional clause "when they/should they deign to function uprightly." This will be mirrored again in an address to Jacob as the redeemed servant, conditional on remembering the teaching (vv. 21–23). As in the passage in Deuteronomy, this conditional covenant is interspersed in our text with affirmations that God alone is God (vv. 6–8, 24–28) and a tirade against idolatry (vv. 9–20). The chiastic arrangement of this chapter underlines this reading. Central to the chapter is the tirade against idolatry. This makes the send-off in verse 28 introducing Cyrus as God's shepherd all the more astounding. In fact this anticipates chapter 45, introduced by a direct address to Cyrus (in 44:28 the address was indirect, in the third person).

Chapter 45 can unequivocally be called the manifesto of universal monotheism. The teaching here is addressed not only to Jacob but to Cyrus! We had heretofore heard that the proclamation was first declared to Jacob (41:27). Now it is addressed in the person of Cyrus to all nations (vv. 1–13). This had already been announced in the program description in 40:5.

Cyrus will cede to the requests of Yahweh on behalf of Jacob without requesting any recompense, any silver (v. 13). This passage (45:1–13), together with the send-off from the previous section 44:28, is perhaps the most decidedly antithetically minded declaration against the priests and the levites of Jerusalem and Judea. It is usual to see the more extreme hostility in Isa 56–66. P. D. Hanson[11] sees in Isa 56–66 a development towards a sharpening of the acrimony directed against the priests and the levites due to the injustices in a failed new Jerusalem. Yes, but this development should be posited antecedent to Isa 40–55. The greatest acrimony is to be found in the source text of the school! It is the postulate of this paper that we have here in Isa 40–55 the master writing at the hub of

---

11 Paul D. Hanson, *The Dawn of Apocalyptic* (rev. ed.; Philadelphia: Fortress, 1979).

the anticlerical group vituperating against the failed Jerusalem. The ultimate put-down is the total silent treatment accorded to the clerical group. It is the ultimate application of the "blessing/curse" of Jacob accorded to Simeon and Levi in Gen 49:5–7, "May I never come into their council: may I not be joined to their company" (v. 6a NRSV). Our redactor will not even address a reprimand. Their council is not the addressee, neither positively nor negatively; it is not their prerogative. No one, he says, may even think to question the potter (Isa 45:9–10. Compare 41:25).

But what has he said to provoke the implied protest? In 44:28 he describes Cyrus as God's shepherd, in conjunction with the divine injunction to rebuild Jerusalem and the temple. This is a kingly designation, as it comes in tandem with the mention of the palace/temple. But God has been declared as the only king and holy place in Israel (43:15) as well as shepherd of Zion/Jerusalem (40:11). Thus he gives the orders, not Cyrus. After all, one can hire a shepherd for one's flock! But already this statement is introduced abruptly against the backdrop of the declaration of God's omnipotence (44:24–27).

What goes beyond this abrupt cold shower is the statement at the head of the new passage addressing Cyrus as God's anointed. While anointment applies to the king in the first instance, by derivation it applies also to the clergy who have to service the king's palace/temple. It is a title that admits of being derivative, and yet is not given to anyone else in this work. It is meticulously withheld from the servant, who in Isa 53 becomes a sin offering. Selfsame will be described as concomitant with God's salvation starting in Isa 49 in anticipation of his work in the second part (chs. 50–55). The designation of Cyrus as anointed of God breaks the very purpose of anointment. Anointment consecrates the appointee, such that he/she will be able to protect the sacral precinct from being defiled from outside. The very logic is destroyed here. The anointed is already the defiled outside. The perspective is inverted. Our writer, after all, is, like Joseph in Genesis, himself in the defiled domain, yet announcing the cleansing words of God to the defiled Jerusalem/Jacob. The servant in Isa 53 will be in the same situation. He will be the desecrated sin offering bringing healing to Israel (53:5). The domain of the clergy, together with clerical prerogative, is totally annihilated in this passage.

But this is not all. We are told that the mediation provided for the redemption of Jacob did not require any recompense/remuneration. More on this as regards the Joseph story will follow in chapter 2 about Joseph. Suffice here to underline that this statement is not simply to undergird the sovereignty of God. We need only read the directive in the book of Numbers (cf. Num 18:24) and the echoes thereof in Deuteronomy against the levites amassing estates, an apart heritage, to see how pointedly pugnacious this statement is in this context. Their sustenance must be assured, we are told in Deuteronomy (Deut 12:12, 18–19; 14:27–29; 16:11–14; 26:11–13), but their services may not be such as to set up a private heritage.[12] Yahweh alone is their heritage.

If the preceding commentary on the first half of ch. 45 is not enough to make us start suspecting that we are at the hotbed of scriptural monotheism, then the second part of the chapter leaves us no choice but to take this suspicion very seriously. In vv. 14–17 the nations acknowledge God as the only god and as the hidden savior. This is in contrast to deities represented with images. God is hidden; he cannot be represented by images. We then have a most amazing statement about this hidden God, a god with no face. He speaks righteousness and uprightness in the open (vv. 18–19). We have here the most succinct description/announcement of scriptural monotheism: A god with no image, whose representation is solely in scriptures enunciating truth and equity. This passage points to a body of

---

12 cf. Paul Nadim Tarazi, "Deuteronomy as a 'Reprise' of Gen 1–2: A Redaction Critical Reading" (Paper presented at ANZATS/ANZSTS Conference, Queens College, Parkville, Melbourne, Australia, July 6, 2004).

"words" that will reveal the hidden deity, effectively the announcement of scriptural monotheism. The chapter ends with a call to the nations to turn to this deity. The teaching of the conditional covenant applies to the nations as it applies to Jacob. This chapter is the chiastic hub of the subsection dealing with the teaching incumbent on the prospective servant (43:1–48:22).

The last part of this subsection, 46:1–48:22, starts with an extended diatribe against idolatry in ch. 46. The next chapter (ch. 47) describes the judgment incumbent upon iniquity at the example of Babylon. Finally the address returns to Jacob in ch. 48. The "new action" (already heralded in 41:15, 25; 42:9–17; 43:18–19) about which Jacob had not been informed before (48:6) is about to be announced. Jacob is reminded of his treachery and iniquity (48:7–8). Yet the offer of salvation stands. Whoever of Jacob gives ear and acknowledges the past acts of God will be beneficiary of the new that is about to be divulged. The final verse (v. 22) curtly summarizes the lesson of the whole subsection 43:1–48:22, "'there is no peace,' says the Lord, 'for the wicked.'" (NRSV).

The first part of the work is nearing its conclusion. It corresponds to the lesson of the book of the Former Prophets. We are about to be addressed concerning the latter and new action of God. Chapter 49 concludes the first part of the work, and prepares for the second part. The second song of the servant comments on the first part and answers to God's call in compliance with it (49:1–6). The servant is still hidden in God, but he can speak now in the first person, and he does so. Like God in the previous passages he addresses the nations. He has been taught by God. His tongue has become a sharp sword, indeed he has been set as a just/select/purged[13] arrow hidden in God's quiver (v. 2). Out of the barren womb of Zion, God

---

[13] The word in Hebrew is *bārûr*, from *brr*. Compare this with the use in Isa 52:11 of the same root in the *nip'al* as a description of the ritual purity requisite of those who bear the vessels of the Lord.

brought forth this servant. This interpretation of the literary figure of his having been called from the womb in v. 1b is justified not only by the imagery of the preceding section but specifically by the statements we will be hearing in the following section. Although Jacob will not be mentioned after this chapter, Zion will be invoked heavily in the subsection preceding the fourth song (cf. 49:14ff in conjunction with 51:3). The imagery from here on and up to the fourth song is that of converting the barrenness of Zion into a garden of Eden, a garden of God. The servant has become the war armory of God. We have a similar metaphor applied to Elijah in the book of the Former Prophets (2 Kgs 2:12). This servant has learned what was incumbent on Jacob to learn in the first section. He has hitherto been hidden in God. This references what we were told in 48:6b, 7. The servant is concomitant with the new to be announced for the first time. Up to now we have heard about the past. Cyrus belongs to the past action of this deity. As in apocalyptic literature, the lesson from the past was the launchpad for the announcement which is new. The mission of the servant is to bring God's solution to the problem God has with Jacob as expounded in part one. The closing verse reiterates what we saw in chs. 45–48. The mission is addressed equivalently to all the nations.

The passage 49:7–13 is an extended commentary on the second song of the servant. It is also a signature of the author/redactor of Isa 40–55. The servant is a despised and abhorred servant of rulers, and yet the recipient of adulation by selfsame. His day is one of salvation. This is the second time that we have the use of the noun salvation in this work after 49:6. It will be used in 51:6, 8, and 52:7, 10. Hitherto we have had the use of the verbal form (to save), including the *hip'il* participle form (savior), to describe the work of God in part one. We will still have a last use of the verbal and participial form in 49:25, 26 together with the last use of the name Jacob in 49:26. In part two Jacob is no longer at work, only the servant. His day of work is called a day of salvation. His day will bring God's salvific work to fruition in contrast to Jacob's bringing to naught God's past actions. He will be a covenant for the people. This is a regal term, however much it recalls the Abrahamic covenant in the book of Genesis. He will parcel out and apportion heritages. This is quintessentially a description of a suzerainty treaty/covenant. He will also release the imprisoned, feed the hungry and bring water to the thirsty. Most importantly he will bring comfort to the afflicted people, fulfilling the program announced at the outset in 40:1ff. At this point it is difficult not to see in 49:7–13 a description of Joseph in the court of Pharaoh. Just as significantly, rather more significantly, the work described here is in fact a description of the implicit design and task guiding the work of the redactor/redactors of the Pentateuch and the books of the Former and Latter Prophets. This is a blueprint for the redaction of those books. These will be the new action and words that God has withheld in the past and is about to blurt out in the latter/current day of our author.

The last passage (49:14–26) echoes the objection of Jacob in 40:27. It stands in contrast to the response of the servant in 49:4 to the same situation. The servant trusts in God's succor, Jacob/Zion bewails the lack of succor. God quotes Jacob/Zion at the end of part one as he did at the beginning. The time of Jacob is over, the time of the servant, of the covenant, is about to begin/resume. Against the backdrop of Jacob's continuing objection, God asserts his intention to continue/resume his program with a new action. The objection in v. 21 becomes that of a barren woman incredulous about giving birth. The image was prepared for already in the response of God to the objection voiced by Zion in v. 14. God there is likened to a nursing mother (v. 15).

The use of Zion to represent Jacob's objection in 49:14 prepares for the transfer from the image of a barren parched land, Zion, to that of a barren woman not expecting children. This prepares for the invocation of the parable of Abraham and Sarah (Isa 51:2) in part two of the book, the solution to the problem expounded in part one. The last verse closes by citing the credentials of the deity, "Then all flesh shall know that I am the Lord your Savior, and your Redeemer, the Mighty One of Jacob." (NRSV). The word *ăbîr* (Mighty One) is used only here as a divine epithet in the composition we are dealing with. In Isa 46:12 it is used only generically. It seems strange that the last word in this part is one that was neither introduced previously, nor will be explained in the following part. In the Pentateuch we find it used only once, in the blessing of Joseph by Jacob (Gen 49:24). In Isa 49:26 we are told that God is the only strongman Jacob needs (cf. Isa 31:1–3, where the school of Isaiah expands on this motif). This word provides a backdrop for the following section.

The verbal root from which comes the name Joseph, *ysp* (to add/increase/provide more), is not used in Isa 40–55 except twice (47:1, 5) at the outset of the judgment of Babylon (in lieu for all Adam, including Jacob) and twice (51:22; 52:1) in the last two judgment pronouncements before the fourth servant song. This use, astride the two parts of the work, marks the import of the transition from part one to part two. God's judgment will fall on the wicked, God will provide for the salvation he intended. This is described as the end of the travail of his people, and as the bountiful increase in their fortune and progeny. The use of the verb, however, is in all four instances in the negative. There will be "no more" of the bad stuff. We should remember that the "bad stuff" suffered by Jacob was described in the first part as resulting from the "bad stuff" produced by Jacob (43:22–28; 48:18–19). This same accusation is repeated in the first verse of part two (50:1). Jacob will not be mentioned by the name Jacob in part two. He, like Babylon, must give way to the servant. His "increase," expressed as treachery in part one (48:8), led to the increase of the "bad stuff." The writer announces in all four instances that there will be no more increase of this type, sounding in Hebrew very close to "no more Joseph." Not only Jacob must disappear in part two. Joseph/Increase of this semantic pedigree must also disappear.

Chapter 1

Excursus: In Gen 30:22–24, Rachel gives birth to Joseph as the culmination of the work and rewards of Jacob. He has acquired wealth and progeny, built himself up, gotten his favorite bride. In a word, he has it made. He is on the increase beyond measure. The birth of Joseph announces the climax of his wheeler-dealing. Indeed, the announcement of the story of the actions of Jacob and their results (Gen 37:2), expressed in the Hebrew text of Genesis as *tôlēdôt*, starts with the Joseph story. He is the summa of all the story/stories of Jacob. The naming of Joseph at his birth by Rachel in Gen 30:22–24 becomes a resume of the passages demarcated by the use of the verbal root *ysp* in Isa 47:1, 5; 51:22; 52:1, astride the two parts of Isa 40–55. Rachel, utilizing a wordplay on the consonance of the two roots *ʾsp* (here in the meaning to remove aside) and *ysp* (to add), describes the significance of the moment. The passage reads: "Then God remembered Rachel, and God heeded her and opened her womb. She conceived and bore a son, and said, 'God has taken away (*ʾsp*) my reproach'; and she named him Joseph, saying, 'May the Lord add (*ysp*) to me another son!'" (NRSV). The verb indicating the end of the bad situation, her barrenness and shame, although from another root (*ʾsp*, in a usage corresponding to the negative of *ysp*), is used as the justification for the name Joseph. It is significant to note that the statement of Rachel underlines also that the appellation Joseph implies that more of the same will come. In other words, Joseph does not only describe the past of Jacob, it describes also the awaited/wished for future perspective, increase upon increase. The function in this passage of Benjamin, the one outstanding son of Jacob not yet born, is to underline the semantic implication of Joseph "more of the same." Left at this point, the story of Jacob will continue as more of the same. The passages we saw in Isa 40–55 say "no more of the same!" Isaiah 40–55 will go on in part two to offer another track. Jacob will be sidetracked.[14]

2.2.2 Part Two: Isaiah 50:1–55:13

The first part described the problem posed by Jacob as Adam redux. Jacob is repeatedly addressed and arraigned. The second part describes God's solution. I called it the Abraham part. Statistically this does not compare with the use of the name Jacob. In fact, statistically the name Abraham is used once in the first part (41:8) and once in the second part (51:2). In 41:8 it is used as a qualifier for Jacob from God's point of view. It anticipates as such the action of God in the second part, which is promised in the first part. In 51:2 it is not Abraham who is addressed. All those who seek righteousness are addressed and told to look at what can only be described as the *parable of Abraham and Sarah*. The word parable is not used, but the function of the statement "look to" is the same. The action will be addressed to Jacob, but it will be in continuation of Abraham. The image of Jacob as a woman initiates this section. The divorce had been due to her own actions. God neither sold her to get credit, nor had he been short of the means to retain her. The plaint of God is voiced, "Why was no one there when I came? Why did no one answer when I called?" (50:2a NRSV).

The answer to the plaint comes from the third song of the servant (50:4–11) initiating God's solution. The third song picks up on the second. The servant has been taught by God and has become a disciple capable of teaching and sustaining the weary with a word. God has opened his ear day in day out to accept teaching. Jacob had stubbornly rejected to hear, to give ear. The servant is described as not having done any of the wrong things Jacob is accused in the first part of having done in this regard. He had suffered every possible indignity and ridicule

---

[14] The question posed in the second chapter of this study project will be: Is the semantic weight of the appellation Joseph in the book of Genesis subjected to modification? Does the storyline effect a semantic transformation on this appellation/type?

and persisted. Here we have again what appears to be a signature of the redactor as in 49:7ff. He stands alone, and sets his face as flint against the indignities of outrageous fortune he must suffer. Yet he continues to lay his trust in God, again in contrast to Jacob. The word that is often translated as flint in this passage is *ḥallāmîṣ*. The four other instances of the use of this word in the OT, Deut 8:15; 32:13; Job 28:9; Ps 114:8, all employ the word to indicate an otherwise forbidding obstacle/wall. But the word in the context of the third song can be heard also as a pun in reply to a to be inferred taunt. One of the indignities our author would have had to suffer would imaginably be that he is a daydreamer. He set his face "indeed as flint/as a man dreaming (the taunt would have been 'the man has been dreaming,' *ḥlm hyṣ*)" and was certain he would not be put to shame. This is, in fact, the taunt Joseph is faced with on the part of his brothers (Gen 37:19). They call him a baal of dreams, meaning a daydreamer. In the story he proves to be an expert in dreams, knowing precisely what will come to pass. In the Joseph story the dream world expresses the reality of the deity. The non-dream world expresses the reality of either Jacob or Pharaoh, while the liminal Joseph stands between the two worlds. Even if the pun is not intended as such in Isa 40–55, the function of the delimiting nature of flint against catcalls and ridicule on one side, and trust in God's "imaginary" reality on the other, is expressed in the Joseph story as the liminality between the dream world and the real world. The notion is the same, the spin-off possibly a pun in reply to a taunt.

In 50:10 the one-man choir of the servant makes of the profile of the servant just presented a lesson and an invitation for whoever would follow. The song ends with an abrupt and ominous warning. Those who play with fire will have to face the consequence of their actions. There is no hint whether fire here points to idolatry as in 44:19, or whether it implies warlike actions as in the ambivalent verse 47:14. In view of the first part of the composition, chs. 40–49, dabbling in idolatry would be the closer meaning at hand, but in view of the fourth song of the servant in conjunction with 49:26, it could be a cryptic reference to those who would take to warlike actions to achieve their gain. In this case Isa 31:1-3 would be a further expansion on this.

God announces his salvation in 51:1-52:12. A crescendo of exhortations to those who would be righteous and wish to join the company of his servant catapults the reader/listener to the ultimate lesson of the fourth song, the well pleasing offering of the suffering servant. The first subsection (51:1-8) of this hortatory section (51:1-52:12) introduces immediately the leitmotif of the whole second part (chs. 50-55).

The lesson of Abraham and Sarah (51:1-8) is the one to be adhered to by those who would pursue righteousness. It is proposed here that this lesson is constructed and expounded for the first time here in the composition we are studying, that is by the redactor of Isa 40-55. As in the case of the appellation Zion for Jerusalem, the lesson about Abraham and Sarah is not borrowed from outside the text, but is the very substance of this text at hand. The renaming of Abram to Abraham in the book of Genesis remains unexplained and unjustified there. The statement that this is because he will become a father of a multitude of nations is not a linguistic one. The pun utilized is rather a reference to the function of the servant of Isa 40-55 to be an emissary of God to all nations. It is an enactment of the lesson of Isa 40-55. The linguistic and pedagogical import of the name Abraham is given in Isa 40-55 and represents the very fabric of the "new" lesson being expounded here. In the following an attempt will be made to demonstrate this.

The book of Ezekiel has no knowledge of Abraham. The one mention in Ezekiel 33:24 is patently a gloss. It comes as an objection voiced mimicking the lesson of Isa 51:1-8 to draw an opposite conclusion to that made in Isa 40-49, that is, that only those pursuing righteousness will be saved. It sounds like a taunt in response to the text of Isa 50-55. The response to the objection is a resume of Isa 40-49. The passage, Ezek 33:24-29, comes sandwiched between 33:1-20 about individual judgment being meted out according to deeds after due notice is given by the prophet, and Ezek 34:1–31 about God as the good shepherd. These passages are most likely the basis for the teaching and imagery we have in the two parts of Isa 40–55. But Ezek 33:24–29 has a different *Sitz im Leben* (situation in life) than the two bordering passages. The occasion indicated in 33:21, the fall of Jerusalem, stands in tension with the *vaticinium ex eventu* of the body of the passage. The mention of Abraham comes in the objection of the people. The objection and the response do not deal with the meaning of the name Abraham, but are an occasion to thresh out the conflicting positions regarding the promise to the one person and the false security of trusting in greater number. Were the invocation of Abraham, as regards content, directly related to ch. 34, it would have been synthetically a construct of that text. But in fact, the invocation is purely incidental to this text and polemical.[15]

The more conceivable literary matrix for the lesson about Abraham and Sarah is Isa 40–55. The redactor will have taken the teaching of Ezekiel about the good shepherd in Ezek 34 to coin or adopt the name. But the lesson is synthetically part and parcel of Isa 40–55. The mention of Abraham as being one at the time of his calling corresponds to the third song of the servant and to the exhortations that follow. The inferred *Sitz im Leben* of the redactor is also reflected in this motif. He stands alone and calls those who would be of like mind to join. The story in Genesis copies this topic and lesson, but the matrix is not original to it. The introduction of Sarah is in continuation of the motif barren land/woman, which, as we have seen in discussing the term Zion, is so fundamental to every sinew of the text of Isa 40–55.

---

15 Cf. Walther Zimmerli, *Ezekiel 2* (ed. P. D. Hanson and L. J. Greenspoon; trans. James D. Martin; Hermeneia; Philadelphia: Fortress, 1983), 191–202. Zimmerli analyzes the incongruities in the flow of the text as it stands, and on pp. 198–199 juxtaposes the use of the mention of Abraham in Ezekiel with that in Isa 41:8 and specially Isa 51:2. Cf. also Walther Eichrodt, *Ezekiel* (trans. Cosslett Quin; OTL; London: SCM, 1970), 456–467.

The main reason for this conjecture, however, lies in the semantic field covered by the name Abraham, and its elucidation in the fourth song of the suffering servant. This name and "song" are the cornerstone of this whole composition, bringing all the strands of argumentation together. Abraham, *'abrāhām* in Hebrew, is to be derived from the Arabic. The fact that the name is said to be shared by the Ishmaelites may indicate an Arabic original also, but the lesson constructed is the teaching of Isa 40–55. The name is made up of *'ab* (father), which is the same in both Hebrew and Arabic, and *rāhām*, which without vocalization becomes the triliteral *rhm*. In Arabic *rahām* refers to a lean and emaciated sheep or goat. It takes also the vocalization *rohām*. The adjective is *rahûm*. Another adjective from this root is *'arham* (more fruitful or plentiful), from *rihmah* (light drizzle). Another noun from the root is *marham*, referring to an unguent or dressing that is placed on a wound to bring about healing.[16] These usages of the triliteral in Arabic correspond to the description and function of the suffering servant in the fourth song. He is down, yet we take healing from his wounds, and the result of his work is a return of plenty and fruitfulness to the barren land/woman. Ezekiel makes of God the good shepherd who goes after and cares for the weak sheep. The composition of Isa 40–55 goes beyond that and makes of the emaciated servant the instrument of salvation. Further down we will see that he is presented as the scapegoat, the living sin offering. It is interesting to note that *rihmah* in Arabic, as well as its plural, means a light drizzling rain lasting a long time. In Hebrew the plural of the word *śā'îr* is used in Deut 32:2 to refer to a drizzle. The same Hebrew word in the singular is at the same time the designation used for the scapegoat in Lev 16, sent out on the Day of Atonement.

This derivation is still only the tip of the iceberg. Abraham becomes the father of this emaciated servant. The servant in the

---

16 Cf. Edward William Lane, *An Arabic-English Lexicon* (London: Williams & Norgate, 1863), 1171–1172.

fourth song becomes the offspring of the story of Abraham. Jacob is bypassed semantically, and the continuation of the Abraham lesson is in the suffering servant. So in fact the apparent discrepancy mentioned above in the sequence of Abraham and Jacob between Isa 40–55 and Genesis, is resolved as such: In Isa 40–55 we have the sequence Jacob son of Abraham followed by the Suffering Servant son of Ab-raham, in Genesis we have the sequence Abraham followed by Jacob son of Isaac followed by Joseph. Abraham cannot be Abraham unless there is a *rahām*/suffering servant of which he would be the father. It is Abraham who is defined by the servant and not vice-versa. The name Abraham in this composition is a referential to the servant. In Genesis the promise of Gen 17:19 to Abraham stands in tandem with the testing of Abraham in Gen 22 (cf. vv. 16–17). Until Abraham is associated with an oblation resembling that of the suffering servant of Isa 40–55, the name Abraham is still not promulgated and the promise is still at risk of being annulled.[17]

This dependency on Isa 40–55 is further highlighted by the wordplay in the Genesis story on Abram becoming Abraham (Gen 17:5). Abram can be translated as the lofty father, the first father, the founding father.[18] This construction is analogous to Hiram, the lofty king of Tyre. One of the implicit reproaches of the Deuteronomic historian addressed against Solomon is that he modeled his temple to that of Hiram and his riches. Abram is also similar to Abiram (my lofty first father). His title to fame in the Pentateuch is that of a Reubenite who joined the rebellion of Korah against Moses and was swallowed by the ground he stood on. Abiram could also be parsed as "their strongman," from the noun *ăbîr* (strongman) with the attached possessive pronoun. In the previous section we had seen our writer end

---

17 Even if, for argument's sake, one were to concede the originality of the mention of Abraham in Ezek 33:24, the expiatory function of the weak lamb reflected in Gen 22 is inherently the synthetic composition of Isa 40–55.
18 Cf. Paul Nadim Tarazi, *The Old Testament: An Introduction: Volume 1: Historical Traditions* (rev. ed.; Crestwood, N.Y.: St Vladimir's Seminary Press, 2003), 92–94.

part one with the affirmation that God is Jacob's "strongman," *ʾābîr*.[19] In conjunction with the fourth servant song it becomes clear that no other source of strength may be resorted to. The abrogation of Abram in the story of Genesis, whether in the meaning of lofty, distant forefather, or in the meaning of resorting to one's own strength or strongmen, corresponds to the teaching and rhetoric running through the redaction of Isa 40–55. This is the implication of 51:1 "Listen to me, you that pursue righteousness, you that seek the Lord. Look to the rock from which you were hewn, and to the quarry from which you were dug." Do not confuse your pedigree. Look to the servant, the new tidings from God, the fabric you will have to conform to in order to become privy to the announced salvation.

The introduction of the name Sarah is also part of the new construction of our author. As we have seen, Jacob is referred to at the beginning of this section in the image of a woman. Jacob will not be used as an appellation in part two. Jacob had been used in conjunction with Zion in part one (Isa 40:9; 41:27; 46:13; 49:14). Zion was the parched land being offered salvation, but like Jacob objecting that she had been forsaken by God (cf. 49:14 echoing Jacob's objection in Isa 40:27 and 44:21). The parallelism between Jacob and Judah was spelled out in 48:1. We followed above the shift in metaphor from barren land to barren woman. The name Sarah corresponds to Jerusalem, a woman's name being appropriate as a designation for a city (both in Hebrew and in Greek). Zion, as a designation for a barren city, will again be offered salvation in the second part, precisely in the section 51:1–52:12 described above as a crescendo of exhortations leading up to the fourth song of the servant. The introduction of Sarah just before these exhortations shows that it functions as an invitation to

---

19 This, in fact, functions as a send-off from part one to introduce the second part juxtaposing the parable of Abraham and Sarah in the second part to Jacob, much as in Gen 17:5 Abram is to become Abraham.

Jacob/Jerusalem[20] to assume a different vocation conforming to the parable of Abraham. This corresponds not only to the role of Sarah in the book of Genesis, but more specifically to the renaming of Jacob in the mysterious passage we have in Gen 32. This will be discussed below in the section on that passage. The redactor of Gen 32 will choose to interpret the name Israel in terms of the verb *śrh*, identical to the name Sarah, thus reenacting in the granting of the title Israel to Jacob the call to Jacob in Isa 40–55 to conform to the parable of Abraham and Sarah and take on the appellation Sarah. As we saw at the commencement of the second part in 50:2, Jacob is addressed as the divine consort (in the sense of a city pertaining to a deity) who was divorced because of her treachery. Jacob now is asked to rectify his divine consort status in order to become Sarah. This appellation, in the context of Isa 40–55, is a pun on the title Israel.[21] "Ab-raham" will modify the appellation Israel.

The first of three emphatic (starting with a double imperative) exhortations in series, the subsection Isa 51:9–16 is addressed to Yahweh but is in fact an exhortation addressed to Zion to remember its deity. The first invocation of Zion in the second part of Isa 40–55 was already in the previous subsection in 51:3. There the tenor and purpose of the repeated use of Zion in this part, Isa 51:3, 11, 16; 52:1, 2, 7, 8, is made clear. Zion, the barren parched wilderness, is about to be converted into a garden of Eden. In this subsection Zion is named twice. In the second invocation in 51:16, the words of exhortation are said to have been placed in the mouth of the prophet by God, saying to Zion "You are my people." The language is reminiscent of the book of Hosea addressed to the Northern Kingdom, and announces the readoption of Jerusalem.

---

20 Indeed to Judah, cf. 48:1. Note that Jerusalem is used in parallel with Zion in both part one and two.
21 More on the implication of the pun and the meaning of the names Sarah and Israel in section 3.2 below.

The second emphatic exhortation in 51:17–23 is addressed to Jerusalem reminding her of her previous discharge. None of her children is up to the task of giving her guidance. In terms of the required function she is in the equivalent situation of a childless woman. This is the central passage in Isa 51:1–52:12. The metaphor of giving birth will be repeated twice after the fourth song of the servant announcing accomplishment. In 54:1 it is with reference to the barren woman. In 55:10 it rejoins the cosmic image of fertilizing the land and making it bear forth, accomplished by agency of God's word, wrapping up the use of this image begun in 40:3.

The other basic linguistic image (cf. section 2.1 above), expressed in the *pi'el* verbal form of *nḥm* (to comfort), is also invoked as a question in this central subsection, "who will comfort you?" After it was set as the leitmotif of the work in the opening 40:1, its use becomes characteristic of the second part of the work. It is picked up in 49:13 in anticipation of the second part, and then repeated in 51:3, 12, 19; 52:9; 54:11 (this last in the passive *pu'al* form).

The third emphatic exhortation, 52:1–6, is expressly addressed to Zion from the outset. In this section we have a reiteration of what we saw in 45:13 and 50:1. The redemption will not require any silver.

The fifth and last subsection of the hortatory section 51:1–52:12, subsection 52:7–12, prepares for the fourth song of the servant. This subsection is a song of the author, the bringer of good tidings. While comfort and redemption are mentioned in v. 9, the vocabulary used in this passage is that of the victorious king bringing salvation and announcing it to all the nations. The redemption of the imprisoned is itself described as a victory at war (vv. 11–12). The terminology is reminiscent of the exodus out of Egypt in the book of Exodus.[22]

It is at this point that we have the culminating passage of the whole work, the fourth song of the servant, 52:13–53:12. The teaching embodied in the fourth song modifies the content of the whole work. It is paradoxically juxtaposed to the passage announcing ultimate victory (Isa 52:7–12). The victory was not achieved by force of silver (Isa 52:1–6), it will not be achieved by force of arms. The polemic is very clear. It is reflected explicitly in Isa 30:1–31:9, which appears to be a commentary by the school of our author. It is interesting that in Isa 30:7 Rahab is mentioned as a name for Egypt, the same Rahab mentioned as a mythological monster in 51:9. These are the only two instances in the book of Isaiah. Given that the mention in 30:7 purports to explain a previous mention, again priority in this instance must be given to Isa 40–55.

The fourth song is again in the third person like the first song. There it was an expression of a wish on the part of God, here it is a judicial ruling after the event. Following the resume of the case in 52:13–15, we have a listing of the facts (53:1–9) and then the pronouncement of God's verdict (vv. 10–12). If the first song was in God's imaginary/wishful future, the fourth song is in the redactor's wishful future. God *will* endorse the work that is being written out. The "Amen" of God will be spoken to the work in progress. It is an expression of the trust in Yahweh by the servant that we were told of in the second and third songs.

The section 53:1–9 starts with a rhetorical question, the function of which is to call disciples to the teaching being expounded, "Who hath believed our report? and to whom is the arm of the Lord revealed?" (53:1 KJV, differently the NRSV).

---

[22] It is in this subsection that we have the last use of the term Zion in this composition. The servant of the following fourth song will bring to an end the barrenness of Jerusalem. The function which Jacob failed to provide, thereby making of Jerusalem for the God of the redactor a figure of a barren ground, is supplied by the servant. The scapegoat will end the drought.

A paraphrase giving a feel of the Hebrew within the flow of the whole composition would be: "Who will say 'Amen' to the pronouncements we have decreed/made to be heard, who has had his eyes opened to see in them the power of the arm of Yahweh?" It is an appeal to would-be disciples to adopt the disposition of the servant as the only well pleasing oblation to Yahweh, in order to have a share in the promised covenant. It is this servant who has been set as a *bĕrît* (covenant) for the people according to the first song (42:6) and the commentary extension of the second song (49:8). What is explicated in the following verses is the very fabric of the eternal covenant that will be referred back to in 54:9–10 invoking Noah, and in 55:3 invoking David. The Abrahamic covenant in part two is an unconditional covenant, in contradistinction to the one with Jacob explicated in part one. Paradoxically the only port of access to it and to a share in its heritage is in the shape of the servant of the fourth song. The notion of salvation/victory is being redefined here such as to be in total contradiction to that held by the opponents! The one servant stands against the many and disjunct from all. Those who would join his company must become obedient to the pronouncement in this section as expressing God's mindset and as defining of the domain of His rule. The word translated as "report" in 53:1 is *šĕmûʿâ* (that which is heard/a report). In the LXX it is translated as ακοη. It is from the same verbal root, *šmʿ* (to hear), as the name Simeon, *šimʿôn*.[23] To hear is to obey in the Semitic usage[24]. Obedience must be given to the teaching of Isa 40–55 exemplified in the teaching about the servant.

In the following verses we are given a profile of the faceless servant. We have already discussed his profiling as a *rahām* with

---

[23] The significance of this appellation will be expanded upon in chapter 2 in connection with the Joseph story. In the Joseph story Jacob must cede obedience to Joseph.
[24] Cf. Kamal Abou-Chaar, "The Two Builders: A Study of the Parable in Luke 6:47–49," *Near East School of Theology Theological Review* 1 (1982): 44–58. Paragraph II.B is relevant to the statement above.

all the possible attached connotations. But this emaciated sheep has also a job description added to his CV and profile. Although he is not called a goat outright, he shares his job description with the scapegoat as outlined in Lev 16. He is, from the point of view of God, an acceptable living sin oblation, rejected outside the land of the living (v. 8). Verse 9 repeats the three things negated in him. He had done no violence, his speech harbored no deceit/treachery, and he was by mistake buried with the rich, implying that he was not by the nature of his job description to be associated with the wealthy/aggrandized.[25]

Verse 7 in this passage has two particularities. The servant is likened to a sheep being led to the slaughter, *ṭbḥ* in Hebrew. The word for sheep used is *śeh*. We translate sheep because it is used in the image of a sheep led to the slaughter. In fact it is a male sheep or goat. Thus the reference to a goat, while not explicit, is maintained. The second matter to be noticed is that in the parallel expression "like a sheep that before its shearers is silent" (NRSV), the word used for sheep in Hebrew is *rāḥēl*. This refers to a ewe, a female sheep. This fits into the shift in the metaphor to that of a barren woman, shorn of her children. The word implies a healthy well off female sheep.[26]

In 53:10–13 trust in the verdict of God is expressed. Although God was pleased to see the servant bruised with blows and left emaciated, he will surely pronounce him not guilty. The restitution involves the many, because his wounds brought healing to those who had been onlookers, his oblation was a sin offering for others, and he made intercession for those guilty of transgression. Thus restitution takes the aspect of enthronement of the victorious. The aspect of his work that triggers all this is that he had made himself destitute of all things to the point of death, caring for the many. This stands in stark contrast to

---

25 This last ambivalence is reduplicated in the liminal character of Joseph in the Genesis story.
26 It is also the name Rachel, mother of Joseph and Benjamin, and favorite bride of Jacob in Genesis.

Jacob, both as he is represented in Isa 40–49, and as he is represented in Genesis, where he makes a grab for anything he can get his hands on, from the heel of his brother coming out of the womb, to the two sons of Joseph, Ephraim and Manasseh, on his deathbed. The two disjunct tracks, the one of Jacob, the other of the servant who, as the emaciated lamb is in continuation of the story of Abraham, the father of the weak lamb, have now been put into total relief.

As to the priests and the levites, their sacred precinct has been declassed by the desecrated servant outside the camp. His sin offering has proved to be the acceptable and effective oblation. The living scapegoat, who carries the sins of others including those of the sons of Aaron and the levites, has made of the offering they present on behalf of their own sins as well as of those of the people a lame duck oblation. Again this is reflected both in Isa 40–49 and in the books of the Former and Latter Prophets as a whole.

The image of the barren woman meets us again at the beginning of the last section of the second part and of the work as a whole, 54:1–55:13. The regalia of the servant have already been described in 52:13–53:12. Now the victory achieved thereby is announced and sung. The image of the divine bridegroom is used in tandem with the image of the barren woman. The over-abundant fruitfulness to come upon her is solely the work of this bridegroom, her God.

The theme of the benefit coming to all nations will be echoed in ch. 55. Central to ch. 54 is the announcement that the new covenant of the servant will be eternal, non-conditional, like the decision to stop the destructive waters at the time of Noah.[27]

---

[27] The invocation of Noah is especially pertinent as his lesson/parable in terms of the nations parallels the lesson given to Jacob as presented in chs. 40–49. Jacob had been practically annihilated as a result of his sins, and yet is being offered an analogous unbreakable covenant. The name of Noah is also to the point. In Hebrew Noah is *nḥ*. This is the same as the unvocalized hollow root *nḥ/nûḥ* meaning "to rest/give rest." While not the same as *nḥm* (to comfort), which is the leitmotif of Isa 40–55, it is a term ("interim" rest) which bears analogy to it.

Chapter 1 51

This is fitting in conjunction with the image of the God of all the earth (v. 5). It also prepares for ch. 55 and the introduction of the nations. Forthwith God will not act destructively. The last verse in ch. 54 reminds us that this announcement of victory and the concomitant covenant applies to the servants of Yahweh. The shape of the servant has already been communicated.

The opening verse of ch. 55 brings forward a central motif, which had been introduced in Isa 40:11 and which we meet also in the Joseph story. In the Joseph story the exhortation is to all who have need to come and be fed. The image used here, however, is that of thirst and water. We are returned to the basic vocabulary of barren land and God of the waters as at the outset in ch. 40, and this will remain throughout this last chapter. No silver will be required. We are told that the new covenant, concomitant with being unconditional, is unilateral and freely given. To underline this, reference is made this time to the hard and fast love of God for David. Central to ch. 55 is the call to return to Yahweh (v. 7). The covenant is unilaterally worked out by Yahweh, but everyone is exhorted to take to heart the announcement so as to enter into its proffered benefits. The work is carried out by the unfailing work of God's word which accomplishes its task and bears fruit (v. 11). The exhortation is a call to hear the communication of the word as regally effective. We had already been told that God alone is king in part one. The reference to David in the last chapter returns this image to the fore, together with the announcement of victory.[28] The

---

28 In accordance with the teaching of part one where God alone is king over Jacob (43:15), David is not called king, he is only a prince/commander. There is no mention of a covenant with him (this is predicated only of the servant in Isa 40–55). The covenant with the servant has the same attribute of being "sure" like the "love" manifested to David by God. The reference to David/Jerusalem, coming after the reference to Noah in the previous passage, makes David's blessings hinge on and subject to the Noahic promise to the nations. This is reflected in Isa 1–39 (Isa 2:2–4; 11:6–9) and runs parallel to the teaching found in the book of Jeremiah (29:7). The surety expressed to David is similar to the surety expressed to the nations, and both

victorious king demands obedience to the reign of his alone effective word. He is gracious and full of mercies. The last verse, indeed the last word, underscores this with a pun. The signs of his victory will never be broken. This is a play on the Hebrew phrase used to express the promulgation of a covenant. In Hebrew the expression is "cut/break (*krt*) a covenant." This is an ominous sign that warns of the consequence incumbent on a breach of contract. The negated passive of the same verb is used here. Strangely it sounds more ominous. It is as if the redactor is saying, "Try as you may, what you may, this covenant will stand unbroken."

3. The Reenactment of the Lesson of Isa 40–55 in Gen 32

The reading proposed above made three principal points. The first is that Isa 40–55 was written as a program launcher for the books of the Law and the Prophets. The second is that it posits two juxtaposed tracks: the one of Adam/Jacob as the problem track, the other of God acting in terms of the parable of Abraham and Sarah as the solution track. The third point made is that the paradigm of the servant-*rahām* presented provides at the same time the basic module with which to effect a literary transformation and thus produce/generate the texts and motifs in conformity with and as required by the project.

Since the basic organization of Isa 40–55 as deciphered above is a contrasting of the actual Jacob with the required servant-*rahām* and an invitation to Jacob to enter into the covenant that is concomitant with the servant-*rahām*, it is a good starting point to test the basic thesis on the passage in the book of Genesis which offers Jacob a new venue by way of the name Israel in

---

find their fulfillment in the covenant that comes concomitant with the servant-*rahām*. The servant, as we saw, has no lineage or progeny. The various to be conjectured "opposing" versions/receptions of the promised divine love for David/Jerusalem (for example Ezek 37:22, 24) are channeled to and subsumed (and critically so) under the covenant of the servant-*rahām*, much as the covenant with Ab-raham in Genesis subsumes all other subsequent actions of the deity with Jacob.

Gen 32. This pericope, as will be demonstrated in the following, describes the conditions requisite for the land to open up to Jacob and for the granting of the title Israel. Israel corresponds to the name Sarah, introduced in the parable of Abraham and Sarah in Isa 40–55. In order to be granted the title and the venue, Jacob will have to "put on" the servant profile as validation of credentials and port of entry into the coveted land of plenty. The chapter runs in "imaginary" time, the time of the wishful thinking of the deity, as can be seen by the immediately subsequent developments setting in with ch. 34 and functioning as a foil to ch. 32.

The names Jacob and Israel play the major role in the chapter. As will be suggested below, the name Israel will be reinterpreted in terms more conducive to the arguments of Isa 40–55. At the same time, it will be seen that a certain polemic can be discerned in the motifs and terminology chosen, which is apparently directed against a "mystery religion" type of religious induction.

3.1 The Name Jacob

Jacob in Hebrew means basically acolyte, adjutant, manservant, someone who follows after someone or something both in a friendly and in a hostile sense. This notion is played upon in Lev 25:42, 55, "For to me the people of Israel are servants: they are my servants whom I brought out from the land of Egypt: I am the Lord your God" (v. 55 NRSV). This comes in an address by God to Moses, Lev 25–26, culminating the Code of Holiness in the book of Leviticus, and recapitulating the basic address of Isa 40–55 to Jacob. In fact the one and only mention of Jacob by name in the book of Leviticus comes towards the end of this address in Lev 26:42. It is reasonable to assume that Jacob pertained to a class providing services but having no domain of their own, and consequently no king. More important though is the wordplay exercised on the name in the texts of the OT. Jacob derives from the Hebrew root *'qb*.

This refers to some thing or action that doubles back up on itself, a protrusion, a heel, a chicane, chicanery, a pursuer, that pursuant upon which (as in the use of *'qb* with the meaning "in consequence of," indicating cause), and thus can be employed with the connotation crooked, treacherous, making a grab for something. This last is highlighted in Gen 25:26 through the explanation of the name Jacob is given at birth. The explanation given is that he grabbed at his twin brother's heel as he came out of the womb. This is reiterated in the plaint of Esau in Gen 27:36. Esau cries out that Jacob lives up perfectly to his name, having taken a grab at and usurped both his birthright and his blessing. We have a similar appreciation of the name in Hos 12:4. An interesting pun on the name is found in Isa 40:4. In a description of the program of God as delineated in Isa 40–55, we are told that "the uneven ground ('crooked' in KJV) shall become level" (NRSV). The "uneven ground" in Hebrew is *'āqōb*, from the same Hebrew triliteral root as Jacob. The Hebrew word translated as "level" is *mîšōr*: this means also "upright," and is from the root *yšr*, from which the adjective and verbal root "to be upright" comes. As we saw above, the problem posed in Isa 40–49 to which an answer is given in Isa 50–55 is precisely how to make of Jacob an upright person!

3.2 The Name Israel

We are provided in Gen 32:29 with a derivation of the title Israel from the rare and obscure verbal root *śrh* (*śry*). This is repeated in Hos 12:4. Another derivation, or possibly an intended pun, is given in Hos 12:5 from *śwr* or possibly *śrr* (to rise as one who would rule), that is from the same root as the name Sarah, *śrh* in Hebrew, (if this last is understood as "princess," the feminine of the Hebrew noun for prince). The basic meaning of this last root, *śrr*, would seem to have the meaning "to rise high."[29] As such the noun Sarah, *śrh*, would be

---

[29] I would suggest that in Hos 12:4–5 we do not have a synonymous parallelism but rather a climactic one which follows the storyline of Gen 32:2–35:15. This explains the two different derivations in vv. 4 and 5.

etymologically distinct from the identically written verb *śrh*. The verbal root *śrh* is found only in the two aforementioned verses, Gen 32:29 and Hos 12:4. Translators, having no other recourse other than these two pericopes to try to surmise the meaning of the word, usually derive contextually the translation "strive with" for want of a more informed translation. This "seems" to fit with the story line, and indeed, the suggested derivation is not an etymological designation but a pun on the name to highlight the teaching of the story (and, as we have seen, it is the identical formal equivalent of the name Sarah even though it is not usual to derive the name Sarah from this root).

The Arabic language provides better help in deciphering the enigmatic use of this verbal root in Gen 32:29. The matrix of meanings associated with the cognate Arabic roots *sry*, *sr*, *srr*, and *srw* match well with the story as in Gen 32. These include secret, night travel, night escapade, concubine (both free or slave), pleasure, a type of tree from which arrows are made, the highest part, to be elevated.[30] All the meanings can be summed under the general heading of either masculine virility or nighttime activity. The possibility suggests itself of a possible use in forms of initiation such as a mystagogical initiation into the intimacy of a supposed higher order. There is a later parallel to this usage in the Islamic tradition about the miraculous night journey/assumption of the prophet Mohammad to the "farthest/ultimate" mosque. It is named *al-isrā'*, from this same root.[31] The analogy from the Islamic use in conjunction with the miraculous night journey of the prophet Mohammad which initiates him into the divine designs of God's address to Israel and Moses and to man in general through the verses of the Qur'an would point to a journey/transposition to a new awareness/insight/body of secrets. On the other hand, if this root were to be applied as a feminine noun, one would expect it to indicate the autonomous domain of a man, in one sense or

---

30 Lane, *An Arabic-English Lexicon*, 1337–1340, 1353–1356.
31 Qur'an 17:1.

another, with the connotation of private or secret. In the parable of Abraham and Sarah, Sarah represents Jacob/the barren Zion, called by the deity to become His initiate/consort city. As such it is a political usage. In Isa 40–55 God's measure of manhood is the suffering servant. The servant has his hidden dwelling in the deity, he expresses the *gratia* of the deity, and his elevation is the work of the deity. It is highly likely that the play on the root *śry* would have been polemically borrowed from a usage by forms of mystery religions and employed as a political term (In line with the teaching in Isa 40–55 that the hidden God is made manifest through His addressed words).

A sociolinguistically more likely original derivation for the title Israel would be from the Arabic *ysr*.[32] The many connotations of the various constructions can be summarized in easy/made easy, well off, left side.[33] It stands opposite to the right side (as indicative of might/power), and to an obstacle course. As such it stands opposite to the "forked" Jacob, and opposite to Benjamin (more below on Benjamin as indicative of a warrior clan/might/power). We could sum up the linguistic meaning, if this derivation is correct, as "making it/being on easy street."[34] The aspiring yuppie Jacob would have his heart's desire set on making it to easy street while remaining subject to the mighty and powerful. This etymology is not made by the text, but it would fit both the sociological class we seem to be confronted with, as well as the caricature of Jacob we have in the Jacob cycle, grabbing every which way in order to "make it." This would be more applicable to a general usage not impacted by Isa 40–55 (The notion of wealth being associated by Isa 40–55 with the wicked and not expressive of well-being). Jacob, if and when functioning optimally, would make it on God's "easy street."

---

32 Cf. the Arabic name Yasser.
33 Lane, *An Arabic-English Lexicon*, 2975–2978.
34 Our texts indeed associate the name Israel primarily with the Northern Kingdom, Ephraim. Ephraim is described as very wealthy and fruitful (cf. Gen 41:52; Hos 12:8–9).

The notion of wealth not being viewed as a measure of success by the redactor of the servant songs, it is very plausible to conjecture that he reinterpreted the title Israel in terms of the root *śry*. This would have served a double purpose. On one hand, he would have downgraded the notion of wealth as a measure of divine success. On the other, he would have polemically countered the attempt to lure "Jacob" into religious practices indicated as Canaanite in the books of the Law and the Prophets, but apparently very similar to what we encounter in the Hellenistic period. That we do have a reinterpretation of the term Israel in Genesis is very likely. In the case of Abraham we have a change of name, which, as discussed above, appears to be a construct of Isa 40–55. In analogy to it we have a change of name for Sarah. The pericope that initiates the change of name for Jacob in Gen 32 introduces a "new" title which is not new. The book of Ezekiel uses extensively the name Israel, and it is a common usage throughout the literature we are dealing with, as well as being attested extra- biblically. The suspicion arises that in fact in Gen 32 we do not have a new designation for Jacob, but a redefinition of the title Israel. The conjectured "original" derivation from the Arabic *ysr* would have been reinterpreted in terms of the root *śry*. It is proposed here that this is the work of Isa 40–55. The analysis in the following sections will try to demonstrate that Isa 40–55 is indeed behind the redaction of the pericope in Gen 32.

The passage in Gen 32 remains enigmatic. As it is central to the redactional scheme directing the flow of the storyline, we must fall back on other elements in the passage to decipher the intended situation. The time of day is given as nighttime before the break of dawn. The action of the stranger who jumps (*nipʿal* of *ʾbq* "jumped him like a sandstorm/engulfed him like fine dust") Jacob is described in terms of a deadly sandstorm (*ʾbq*), like the plague that hits Egypt in the book of Exodus (Exod 9:9). It is a very severely testing situation. The use of the pun on the obscure root *śrh*, which I summarized from Arabic under the general title of "masculine virility," after Jacob had left himself naked of all goods and alone, would point the attention to a testing expressed in terms of a rite of passage, or possibly of an induction testing of a mystery religious type. The highlighting of the ford of Jabbok (to be derived from the root *bqq*) as the location for the story shows that it is a testing in terms of a passage into another order. The sparsely used Hebrew root *bqq* would appear to highlight the notion of a destructive testing. The Arabic usage of *bqq* in the sense of dividing and consequently opening a breach would support the notion of opening a passage. The Arabic root *bqy* in the sense of remain/prove to be perdurable goes also in the direction of a proving testing. Indeed, the root *bq*, *bqy* in Syriac includes outright the meanings to try/prove/examine/inquire into and trial/investigation.[35] The meaning of the passage would seem to be that Jacob undergoes a very severe testing (*śrh* would have to be understood as such rather than as "to strive.") He persists until he proves himself, and becomes a proved inductee. The acolyte has come of age and become the initiate of God, "Israel." How this functions within the wider context will be discussed in the following sections 3.3 and 3.4.

3.3 Mahanaim

The master location given for the events of Gen 32 is indicated in v. 3 as Mahanaim. This sets the framework for the ensuing events. Jacob recognizes the place as God's encampment, and uses the dual form of the word encampment as the name of the locale. We are theatrically in God's location and in God's time. The use of the dual/plural is to be expected in a toponym. But in view of the developments described in Exod 33 (following the events surrounding the worship of the golden calf by all the people led by Aaron, whereby God removes His tent of meeting/tabernacle to a tent outside the encampment of Jacob so as not to destroy Jacob), the name

---

[35] Cf. J. Payne Smith, ed., *A Compendious Syriac Dictionary: Founded Upon the Thesaurus Syriacus of Robert Payne* (Oxford: Clarendon, 1903), 52.

Mahanaim assumes a critically important redactional function. The location is described as at a time and place where and when Jacob can encounter the deity face to face and survive (compare Gen 32:31 with Exod 33:20–23), effectively a time and place where the encampment of Jacob and the tent of meeting are located in the same place.

3.4 Genesis 32: Reenactment of Isa 40–55 and Reinterpretation of the Title Israel

The story of Jacob in Gen 32 comes as the culmination of his exorbitant increase, symbolized by the birth of Joseph, on the eve of his return to the land where his fathers sojourned. It is equivalent to the situation of Jacob/Israel at the end of the Pentateuch, with Moses looking across the Jordan to the promised land. Jacob in Gen 32 paradigmatically does what is required in order to be granted access to the land, and consequently to have the name Israel bestowed upon him.

In vv. 4–9 Jacob divides his camp defensively into two camps. He is apprehensive about the reception his brother Esau prepares for him on his crossing the Jordan.

In vv. 10–13 Jacob prays to God for succor in order to be allowed reentry into the land. This elucidates fully the topic of the pericope.

In vv. 14–21 Jacob prepares a gift to appease his brother and gives exact commands to the leaders of the companies sent as to what to say to Esau.

Having done all actions that are humanly advisable, military/defensive, diplomatic, and most importantly presented supplication to the deity, Jacob is still where he is in his own camp, outside the land. We are reminded of the parable of the rich man in the gospel of Mark 10:17–27. Jacob still has to find a way to pass through the proverbial eye of the needle! It is at this point that we have the reenactment of the role of the servant of Isa 40–55. The deity from whom he requested succor has very specific requirements before the requested succor is provided and safe passage and entry are ensured. He must be severely tested to determine if all requirements are satisfied, and he may become the inductee of the deity into the promised land.

The environmental circumstances surrounding the events in this pericope set the tone for the developments. It is nighttime and obscurity is the dominant motif. A cloud of darkness and mystery engulfs the players. These circumstances bring together two different sets of topics. We have a double motif. One set is the set of topics associated with testing and mystagogical induction. The other set is the syntactical presentation of Isa 40–55. The God of the servant is a hidden God, and the servant is trained for his public service while hidden in the hiddenness of God.

In Gen 32:23–32, Jacob acts out the servant of Isa 50–55. He first makes himself bare of all that appertains to him of wealth and children, (Joseph emblematically being the last one to be let go off as we will be informed in the immediately following passage in 33:2 describing and enacting the entry). Then he stands alone with the faceless and nameless figure of the deity, taking all blows from God and man, and remaining till the early hours of the morning, not releasing nor rejecting the deity until he is blessed by this deity and morning dawns. His "flag" remained up all through the night, enduring all the blows, not relenting to despair, and so he "earned" the title "Israel." The land, represented by his brother Esau/Edom, opens up to him. This is the work of the servant in Isa 50–55 standing opposite to that of Jacob in 40–49. Genesis 32 expresses the imaginary time of the deity of the redactor of this text, his unrealized wish as expressed in Isa 40–55. Only by denuding himself of all his possessions, and taking the shape of the suffering servant, enduring all possible injury from men and the deity, and holding on to hope in the blessing of the nameless and hidden deity does he achieve entry into the land/blessings of the covenant. The verb *śry* proves to mean in this context: Going the road with God, being tested and proven, and becoming intimate of God![36]

As fates would have it here, determined by the redactor, this is made possible for Jacob because Benjamin has not yet been born to him. He still does not have a warrior clan (I derive Benjamin from the Arabic root *ymn* indicating the right hand/good fortune, in the sense of those wielding power by means of a mighty right arm/having the upper hand).[37] Our writer, after all, wishes to understand the name Israel in this pericope as derived from *śrh*, as indicating becoming intimate of the deity and initiate into the realm of God (in other words he proved himself into the realm, not as over and above God). God, the stranger who jumps him and has the upper hand, will function as his strongman and as his king, again exactly as in Isa 40–55. The inductee will function as subject to and under the protection of the inducting stranger/deity. This is why he insists on receiving the blessing from the stranger, and names the locale as the locale of the meeting with the nameless deity and surviving. It was not by his strength that he passed the test, but by his holding on to the stranger and sustaining all the bruising from God and men. Hosea will understand it as repentance to God, as weeping and entreating the deity (Hos 12: 5), thus becoming proven, and making the Jacob clan the addressee of God and recipient of His word. "Real" time resumes in Gen 34–35 where we have the beginning of the story of the collapse of Jacob, expressed as the sins of the sons of Jacob. The birth of Benjamin, the warrior clan, in Gen 35:18 puts an end to Jacob's good time with Rachel.

---

[36] The mysterious blow Jacob receives on his hip joint in v. 26 appears also to be an assimilation to the profile of the servant in the fourth song. The hip would stand for the procreative capacity of a man. The servant appears to have no progeny who would keep his memory (Isa 53:8).

[37] More on the name Benjamin and its redactional value in Genesis will follow in chapter 2.

4. Interim Conclusions

The thesis being argued is that Isa 40–55 was written as the project launcher for the books of the Law and the Former and Latter Prophets. It presents the basic scheme of scriptures as the parable of Abraham and Sarah in conjunction with the songs of the servant. At the same time it functions as the "transform/transformational paradigm" to be applied on the material being redacted, making of the various passages and pericopes modules reflective of this scheme. I borrow the term transform from mathematics, and employ it in the sense of a predisposed literary transformation to be applied to the material. Isaiah 40–55 is thus the redactional implement launching and delineating the redactional work required. The primary structuring element is the setting up of two tracks of action, in dialogue with one another but disjunct; the one of Jacob/Adam representing the sins of all Adam, the other of God/God's word delineated by the servant-*rahām*. Together with this, it traces graphically the paradigmatic form of this servant-*rahām*, providing the rule/canon for the promulgation of the covenant with this deity and for arriving at the solution/salvation to the problem posed by Adam/Jacob.

This servant stands outside the camp of Jacob, and consequently stands opposite the clerical organization being attempted by the opponents.[38] The elucidation of the major elements of this thesis will require the study of several texts and motifs in the books of the Law and the Prophets. The central argument comes in a second part, chapter 2 of this book, discussing the Joseph type and its transformation in the Joseph cycle in the book of Genesis. The illustration of the thesis in the analysis of Gen 32 and the reinterpretation of the title Israel in this chapter is proposed as emblematic of the program and procedure put forth by Isa 40–55 and implemented in the

---

38 Cf. Paul Nadim Tarazi, "The Book of Jeremiah and the Pentateuchal Torah," in *Sacred Text and Interpretation: Perspectives in Orthodox Biblical Studies* (ed. Theodore G. Stylianopoulos; Brookline, Mass.: Holy Cross Orthodox Press, 2006), 7–36.

production of the corpus of texts of the Law and the Prophets. The unity of the corpus is one proposed, launched and generated by the text of Isa 40–55. The verification of the thesis awaits the analysis and the argumentation of key texts, types, and structuring elements in the upcoming parts/chapters of this study. The following chapters of this monograph chart paradigmatically, rather than exhaustively, the work required by the proposed thesis as presented in this first part/chapter.

4.1 Postscript

The thesis underlying this paper is that the Pentateuch and the books of the Former and Latter Prophets are a redactional project initiated by the redactor of Isa 40–55, and completed by his school. The work presupposes and is founded upon the corpus of the work and the approach of Paul Nadim Tarazi, accessed both through his written works, as well as through his oral teaching and discussions. In several recent works he has postulated the book of Ezekiel as the writing from which and around which Scripture formed. He has expressed this in different ways,[39] including description of the book as the blueprint[40] for the Law and the Prophets. In two other instances he mentions Second Isaiah in conjunction with Ezekiel.[41] The priority of the book of Ezekiel is concurred to and premised in this paper. It is also premised to be the bone of contention between the Isa 40–55 group and their opponents with primarily a priestly and levitical posture.[42] On the other hand, I propose Isa 40–55 as deliberately and technically the

---

39 Cf. Tarazi, *The Old Testament: An Introduction: Volume 1: Historical Traditions*, 23–25, 29–40.
40 Paul Nadim Tarazi, "Paul, the One Apostle of the One Gospel," JOCABS 2.1 (2009): 15–18. Cited 23 September 2010. Online: http://ocabs.org/journal/index.php/jocabs/article/view/40/15.
41 Paul Nadim Tarazi, *The New Testament: An Introduction: Volume 4: Matthew and the Canon* (St Paul, Minn.: OCABS Press, 2009), 48 n. 9, and Tarazi, *Genesis*, 32–33, where Ezekiel and Second Isaiah are named as the two "fathers of scripture."
42 This position is given expression to and argued at length, as regards the Pentateuch, in: Tarazi, "The Book of Jeremiah and the Pentateuchal Torah."

blueprint, or proposal, for the redaction of the full corpus we know as the Law and the Prophets. It is part and parcel of the "new" that "will be heard for the first time" (Isa 48:6–8). The centrality of Ezekiel is that it is the text that is being reclaimed, after having been misappropriated by the temple group[43] according to the Isa 40–55 group. The new corpus is being proposed as the "place" within which Ezekiel is to be read, as opposed to the temple. Moses becomes the frame of reference for the reception of Ezekiel, not the temple and the priesthood. P. D. Hanson in his seminal work[44] sees in Isa 56–66 a development towards a sharpening of the acrimony directed against the priests and the levites due to the injustices in a failed new Jerusalem. He projects this as having occurred after Isa 40–55. I shift this conjectured development to the interval of time between the book of Ezekiel and Isa 40–55 (cf. section 2.2.1 above).

The attempt was made above, in the first three sections of the paper, to show the impact of Isa 40–55 on the redaction of Gen 32 and the reinterpretation of the title Israel. This remains only an initial piece in the jigsaw puzzle, albeit a paradigmatic one. The cornerstone of the argument will come in a discussion of the Joseph type and its transformation. Much of the evidence adduced could point to an inverse theory to the effect that Isa 40–55 is a resume of Scripture. I believe enough evidence was cited to start questioning this. A final decision would await a survey of all the Law and the Prophets. It should be pointed out that if Isa 40–55 is seen as a "perfect" resume of Scripture, then it is practically equivalent to stating that it expresses the design behind the work. Still, technically, the thesis presented here is that it actually is the blueprint composed to set off work on the project.

---

43 Ibid.
44 Hanson, *The Dawn of Apocalyptic*.

Chapter 2
The Impact of Isa 40–55 on the Joseph Type and Its Transformation

Preamble

This is the second part of what initially had been a single paper prepared for the Festschrift celebrating the forty-year milestone in the teaching career of Professor Paul Nadim Tarazi. Space limitations incumbent on the Festschrift made it necessary to cut the material and reedit a first part of the paper for publication in the Festschrift. Here, the rest of the original material has been recut and reedited for publication as chapter 2. This second chapter must be read conjointly with the first part. It presupposes the first part and cannot be understood without it. It had been interwoven with the material in the first part, and, indeed, much of the material will be re-invoked in the following, and some of it will be repeated. While the material for this second part has been cut, reedited, and rounded up, it remains essentially as it stood in the draft written in 2010, albeit published now on the year following on the Jubilee commemoration of Professor Tarazi's teaching career.

Chapter 2 is in continuation of the thesis presented in chapter 1. The basic thesis thus constitutes the main title heading of this monograph as well. Chapter 2 is a study of the Joseph type in Scripture. In part/chapter 1, it was announced as the cornerstone of the basic argumentation of the thesis presentation. It involves an analysis of the story of Joseph in the book of Genesis (Gen 37–50) in function of the analysis made in part/chapter 1 of Isa 40–55. The introductory remarks on the proposed reading and method in the first section of chapter 1 must be kept in mind here as well. Additionally, the following remarks are incumbent specifically regarding the Joseph story and the study of the Joseph type. The Joseph story in Gen 37–50 is a novella. It differs in literary form from the preceding and subsequent passages in the book of Genesis and the Pentateuch. This has led critics to see it as a borrowing from an extra-scriptural source that is to be determined, some critics suggesting it might be a borrowing from an Egyptian source. It may be a borrowing, but what is important for this study is the redactional work that can be inferred within the context of the scriptural literature at hand. Being a novella, it is quintessentially, in terms of its literary form, fictional literature. In the context of scriptural literature, it must be understood as pedagogical literature. In both pedagogy and fiction, the characters in the story play a paradigmatic role, they become types, and the appellation of the character becomes an invocation of a type. The "imaginary" in the mind of the author is the "reality" in literature. In the wider sense, it functions as a parable, metaphor, or paradigm, and, pedagogically, these become carriers of the teaching. The study of the type becomes an attempt to explore how the author or redactor "images" the world through the narrative line, the paradigms, and the characters/types therein, that is, the "imaginary" time and world in the mind of the redactor, the teaching therein. The author or redactor, in the creation of the narrative, has recourse to the full gamut of literary utensils. Unlike a scientific description, literature provokes interaction with the mind of the reader employing the manifold tools of literary artifice. But just like in science and mathematics, this can lead to a complex construction/creation that is to be deciphered and explored in the analysis/deconstruction.

1. The Apparently Conflicting Use of the "Joseph" Type/Appellation in the OT

The use of the appellation Joseph in the Joseph story in the book of Genesis for a personage presented as a major positive agent for the deity's work in the book stands in sharp contrast to the negative references to Joseph and the Joseph tribes in the books of the Former and the Latter Prophets and in some passages in the book of Psalms. A source critical resolution of this contrast, as well as a historicizing fundamentalistic one, bypasses the literary and redactional function of an appellation in a given text or corpus and its use as a type. Names in literary texts play a primary role in the argument of a storyline. They predispose the articulation in a given direction, and function as focal points, as attractors propelling forward the argument/action. Both the Books of the Former and the Latter Prophets are generally assumed to stand in an interlocutory relationship with the Pentateuch, regardless of how one may construe this relationship and the consequent dependency. This paper studies the interrelation of the redactional treatment of the Joseph story and the redactional structure of Isa 40–55. The study will be done in an attempt to show that there is an intentional redactional design behind this discrepancy in the use of the appellation Joseph aiming at producing a transformed type. At the same time it will shed light on the impact of the composition of Isa 40–55 on the redaction of the Pentateuch and the books of the Former and Latter Prophets.

1.1 Conflicting Usages

The most outspoken contrast in the use of the appellation Joseph can be seen in Psalm 78, "He rejected the tent of Joseph, he did not choose the tribe of Ephraim;" (Ps 78:67 NRSV). The book of Amos is also outspoken in this respect. "Seek the Lord and live, or he will break out against the house of Joseph like fire, and it will devour Bethel, with no one to quench it." (Amos 5:6 NRSV). "Hate evil and love good, and establish justice in the gate; it may be that the Lord, the God of hosts, will be gracious to the remnant of Joseph." (Amos 5:15 NRSV).

This discrepancy becomes more acute when we see the treatment of Ephraim and Manasseh in the books of the Former and the Latter Prophets. The book of Hosea is one lengthy diatribe against Ephraim. The books of Kings are again an extended listing of the sins of Samaria, representative of the Northern Kingdom of Israel, basically Ephraim.

Joseph, identified with Ephraim, is the most unlikely personage to be portrayed as a saintly type, betrayed by the other sons of Jacob while bringing them salvation. Quite the contrary, as exemplified in the Elijah/Elisha cycle and in the book of Hosea, Ephraim, as the Northern Kingdom of Israel, leads the tribes astray going after Baal.

As to Manasseh, it is very much to the point that after Samaria and the Northern Kingdom collapse due to their apostasy according to the writers, the name of the king of Judah who will seal the fate of Judah and the Southern Kingdom by his apostasy is Manasseh! It is as if the types of both the sons of Joseph, Ephraim and Manasseh, are figures of apostasy and doom.

The name Joseph is derived from the Hebrew triliteral root *ysp* (to add, increase). The content and nature of the increase remains ambivalent until specified. It requires a complement. Ezekiel already correlates between Joseph and Ephraim (Ezek 37:16, 19). The Pentateuch makes of Ephraim and Manasseh the "sons" of Joseph (Gen 41:51–52). How do the names Ephraim and Manasseh inform the appellation Joseph?

1.2 The Name Ephraim

The name Ephraim is derived from the Hebrew triliteral root *prh*, meaning to bear fruit, to be fruitful. This is indicated as such in Gen 41:52 and Hos 13:15. Thus, Ephraim would indicate fertile acres and pastureland. It is a rich domain. This can connote blessings, but it can, in the context of the prophetic diatribe against wealth, also connote apostasy.

1.3 The Name Manasseh

The name Manasseh is commonly derived from the Hebrew triliteral root *nšh*, meaning to forget. At the name giving of Manasseh in Gen 41:51 this is the meaning given, the form being read as a *piʿel* participle of this root, "to cause to forget." It is astounding that critical scholars and lexicons accept this explanation at face value. In practically every other instance involving etymological explanations in the Hebrew text, selfsame critical scholars dismiss the explanation given in the text as popular, or describe the passage as etiological. In this case, although formally the parsing of the form is correct, no consideration is made for the fact that, for a tribal patronym, this explanation leaves the reader in want of an etiologically convincing etymology. As a literary ploy, it would be definitely disingenuous. The passage is a very pregnant passage in the flow of the Joseph story. The names of Ephraim and Manasseh would be expected to impart a semantic weight to the name Joseph as he is set to embark on his major work, and in conjunction with the name of his wife and his father-in-law give a specific spin to the storyline. More on the function within the storyline will be discussed later below.

Useful towards investigating the possible etymology of Manasseh would be a wider view of the triliteral root. It is in fact a *lāmed yôd* root, *nšy*. From this root we also have the noun *nāšeh*, which, in conjunction with the word *gîd* (nerve, sinew) in Gen 32:23, is usually understood to refer to the sciatic nerve. In the same verse it is used also in conjunction with the hip joint, *kp hyrk*. The hip, *yrk*, is often a reference to the procreative region of the body. It is interesting to note that this verse relates to a weakness imparted to Jacob by the deity at the occasion of his being given the name Israel. Also apparently cognate with the root *nšy* is the noun *nāšîm*, the plural form used for *ʾššāh*, woman. One could conjecture that the topic relating that which pertains to women and procreation on the one hand and to forgetting on the other is the common motif in masculine dominated societies that preoccupation with women and procreation leads to forgetfulness.

Pertinent to the tribal etiological investigation of this question are two related passages in the book of Numbers, 27:1–11 and 36:1–12. Both are petitions by a prominent man of the tribe of Manasseh. Both are posed to Moses in view of the immediately following end of his work as far as the book of Numbers is concerned. It is amazing that the concern given expression to in these petitions is considered so vital as to have to be dealt with before the passing of Moses (Num 27:12–13)! It is also interesting that in both cases the tribe of Manasseh is invoked, and in the second case Joseph also is invoked, escalating the issue to become pertinent to the whole house of Joseph. The issue, as explained in the first passage, is the heritage of the tribe and its preservation. If a man dies and has no sons, then provision must be made for his inheritance to be preserved so that his memory/remembrance would not be lost. In this case the inheritance would fall to the daughters as adjudicated by Moses. The second passage follows up on this decision in order to prevent the loss of tribal territory. Since a daughter receiving her father's inheritance could marry outside the tribe, exogamy would lead to the loss of tribal territory. Moses adjudicates that in this case the daughters would be obligated to marry within the tribe in order to preserve the domain. The topics of remembrance, procreation, inheritance and preservation of domain all join together here. The commanding tribal figure is Manasseh. The significance affects the house of Joseph. This is all the more astounding when we take into account that it is usually through Ephraim that the invocation of Joseph occurs. We can conjecture that the Joseph tribes were wont to reject exogamy. They were a rich tribe, with fruitful pastures and fields, Ephraim! The tribal riches were to be preserved in the family. The domain had to be kept safe from intrusion. The patronym Manasseh would give expression to this practice in Joseph. It could be a compound of the preposition *min* (from), and either the expression "his women," or "his procreative sciatic sinews." This is a concern that occupied the mind of both Sarah and Rachel in the same book of Genesis from a feminine side of the fence. It could be a reference to the practice of endogamy in the tribes of Joseph. Having a rich domain, Ephraim, Joseph would need to protect it and assure a continuance of remembrance through endogamy, Manasseh.

This would give both a sociological etiology for the tribal patronym, as well as a more ingenuous literary construction by the redactor of the story. It has always been noticed that the explanation for the name given in Gen 41:51 is peculiar in that it indicates that the birth of the child will make Joseph forget not only all his tribulations, but also his father's house. Translations are proposed to mitigate this apparent problem.[1] If read with the above conjecture in mind, it becomes a very suggestive and foreboding text. That by which remembrance was to be achieved, progeny, will in the book of the Former Prophets lead to forgetfulness and oblivion. The riches of Solomon and his promiscuity will lead to the fall of his kingdom. The Northern Kingdom, basically Ephraim, will come to naught because of its preoccupation with its riches leading it to apostasy. King Manasseh, representing the concern of the Davidic kingdom to procure progeny and preserve the dynasty, is led by this concern to apostasy, dooming the Kingdom of Judah to destruction. That which was supposed to preserve one's remembrance, progeny, becomes a trap to apostasy, causing to forget the ordinances of the God of the fathers, 2 Kgs 21:2–16, and thus to total destruction.

1.4 The Question to Be Posed

The question to be posed at the end of this section becomes the following: If there is literary artifice in the use of the semantic weights implicit in the employment of appellations,

---

[1] Cf. Gerhard von Rad, *Genesis* (trans. J. H. Marks; rev. ed.; OTL; London: SCM, 1972), 379. Claus Westermann, *Genesis* 37–50 (trans. J. J. Scullion; London: SPCK, 1987), 97.

and if there is a double meaning intended by the redactor or redactors of this literature in both the use of Ephraim and of Manasseh as semantic weights informing the appellation Joseph, then what is the redactional design that can be deciphered behind this double-edged use of the appellation/type Joseph? In the following section there will be an expansion showing that there is a double liminal aspect to the character of Joseph in the story in the book of Genesis.[2]

2. An Attempt at Deciphering the Impact of Isa 40–55 on the Joseph Type

One of the most difficult tasks that face exegetes in dealing with Isa 40–55 is that it is very difficult to ascertain which passage speaks of the Servant, and which passage speaks of Jacob/Israel. Is the servant Israel, or does he/she stand opposite and in contrast to Israel? In no other work does this confront us as such and in a totally analogous manner, as it does in the Joseph story. Is Joseph Jacob, or does he stand opposite and in contrast to Jacob? The passages can be easily sorted out, but the situation is the same. Joseph functions as a liminal figure between Jacob and God. He also functions as a liminal figure between Jacob and Pharaoh. The double ambivalence of his person leads also to confounding the visage of Pharaoh with that of God. They share after all the same polar position opposite to that of Jacob through the superposition of the double liminal functions of Joseph, much as the functional roles of the God of the servant and Cyrus appear to become confused. In fact the literary subtlety of the Joseph story in the book of Genesis is often more difficult to fathom than the apparently confounding passages of Isa 40–55. This happens due to the assumption often taken that it is a naive straightforward story compiled from two

---

2 In the original write-up, the exposition and analysis of Isa 40–55 was intercalated here before the following expansion on Joseph. At the latest at this point, the reader should read and have in mind, if not already done, Chapter 1: Analytical Reading of Isaiah 40–55 as the parable of Abraham and Sarah and its Reenactment in Genesis 32.

sources, and its function is simply that of transitional comic relief providing cover for changing stage props. An attempt will be made in the following to elucidate the centrality of the function of the story, the transformation of the character type Joseph that is worked by the story flow, the subtlety of the interchange of character roles that enter into play, the dramatic complexity of the characters and the multiplicity of ambivalent connotations that the motifs in the story take on. An attempt will be done to show that this process in the story runs parallel to the redactional framework deciphered above[3] in Isa 40–55, not in sequence, but in function and inferred redactional situation. The question of literary priority will be posed and answered, as the title of this paper indicates, in terms of the impact of Isa 40–55 on the transformation of the type Joseph effected by means of the story in Genesis.

2.1 Joseph and the tôlēdôt of Jacob

At the beginning of the story in Genesis Joseph is equivalent to the Jacob who has it made. He is expressive of the penultimate increase that Jacob has achieved. The story of Joseph is introduced as the *tôlēdôt* (generations) of Jacob, the story incorporating/unfolding what Jacob has done. It is the story of what was born of the actions of Jacob. The Hebrew word is derived from the root *yld* (to give birth). Its use is very distinct in the Pentateuch. It is different from the question of giving birth to children, with which it is often confused. The translation of the word *tôlēdôt* as "generation," "genealogical table," "progeny" are all wrong. In the Pentateuch it means the resultant developments from the actions of the subject of the action. Whereas God works his actions by addressing with his word, the actions distinct from his actions are portrayed as a deterministic series of engendering, analogous to the mythological depiction of deities and their actions in ancient mythological stories. For example, God creates in Gen 1 with

---

3 Cf. Chapter 1.

his word, but in 2:4 we are told, at the beginning of the Yahwist report, that we are going to hear about the *tôlēdôt* of the heavens and earth on the day God had created them. Thereupon it is insisted in verse 5 that God had not begun to function as supplier of the life giving waters, the heavens and earth are left to their own devices. There follows a lengthy parenthesis, in a mythological figurative language, about the setting of Adam and Eve in the garden of Eden, indicating God's intention in the matter; whereupon, instead of God's intention coming to fruition, the serpent in concert with Adam and Eve disrupt those intentions. Parallel to the perfection of God's work in 1:1–2:3, another track of action, disruptive of the first is introduced by the word *tôlēdôt* in 2:4. The Yahwist "creation story" is in fact not a creation story, but the story of the inception of evil into the created order, known from the Epic of Gilgamesh. Another example is the mention of "the *tôlēdôt* of Aaron and Moses" in Exod 3:1. It is manifestly impossible that the reference would be to a common engendering of progeny by Aaron and Moses! What follows, in fact, is the setting up of the levitical office, expressed as a lineage. The redactor of the Pentateuch is eminently opposed to the priestly and levitical office as it developed as a prerogative and a lineage derived from Aaron and apparently endorsed by Moses.[4] In this case, *tôlēdôt* indicates an undesired development due to the misappropriation of Moses by a group claiming their lineage from Aaron. The other Moses, opposed to this Moses, will be the Moses of Joshua, who will not have a *tôlēdôt*, but more on this later. A third example is that of Abraham. He gives birth to many children, but no *tôlēdôt* is mentioned for him. His work is

---

4 Cf. Paul Nadim Tarazi, "The Book of Jeremiah and the Pentateuchal Torah," in *Sacred Text and Interpretation: Perspectives in Orthodox Biblical Studies* (ed. Theodore G. Stylianopoulos; Brookline, Mass.: Holy Cross Orthodox Press, 2006), 7–36.

considered God's work, and consequently ascribed to the first track, God's creation in Gen 1.[5]

2.1.1 The Name Benjamin as a Motif in the Jacob Story

The name Benjamin, like the name Israel[6], must also be deduced from the cognate Semitic usage. It could simply mean "son/sons of the South." Alternately it could mean "son/sons of the right hand." The Arabic root *ymn* indicates good fortune, in the sense of having the upper hand. One could conjecture that it implies a warrior clan, in the sense of those wielding power by means of a mighty right hand/arm. This would fit in well with the biblical stories about Benjamin. As such it would stand disjunct from the term Israel if the last is derived from the Arabic *ysr* "left hand/easy street."[7] Benjamin would be the warrior class, on top of it all, claiming power and kingship. Israel would be the merchant and clerical class, following (as in the name Jacob)[8], servicing and subjacent to the warrior class. While in Israel the introduction of the kingship is a huge problem in the biblical literature, it is the Benjaminite Saul who becomes the first king in Israel.

A very interesting case in the story line we are trying to decipher is the sequence of the giving of the name Israel to Jacob in Gen 32 and the birth and naming of Benjamin in Gen 35. The following are excerpts from the conclusions drawn above in chapter 1, section 3.4 regarding the giving of the name Israel to Jacob:

> The story of Jacob in Gen 32 comes as the culmination of his exorbitant increase, symbolized by the birth of Joseph, on the eve of his return to the land where his fathers sojourned. It is

---

5 For an analysis which has points both of convergence and divergence from the one given in this paragraph, cf. Paul Nadim Tarazi, *Genesis: A Commentary* (The Chrysostom Bible; St Paul, Minn.: OCABS Press, 2009), 27–89, 173–181.
6 Cf. Section 3.2 in chapter 1.
7 Ibid.
8 Cf. Section 3.1 in chapter 1.

equivalent to the situation of Jacob/Israel at the end of the Pentateuch, with Moses looking across the Jordan to the promised land. Jacob in Gen 32 paradigmatically does what is required in order to be granted access to the land, and consequently to have the name Israel bestowed upon him.

In this pericope Jacob is the servant of Isa 50–55:

> He first makes himself bare of all that appertains to him of wealth and children, (Joseph emblematically being the last one to be let go off. . .). Then he stands alone with the faceless and nameless figure of the deity, taking all blows from God and man, and remaining till the early hours of the morning, not releasing nor rejecting the deity until he is blessed by this deity and morning dawns. His "flag" remained up all through the night, enduring all the blows, not relenting to despair, and so he "earned" the title "Israel." The land, represented by his brother Esau/Edom, opens up to him. This is the work of the servant in Isa 50–55 standing opposite to that of Jacob in 40–49. Gen 32 expresses the imaginary time of the deity of the redactor of this text, his unrealized wish as expressed in Isa 40–55. . . .
>
> As fates would have it here, determined by the redactor, this is made possible for Jacob because Benjamin has not yet been born to him. He still does not have a warrior clan. . . . Our writer, after all, wishes to understand the name Israel in this pericope as derived from *śrh*, as indicating becoming intimate of the deity and initiate into the realm of God (in other words he proved himself into the realm, not as over and above God). God, the stranger who jumps him and has the upper hand, will function as his strongman and as his king, again exactly as in Isa 40–55. The inductee will function as subject to and under the protection of the inducting stranger/deity. This is why he insists on receiving the blessing from the stranger, and names the locale as the locale of the meeting with the faceless deity and surviving. It was not by his strength that he passed the test, but by his holding on to the stranger and sustaining all the bruising from God and men. Hosea will understand it as repentance to God, as weeping and entreating the deity (Hos 12: 5), thus becoming proven, and

making the Jacob clan the addressee of God and recipient of His word.[9]

After the reception of Jacob in the land in Gen 33, both by his brother Esau, and the "nations" in the Shechem area, we have the beginning of the story of the collapse of Jacob in Gen 34–35. It starts with the sin of Simeon and Levi (Gen 34), who manage to both break the covenant of Abraham, and the concomitant harmony with the nations (represented here by the Shechemites) promised by the covenant. The covenant is dented. Jacob is reminded by God of the covenant and told to go to Bethel (35:1–15). The place has become a place for weeping, for repentance (v. 8). Just as the Jacob company get back on the way to the prospect of a fruitful abode, Ephrath, Rachel gives birth to Benjamin. Jacob takes it as good news, but Rachel has a premonition that it forebodes ill. She calls him "Ben-oni" from the Hebrew ʾwn. This can have one of two meanings which appear to be opposite. The context is usually used to determine the choice of translation. The range of possible translations comprises "sorrow," "undoing," "iniquity," "strength." In Arabic the cognate roots ʾww, ʾwn, ʾwh have the same range of meaning[10]. One could paraphrase this range as including disaster and its resultant grief, as well as the power or mischief which inflicts it. In the passage in Hosea we have seen, Hos 12:4–5, it indicates the coming of Jacob to the full vigor and strength of manhood. The context in Gen 35:18–19, in conjunction with Rachel expiring and dying, indicates that Ben-oni is foreboding of ill to come, and the expiry of Jacob's good time with Rachel, for whom he labored so much. Jacob is oblivious to all that, and revels in acquiring a warrior troop. Rachel is buried in Bethlehem, the house of

---

9 The two preceding paragraphs resume what was expanded upon in section 3 of chapter 1, repeating the conclusions as formulated in section 3.4.
10 Cf. Edward William Lane, *An Arabic-English Lexicon* (London: Williams & Norgate, 1863), 123, 129–131.

Bread. In the Joseph story Jacob will not have bread again until he loses Benjamin.

Before we can leave this cycle of the collapse of Jacob, the redactor will give us the "fortuitous" report about Reuben's sin with his father's concubine. The eldest recapitulates the sins of Jacob/Jacob's sons.[11] Jacob now is at full "strength." The twelve sons are listed just before we embark on the Joseph story.

2.1.2 The Name of Simeon as a Motif in the Storyline

In the Joseph cycle we hear that Jacob had to lose Simeon after he had lost Joseph and before finally being asked to lose Benjamin (Gen 42:36). He progressively has to do here by force what he had done by choice in Gen 32 in order to enter the land. But why is Simeon singled out alongside Joseph and Benjamin? Simeon is very enigmatic. He is very recessive in the texts we have except in chapter 34 where in conjunction with Levi he becomes uncharacteristically and unexpectedly aggressive. The name comes from the common Semitic root $šm^c$ (to hear). As was hinted at in section 2.2.2 of chapter 1, the suggested translation being proposed here is: "title to mandate obedience/a domain where one has the say." To hear is to obey in the Semitic usage.[12] The triliteral root here is construed as attached to the third person masculine plural suffixed pronoun in its late Aramaic form[13] functioning as object complement.

---

[11] Cf. Ezek 33:24–29 where the sin of the Israelites precluding salvation is summarized as violence and adultery. The passage, as analyzed in chapter 1, section 2.2.2, is apparently a gloss echoing the teaching of Isa 40–55, and responding to an objection provoked by Isa 51:1–8. The two aspects of the sin are indicated in Isa 40–55 by the repeated use of the one root $pš^c$ (meaning to transgress, go out of line, both in the political and in the sexual sense) as a verbal form (43:27; 46: 8; 48:8; 53:12 twice) and as a noun (43:25; 44:22; 50:1; 53:5, 8).

[12] Cf. Kamal Abou-Chaar, "The Two Builders: A Study of the Parable in Luke 6:47–49," *Near East School of Theology Theological Review* 1 (1982): 44–58. Paragraph II.B is relevant to the statement above.

[13] Cf. Stanislav Segert, *Altaramäische Grammatik* (Leipzig: VEB, 1975), 107 Paragraph 3.7.1.2.

Thus it would indicate the domain where "their" word would have regal power, the place where obedience is accorded to what "they" broadcast, to that which is heard from "them." This may seem stretched, but three different instances of its usage will illustrate that this, in fact, is the redactional role it plays in the Pentateuch and the books of the Former Prophets.

- In Gen 34, the semantic conjunction of Simeon with Levi leaves us with Levi wielding the sword, applying his rule, and thereby usurping the mandate of Jacob, and breaking the Abrahamic covenant. Levi effectively claims to rule, and make his word stand by force.

- In the books of the Former Prophets, when Judah has the kingship, Simeon's territory is subsumed under that of Judah.

- The most telling proof/application of this rule is in the blessings of Moses at the end of the book of Deuteronomy. In the course of Deut 32–33, encompassing the song/curses of Moses (32) and the blessings of Moses (33), we have thrice (32:15; 33:5, 26) the use of the word $yšrn$ (Jeshurun). These instances, together with the use in Isa 44:2 are the only instances of this word in Scripture. As was shown in section 2.2.1 of chapter 1, it functions as a conditional clause applied as an epithet to Jacob, to the effect that what is predicated as blessings is conditional on the fulfillment of this condition, the condition being that Jacob function uprightly. The situation that must exist for this to be the case is given in Deut 33:5. In the imaginary time of Deut 33 the situation is defined by the reign of God as King in Jacob "and He (God) was King in Jeshurun, when the heads gathered of a united people, the tribes of Israel" (v. 5 my translation, similarly the RSV, whereas the NRSV goes its own way here). The point is that for the blessings to be effective, God must be King in Jacob/Israel. The eschatological oneness envisaged in Ezek 37:19, and the condition set in Isa 44:2 as well as all of Isa 40–49 are both invoked here. What is amazing is that there is no mention of Simeon in the blessings bracketed by the use of the appellation Jeshurun in 33:5, 26. When God is King, Jacob does not have the regal say, the semantic quantity Simeon does not appertain to Jacob/Israel.

In the Joseph story, Simeon must be withheld from Jacob when Joseph has the say, both in the name of Pharaoh, and in the name of God. The regal word to which obedience is mandated is in the hands of Joseph. It is sequestered by Joseph.

2.2 Joseph the Dreamer and the Hidden Redactor/Servant of Isa 40–55

As we saw in chapter 1, section 2.2.1, God in Isa 40–55 is described as hidden (45:15), and consequently faceless. He is manifest in his words declared through the redactor/prophet. In the Joseph story the reader immediately gets the impression that the storyline is somehow different in texture from the other sequences in the Pentateuch. God does not appear except by mediation and inference. Dream interpretation becomes in the Joseph story the major vehicle carrying forward the storyline (cf. chapter 1, section 2.2.2). The suspicion arises that it is possibly a borrowed "secular" moralizing story. Attempts have been made to find an Egyptian wisdom story origin for it,[14] which could be a possibility. What adds to the "flat" impression, given the very mythological character of the other Pentateuchal cycles, is that Joseph actually does nothing, at least not in the first part of the story, other than report dreams and their

---

14 Cf. Von Rad, *Genesis*, 433–40.

translation. He is totally overwhelmed by the storyline and the other characters, and becomes in what befalls him the proxy for the functioning of God's will.

In fact, the communication to him in dreams corresponds to the training in secret of the servant by the deity in Isa 40–55 (49:2). He appears uncannily to be how people would look on and behold the redactor/servant in Isa 40–55. The representation of the Joseph character easily corresponds to a biography or autobiography of the redactor of Isa 40–55, who identifies his message with that of God, and whose person seems often to be interchangeable with that of the servant. For this reason, I prefer to take the dream motif together with the motif of the *Deus Absconditus* in the Joseph story as a reply to the sarcasm and rejection faced by the redactor of Isa 40–55. He presented a preaching claiming that it is divine, against all what appeared to be common sense. He would have been put down as a dreamer (cf. chapter 1, section 2.2.2 and the comment on the word *ḥallāmîŝ* in Isa 50:7). The response in the Joseph story takes up on the derisive taunt. Joseph's brothers call him a "*baal* (used here in the sense of 'an espouser of') of dreams," meaning a daydreamer (Gen 37:19). Yes, indeed, comes the response, he is an exact scientist as far as dreams are concerned, and his dream interpretation never fails to come true!

2.3 Analysis of the Dramatic Flow of the Joseph Story (Gen 37–50)

The name Joseph is derived from the Hebrew triliteral root *ysp* (to add, increase). As we saw above (section 1), the semantic filling of this appellation are the "engendered" Ephraim and Manasseh, the fullness of acquired wealthy fruitful estates as well as progeny through whom one will be remembered. This is the situation of Jacob at the beginning of the Joseph story. Joseph is the alter ego of Jacob. As the story evolves they will go two different ways, Jacob will still end up like the initial Joseph, after undergoing a peripeteia that "doubles up" on itself. The peripeteia of Joseph will undergo a very different and more complex development. At the end Joseph will not be "Joseph" as at the beginning. He will acquire as a result of his double liminal role both the aspect of Pharaoh, and that of God/God's servant. Jacob will be Jacob, but Joseph will not be Joseph.

2.3.1 Chapter 37: Joseph is Jacob at the Outset of the Story

The initial chapter (37) introduces the "inside" story on the real Jacob. The subtlety of the story telling which carries a double-edged connotation throughout should not be overlooked because of what appears to be a straightforward storyline. Joseph at the outset is seventeen years old. He is not yet of full age to be in the company of his "full-blown" brothers. He is still in the company of the children of the servant "brides" of Jacob. This will also be the "age" of the stay of Jacob in Egypt. We will be told that he will die in Egypt seventeen years after his entry into that land (Gen 47:28). He will be technically in the servant quarters of the Egyptians, his aspiration to have a "house" of his own still unrealized. This is the situation at the outset. The story will relocate Jacob to Egypt, thereby "correcting" the initial mistake of the positing of Jacob on what appeared to be his own ground. This corrective transposition is the only change that is effected by the storyline on the character of Jacob. The story of Joseph is in fact the story of the revelation of the character of Jacob's story, whereby God allies his position to that of Pharaoh, as happens in the books of the prophets generally (compare the function of Nebuchadnezzar in Jeremiah, Cyrus in Isaiah 40–55). This is the exact perspective of Isa 40–55.

The aspiration to kingship in Jacob is reflected in the presentation of Joseph. He is a shepherd, the traditional description of a king. The mysterious piece of clothing supplied to him by Jacob is described in the only other use of it in 2 Sam 13:18–19 as "how the virgin daughters of the king were clothed in earlier times." He dreams of becoming king over his brothers. An obscure statement in verse 2 is interesting in this regard. This is usually translated similarly to what we have in the NRSV, "he was a helper to the sons of Bilhah and Zilpah, his father's wives; and Joseph brought a bad report of them to their father." The root of the name Bilhah, *blh*, refers to becoming worn out, corrupt. The root of the name Zilpah, which we do not have in the Hebrew scriptures, means in Arabic to be obsequious, to put on airs, to try to overtake or take in. These credentials already tell a story. What is most strange is the clause translated as "brought a bad report of them to their father." It stands absolutely without follow-up. It could be explanatory of the import of the names of Bilhah and Zilpah, "bad news." But Joseph is described as "bringing into their father's house" this bad news. He is actively subject of the action which lands the bad news inside the house of Jacob. Wealth and progeny have introduced bad news into Jacob's house. The epithet "bad" actually comes appositive to "rumor/news," "Joseph brought rumor, a bad thing, into their father's house." Given the imagery of shepherd/king in this passage, it is important to note that in Hebrew there is full consonance between the word shepherd, *r'h*, and the word translated as a bad thing, *r'h*. Only the vocalization differentiates between them. The aspired for kingship is a bad thing. The same clause can be parsed differently if we take only the unpointed Hebrew text. We can read "Joseph entered with a full-grown bear/beast (*db tm*), a bad thing, into their father's house." This would be a variation on the motif of the aspiring kingly lad killing the beast as title to assuming the throne. The result is the same. In this case the "bad news" becomes the "bad news bear/beast."

The ensuing dreams have a climactic structure. The first indicates that Joseph will reign over his brothers. The second makes him over and above Jacob and Rachel as well as his brothers. This second dream is the first sign of a divorce between Jacob and Joseph, which will be consummated by the end of the story. At this point it is kept in the "hidden" remembrance of Jacob, a premonition of things to come.

His father sends him to see "how goes"/how things are going with his elder brothers, literally "looking for the peace (*šālôm*) of his brothers." They are not where they are supposed to be in the open city of Shechem, but in Dothan. In the Hebrew we have this location mentioned only one other time in 2 Kgs 6:13. The story of Elisha there wraps the locale in an aura of a secret hideout. The forces waiting to assist Elisha are invisible, hidden from sight. A derivation from Aramaic would support this. The term *dt* in Aramaic means decree/law. It is used in the Hebrew and Aramaic parts of the book of Esther, and in the Aramaic parts of the book of Daniel. The name Dothan can be parsed in Aramaic as "their law." It would indicate an outlaw hideout. The activity of the brothers is described as shepherding. The locale can be understood as a clandestine center for the organization of an insurgency. Both the mission of Joseph and that of his brothers would be to achieve "peace" by means of an armed rebellion/insurgency. Joseph, after all, is described in the same terms as Saul the Benjaminite is described in 1 Sam 9:1–5, a comely lad sent in search of a donkey/kingdom, wandering and lost in the regions of Ephraim.

The duality of the roles of Reuben and of Judah interjected into the storyline is often taken as an indication of two divergent source documents[15]. In fact Reuben functions here in lieu of Joseph/Ephraim since Joseph is tied down to another role at this point of the story. Ephraim/Samaria, represented here by Reuben, had hoped to hoard the wealth in its wells (cf. books of Hosea and Amos), Judah sells out (Ezek 16:33). The sale is to the Ishmaelites/Midianites. The kingly way is that of the Ishmaelites (which means "God will hear"). This is an indication that God will redirect the intended treachery to his

---

15 Cf. Westermann, *Genesis* 37–50, 19–20, 31–45, for a concise overview of the source critical question and the various proposals that have been made for and against it, as well as his analysis of ch. 37.

own end, as we will hear in 50:20. The term Midian/Midianites derives from the same root, *dîn*, as judgment/to judge. Those who did perform the treachery nevertheless stand under judgment.

The last passage in this chapter, vv. 31–36, sets the tone for this whole cycle from the point of view of the deity, the divine track. Reuben, aptly the first born, has already expressed the anguish that the treachery will have brought to naught the whole house of Jacob (v. 30). The cover-up in vv. 31–36 proves very revealing. The coat of Joseph is dripped in the blood of a he-goat, *śʿîr*. This is the term used in Lev 16 for the scapegoat, the living goat who is dispatched into the wilderness as a sin offering. Joseph is installed into a new office, that of the scapegoat, an office otherwise shared only by the servant of Isa 53.[16] The Joseph story goes on to highlight this scapegoat function in v. 36. Joseph is taken to the head executioner/slaughterer. (This is the derivation of the Hebrew term usually translated as head cook or head of the guard.) The designation is derived from the Hebrew root *ṭbḥ* (to slaughter). Jeremiah also is taken by the chief slaughterer/executioner Nebuzaradan together with all the people of Judah (Jer 40:1ff). The motif, as applied to an individual, is a reproduction of Isa 53:5–7, where the noun *ṭbḥ* (slaughter) is used, together with the expiatory function for the servant. The servant is described as a

---

[16] A careful reading of Lev 16 will show that in fact the living offering of the scapegoat one-ups the service of Aaron in the temple on the Day of Atonement. He is let loose for Azazel. In addition to atoning for the sins of the people, which Aaron carries out for his own and the people's sin, this goat also does it for Azazel. This name is not used in this text as a name for the goat, which could then have meant scapegoat literally from the combination of *ʿz* (goat) and *ʾl* (go away/disappear), but as the locale/end for which he is sent, this being "for the greatness of God," derived from the Hebrew and Arabic root *ʿz/ʿzz*. The scapegoat in Lev 16 is reinterpreted, in the sense of Isa 53, and used as an introduction to the Holiness Code, which spells out the conditions for a return and redemption of the land. Compare this with what Joseph says to his brothers in the concluding part of his story in Gen 50:20: "Even though you intended to do harm to me, God intended it for good, in order to preserve a numerous people, as he is doing today" (NRSV).

sheep/goat led to the slaughter because of the transgressions of the people.[17] Joseph starts to become the servant of Isa 40–55.

2.3.2 Chapter 38: Judah as Jacob

Chapter 38 introduces the implement needed for the ultimate transformation of Joseph which will be employed later in the story. The terms used and the framework of the situation presented is a legal proceeding, or a series thereof. The Adullamite functions as a sort of judge or public notary. The name Adullamite/someone from Adullam can be derived from either the Akkadian or the Arabic usage. As a semantic weight within this chapter only one comes into question, the Arabic root, ʿdl, meaning to be just/to administer justice. His name, Hirah, if derived from the Hebrew ḥûr would indicate whiteness, or white linen. This could be an indication of office. The name of the father of Judah's bride is Shua, which is actually the Hebrew root šwʿ. This is a difficult root to analyze. From it we have the name Joshua/Jesus. The usages of this triliteral in the texts we have are mainly in the meaning "cry for help." This is more often than not in the sense of a legal plaint[18]. The other use is to denote a highly placed person. If we combine these usages, we could see a common topic in the English expression "to raise a court case." A legal plaint to be presented as such must be presented to a high-positioned tribunal. While the plaint more often than not would be that of lowly people, those who are highly positioned would have their case more readily access the tribunal and be adjudicated. The verbal use of šwʿ indicates "raising" a plaint. The noun from the same triliteral indicates someone or something in a raised public position, cf. Job 34:19; Isa 22:5; 32:5.

The proceeding involves the plaint mainly of Tamar. She proves to be righteous (v. 26), whereas Judah proves to be a liar in the matter of not holding to the obligation of his son Shelah.

---

17 Cf. chapter 1, section 2.2.2.
18 J. Hausmann, "šwʿ," TDOT, 14:532–36.

Shelah, in fact, is said to be born in Chezib (v. 5), which is derived from the Hebrew *kzb* (to tell a lie). The obligation not met by Judah is that of the levirate law. This is introduced here for the first time by way of the story. But why do we have this protocol of this proceeding at this point in the story of Joseph? I believe the reason is that it lays bare the legal implications of the adoption of Ephraim and Manasseh by Jacob which is so essential for the outcome of the Joseph story. The importance of this motif is underlined by its recurrence in a third variant in Gen 42:37. Reuben requests from his father Jacob that he hand over Benjamin to be taken to Egypt so that the sons of Jacob would get audience in Egypt and be able to purchase wheat. As collateral he offers him his two sons to kill should ill befall Benjamin! The trade in the two firstborn sons in the house of Jacob seems to be endemic. Judah defrauds not only Tamar. He defrauds his first son Er by failing to honor the levirate obligation to provide surrogate sons for him, who, had they been born of Shelah, would legally belong to the house of Er. Onan refused to honor the obligation because he construed it as pure loss with no return for him. The restitution made by Jacob to Tamar is restricted to Tamar. She gains entry into the house of Judah. But the end effect is that Judah has stolen the progeny of Er. He adopts legally the sons of Tamar thereby establishing his own house. Had this been possible to Onan he would hardly have refused. Effectively, Judah legally "uploads" the twin sons of Er to himself. Later in the Joseph story Jacob legally "uploads" the sons of Joseph to himself, thereby "stealing" the sons of Joseph. The offer of Reuben to have his sons killed shows that the matter from his point of view is not benign, but is "murder." Anyhow, the deity of the writer of the passage has already applied the capital punishment on Onan for this crime. The question of the adoption of Ephraim and Manasseh later on in the story is not a moot legal argument to establish the right of the Joseph tribes to two portions of heritage. One hardly needs to take Joseph to Egypt for that. The storyline is not arguing apportionment, it is telling of the dispossession of Joseph. If the text were making reference to David in the person of Judah, as is often suggested, then it would be to the David going after his sons to kill them, not the ascendency to the throne. This chapter is placed here to prepare for the divorce in progress between the role of Jacob and that of Joseph.[19]

2.3.3 Chapter 39: Joseph and Isaac

The dispossession of Joseph is still in progress in chapter 39. Not only was he treacherously sold out in the house of Jacob. He is treacherously dealt with among the nations. Initially he is still very comely we are told, "Now Joseph was handsome and good-looking" (v. 6 NRSV), exactly like his mother Rachel (29:17). He is not yet like the servant of Isa 52:14; 53:2. Here we have a further episode of his denudation. Graphically he will leave his garment in the hand of the Egyptian lady and run (Gen 39:12). We had already seen his brothers strip him of his kingly robe and throw him into the pit (37:23–24). Here he will be thrown into Pharaoh's prison (39:20).

A very indicative trait in this passage is the use in 39:14, 17 of the verb *ṣhq* (in the *pi'el* form), translated in the NRSV as "to insult," but explained in the text as "He came in to lie with me." This is the root from which we have the name of Isaac (in the *qal* form). The suggested (and possible) translations of this verbal root in the Pentateuch try to mitigate the verbal action implied in the *pi'el* form. All give an aspect of the triliteral *ṣhq*. Lexically the triliteral can indicate in the *qal* form "to smile," "to laugh"; in the *pi'el* form "to grievously insult/mock," "to revel," "to crush," "to engage sexually." The last three come closest to

---

[19] The name of Perez, Judah's son from Tamar is also indicative. He has already doubled up like Jacob on his twin brother coming out of the womb. His name derives from *prṣ* (to make a breach/break out). In this it is similar to *pš'* (to transgress/go out of line). In conjunction with his mother's name, Tamar (derived from *tmr*, meaning fruit, especially of the date palm), Perez parallels an aspect of the name Ephraim, from *prh*, (in the sense of to break out as a fruit or shoot). Perez stands in a line of scion upstarts on the line of both Adam and, here, specifically Judah as Jacob.

explaining the use that we have in the scriptural passages, and that we have in Arabic. What we have initially (Gen 17:17; 18:12, 13, 15) and at the naming of Isaac (Gen 21) is the benign qal form. Matters quickly take on morbid overtones with the use of the *pi'el* form in the following. Sarah herself is taken aback in Gen 21:9 seeing Ishmael exercise this verbal action. (Please note that there is no mention of his practicing this action on Isaac as the NRSV would suggest.) It is used as it is usually used in the absolute, without a complement. As a result Sarah demands that Hagar and Ishmael be dispatched out of the territory of her son Isaac. Already in Gen 19:14 we are given a premonition of the possible implications attached to this verbal action. Lot is perceived by his prospective sons-in-law as someone who is putting on airs of embarking on this verbal action, and his call to leave the city is disregarded by them. This misconception on their part follows on his statement to them saying: "Up, get out of this place; for the Lord is about to destroy the city." (NRSV). This scene unfolds in Sodom. In the story of Samson, when the Philistines bring the blinded Samson out of prison to have him perform this action, he does so for them (Judg 16:25, 27).[20] Thereupon he is made to stand between the pillars of their temple, just before he brings the house literally down on them and on himself.

The most telling usage is in Exod 32:6, the day after the festivities around the golden calf with Aaron joining in, "They

---

[20] In this passage of the book of Judges, two forms of this verb are used: *šḥq* (with *ṣādê*) and *śḥq* (with *śîn*). In the Pentateuch, both for the general use of the verb and the name of Isaac the form with *ṣādê* is employed. In DH, for the general use of the verb the form with *śîn* is employed while for the name of Isaac the form with *ṣādê* is employed. The one exception in DH is in the passage of Judges in question. In Judg 16:25. 27, two instances of the verb employ the form with *śîn* (once *pi'el* and once qal) while one instance of the verb (*pi'el*) uses the form with *ṣādê*. There appears to be intent to invoke the connection with Isaac. The usage in DH is replicated in the books of the Latter Prophets and the third part of the canon. One exception to this is the use of the verbal noun in Ezek 23:32 with *ṣādê* (the only time that this root is used in either form or spelling in Ezekiel). Further, in three cases (Ps 105:9; Jer 33:26; Amos 7:9, 16) we encounter the name Isaac spelled with *śîn*. In chapter 3, section 2.6, this diverse use is discussed in detail in an excursus.

rose early the next day, and offered burnt offerings and brought sacrifices of well-being; and the people sat down to eat and drink, and arose up to revel (*lshq*)." (NRSV). What appears innocuous as the last word in this passage is precisely the verbal action at issue. It seems to sum up all their sin for the redactor, who has God tell Moses to reject the people; they can no longer be a vehicle for his actions. The "Isaac" action appears to be an impossible action for God's track to continue. It is a total dead end. In the ensuing passages Moses prevails on God to put a hold on total dismissal. God has to come up with a solution to deal with this impasse. He decrees that he cannot remain in the Israelite camp without destroying it. He sets up a separate camp, a tent outside, and now we have two encampments, one for God and one for Israel. The divorce is the sine qua non for the non-destruction of the people. Moses will act as the go-between between the two camps. He brings the plaint of the people to the tent of God, and returns to the people with God's communication. The book of Moses will be the only access the people will have to this deity. Just by way of a casual closing remark we are informed that Joshua son of Nun would remain 24/7 inside the tent of God's tabernacle. Moses himself would come only for a brief stay, but Joshua is at home with the Ark of the Covenant containing the redone tablets of the Ten Commandments. It is not Moses, but the Moses of Joshua that is addressed to the people gathered together with Aaron in their own sinful camp. Joshua son of Nun is in God's camp, hidden in God's tent, just like the servant of Isa 40–55. We have now two conflicting tracks: Jacob in one camp, Joshua, the servant of Moses, in the other. We will come back to this later, to see how the fully transformed Joseph will fit into this.

Now, why must Joseph not be an Isaac in chapter 39, why must he not perform the "Isaac" action? We need to take another look at the Isaac story. Abraham and Sarah laugh at the suggestion that Sarah can have a biological child. They are not on God's line of thought. God's announcement to Abraham is that he will procure for him a child from Sarah. He will address the problem of Sarah's barrenness, just as later he will address the problem of Rachel's barrenness. From God's point of view this is an "unnatural" development, implicating the agency of God. In this he sees the reality of the situation as clearly as Abraham and Sarah. The point for God is that this "unnatural" development will bring Abraham and Sarah about to his line of thought regarding the promise, the line of action he addressed to Abram changing his name to Abraham. Sarah continues to have one thing on her mind, a natural biological son who will vindicate her. The agency is incidental to the result. When Ishmael set about to do the "Isaac thing" within the domain she thought would be her own, she forces Abraham to send Ishmael away. She does not want Ishmael to be a co-heir with her son Isaac. Abraham is distressed, after all both Isaac and Ishmael are natural sons for him. A tug of war develops between Sarah and God. The promise given to Abram was to change his function and make him the father of the sacrificial *rahām*. Until there is a *rahām* Abraham has not become Abraham.[21] In Gen 22 there is an attempt to make of Isaac a *rahām*. But with everyone apprehensive about the fate of Isaac lest Abraham should lose his "new found" domain, including the reader of the story today, Isaac is decommissioned at the last minute, and a temporary substitute is found. That a disjuncture is incumbent semantically which would maintain Abraham and God's promise within God's domain eludes most readers. The redactor has this disjuncture built into Isaac's name. Because he is an Isaac, he cannot be a *rahām*. Abram/Abraham's status of being on/expressive of God's line of thought, God's track, is still conditional, semantically, on a *rahām* being found to consummate his change of name. In fact we will only have an Abraham after we have a *rahām*. By accepting to return his domain to God in Gen 22, Abraham acquits himself of the "Isaac" action that he did, albeit in the benign *qal* form, when he "fell on his face and laughed" in Gen 17:17 (as Sarah also

---

21 Cf. chapter 1, section 2.2.2.

does in 18:12, 13, 15; 21:6). Only as a result of the Abraham domain being effectively returned to God's domain is the promise and covenant reinstated in Gen 22:16–18.

Isaac, on the other hand, is now free to go his own way. He has been decommissioned. He will go the way of all Adam. In Gen 26:8 he does the "Isaac" action with his wife. This is a rare instance of the verb *ṣḥq* being used with a complement. Abimelech sees them, and in 26:16 he decides, like Sarah in Gen 21, that this is too much for him. It constitutes too much of a threat to his domain, and he requests that Isaac leave his domain. As such, the "Isaac action" seems to imply to set up one's domain/territory in such a way that it is delimited from that of anyone else. The delimitation functions equally as regards other men, as in the case of Ishmael and Abimelech, as well as regards the deity. Concomitant with doing the "Isaac action" is the generation of one's own story/history of implicated developments. In the Pentateuch this is expressed as *tôlēdôt* (generations). Sure enough, before Isaac does "his thing" the passage is introduced in 25:19 as the *tôlēdôt* of Isaac. Isaac will now have a story like Ishmael. Indeed the *tôlēdôt* of Ishmael immediately precede those of Isaac. Isaac's sons will each have a *tôlēdôt*. Esau/Edom functions as Adam redux. Jacob recapitulates the sins of all Adam. This is the content/teaching of Isa 40–49, the sins of the nations and of Jacob. With Esau and Jacob we are back to the story as before the intervention of God with Abram. Abraham on the other hand, in spite of all the sons he will have, (he is after all the father of many nations), will not have a *tôlēdôt*. In fact we are told in Gen 25:5 that he gave all he had to Isaac. He has passed on the abundance of God's blessings to Isaac, but he has also thereby left himself without a domain. His domain is coextensive with a multitude of nations, similarly to Adam, but in function of God's promise/God's domain. His parable can only be continued within God's line of thought. The agency of God is incumbent on the continuation of Abraham's story, and this entails that Abraham should not have a domain of his own. His story started after all as a call to leave his father's house in total measure. The domain of God cannot be but God's domain. God is God. The parable of Abraham, the storyline of God's work, will continue/be defined when a *rahām* is found. Joseph in Gen 39, while in the "natural" line of Isaac, does not do the "Isaac" action. He still has a foot in Jacob's camp, but the other foot is getting further away. The denudation is still in progress, the denouement is still ahead in the Joseph story. The *rahām* like Abraham cannot have his/her own domain if he/she is to fit into the tent of God, into God's tabernacle.

2.3.4 Chapters 40–41: Crisis and False Denouement

Chapters 40–41 introduce a new ambivalence to the character of Joseph. The liminal ambivalence had involved until now the polarity between Jacob and God. Now we have a polarity between Pharaoh and non-Pharaoh. This last will involve in the following chapters both Jacob and the Egyptians. Jacob (in the person Joseph) will be confounded with Pharaoh while still being Jacob. Jacob and the Egyptian population will be confounded while being disjunct. Worst of all, God and Pharaoh become confused through the double agency of Joseph.

Joseph rises here from the lowest to the highest position in Egypt. His actions, he protests, are God's. Pharaoh makes of his actions Pharaoh's actions! Instead of a denouement the plot becomes more involved and complex. Joseph reduplicates the success of Jacob which had been summed up at the outset. The developments appear to roll back the developments of the first chapters. The roll back is in fact in the reverse order of the rise of Jacob. Jacob had worked seven lean years for Leah, and then seven years for the beautiful Rachel. In contrast, the seven fat cows, described as beautiful to the sight (41:2) in terms similar to the description of Rachel (29:17), come first. The roll back in fact ends up being a roll back on Jacob. Joseph transfers his semantic traits to Egypt, and Jacob ends up bereft of selfsame. Joseph does not change position in this with God, but he becomes completely at the polar opposite of Jacob. While the selling out of Joseph affected the situation of the house of Jacob in the same way, the rise of Joseph produced a see-saw effect, with Joseph rising and Jacob dipping. Instead of Joseph approaching the servant profile, Jacob appears to be going in that direction now. With Joseph and Egypt at the height of plenty and wealth, we have two passages describing the marriage of Joseph and then the birth of his two sons, immediately before the famine sets in. (Just as Joseph came as the culmination of Jacob's story, immediately before Jacob's decline began with the birth of Benjamin following on the sin of Simeon and Levi (Gen 34–35), Ephraim and Manasseh come as the culmination of Joseph's story before the decline.)

The first passage is the coronation of Joseph as viceroy (Gen 41:44–46). He is solemnly declared as practically Pharaoh's son (v. 44), given a regal name by Pharaoh, given a wife by Pharaoh (v. 45), and in culmination declared of regal age, that is thirty years old, and consequently assumes the office (v. 46). His trajectory, which was truncated in Israel, is completed and surpassed in Egypt. What might the acquired name, Zaphenath-paneah (*ṣpnt pʿnḥ*), mean? The first part of the name, *ṣpnt*, has the characteristic Hebrew letters for North, *ṣpn*, together with an attached "*t*." In Isa 41:25 God says "I stirred up one from the north (*mṣpn*), and he has come (*wyʾt*), from the rising of the sun he was summoned by name. He shall trample on rulers as on mortar, as the potter treads clay." (NRSV). It is not clear whether the servant or Cyrus is intended. The words "from the North" and "he has come" follow each other in the Hebrew and look attached and not vocalized as such: *mṣpnwyʾt*. The *m* is the prefixed preposition "from," the *wy* are the waw consecutive with the imperfect prefix for the third person singular. If we isolate "north" and attach the verb "came" we would have: *ṣpnʾt*. I would translate the first part of the name given by Pharaoh to Joseph as "(from) the north came" in a direct reference to Isa 41:25. The second part of the name, *pnḥ*, I would analyze as a composite of *pḥ* (cry of a woman in travail) and *nḥ/nûḥ* (give rest). In Isa 42:14 God says "For a long time I have held my peace, I have kept still and restrained myself, now I will cry out like a woman in labor (*pḥ*), I will gasp and pant." (NRSV). God will release now a cry, the words he had withheld, like a woman giving release/giving birth to a child. The word for "a cry like a woman in labor" is *pḥ*. As to the verbal root *nḥ/nûḥ* characteristic use of it can be seen in the related texts Gen 42:33; Isa 63:14. This last belongs to the school of Isa 40–55. Moreover, in Hebrew the name Noah is *nḥ*. This is the same as this hollow root *nḥ/nûḥ* meaning "to rest/give rest."[22] The suggested translation of the full name is: "(from) the north came a cry of travail for release to rest."[23] I would take the name given to Joseph as a direct reference to the message of Isa 40–55. The two verses (Isa 41:25; 42:14) indicated above come practically bracketing the first song of the servant, and describe the disposition of God as he embarks on His new plan. The reference to the covenant with Noah comes towards the end of Isa 40–55 in chapter 54, where it is cited as analogous to the action that God was about to do through the servant. The two parts of the name given to Joseph suggested here bracket the full presentation of the servant in Isa 40–55 from chapter 41 to chapter 54. As elaborated in chapter 1, the plan of the deity as introduced in Isa 41–49 appears to refer to a project to produce a body of "words" that will reveal the hidden deity. Chapter 54 presents the "relief" given at the time of Noah as surety that God's "new" project, which will comfort Jacob and bring salvation to Jacob and the nations, will be realized. Chapters 54–55 read like the script used for the redaction of the Joseph story as it unfolds following the name giving.[24] As is fitting for

---

22 Cf. chapter 1, section 2.2.2, particularly footnote No. 27.
23 In the summation in section 3.1 below in this chapter, a variation of this translation is proposed that builds on the same arguments.
24 How Joseph in the Pentateuch is brought into connection with the Tablets of the Law given on Sinai will be elaborated further below. (It has already been hinted at in chapter 1).

this passage in the Joseph cycle, where God and Pharaoh become confused, this name for Joseph is declared by Pharaoh in lieu of God.

The name of Joseph's wife is Asenath, *ăsĕnat*. The Hebrew word *ăsôn* (evil, ill) has the same consonants, less the feminine ending "*t*." It is found in the whole of scriptures only five times, three of them in the immediately following chapter of the Joseph story (42:4,38; 44:29), while the other two are found in Exod 21:22–23. In Gen 42:4 we are told, "But Jacob did not send Joseph's brother Benjamin with his brothers, for he feared that harm (*ăsôn*) might come to him." (NRSV). Similarly in 42:38; 44:29. The redactor is telling us that this wife is bad news.

The name of Asenath's father is Potiphera. This is usually translated from the Egyptian as "he whom the Ra gave."[25] If we want to make a Hebrew derivation for the storyline, then a more likely translation would be "a Libyan (?) offshoot/upstart" (from *pwṭ* "Libyan (?)"[26] and *prʿ* "offshoot").[27] A more interesting question is his office. He is a priest of On, *ʾn/ ʾwn*. The term was discussed above when dealing with Rachel giving birth to Benjamin. It is an ambivalent term/root, but the prevalent meaning would tend towards "unrestrained strength/vigor" resulting in "calamity/falsity." I interpreted it above in section 2.1.1, given the context, as a "foreboding of ill to come, and the expiry of Jacob's good time with Rachel." Given the name of Asenath in the current context I would draw the same conclusion here, substituting Joseph for Jacob. What will issue from this marriage, Ephraim and Manasseh, forebodes ill. This

---

25 Cf. BDB 806.
26 There is little agreement as to which location is intended. The LXX translates the word as Libya. Whatever might be said regarding the derivation of the name and the provenance suggested here, compare this passage and what follows with what is said in Isa 45:14.
27 The triliteral "*prʿ*" also commences the rendering of "Pharaoh" in Hebrew (*prʿh*). This triliteral in the Semitic languages can variously be rendered as: "branch, offshoot, hair locks, progeny, leader, leadership" and as verb "to uncover, branch out, free oneself of encumbrances, let loose."

fits in with what I otherwise interpreted for this passage, namely, that Joseph returns here actually to the trajectory of Jacob.

The second passage, Gen 41:50–54, reports the birth of Ephraim and Manasseh very ominously: "Before the years of famine came, Joseph had two sons, whom Asenath daughter of Potiphera priest of On, bore to him." (v. 50 NRSV). We have commented on the name giving to Manasseh above (cf. section 1.3). Progeny makes Joseph forget everything including his father's house: "Joseph named the firstborn Manasseh, 'For,' he said, 'God has made me forget all my hardship and all my father's house.'" (v. 51 NRSV). Progeny which was supposed to help keep in remembrance provokes instead forgetfulness. The name giving to Ephraim is reported even more ominously: "The second he named Ephraim, 'For God has made me fruitful in the land of my misfortunes.' The seven years of plenty that prevailed in the land of Egypt came to an end;" (vv. 52–53 NRSV). That which was supposed to make fruitful signals instead the end of plenty! We are reminded of the irony implicit in v. 49, "So Joseph stored up grain in such abundance—like the sand of the sea—that he stopped measuring it; it was beyond measure." (NRSV). The promise to Abram/Abraham of progeny without measure is distorted here to stored wealth without measure. The original semantic matrix of Joseph, Ephraim and Manasseh, is indicated here as being extremely bad news. Joseph here is both God and devil.

2.3.5 Chapters 42–45 Inversion of Roles: Jacob as the Servant

The following chapters, 42–45, reverse the tide. We saw at the end of chapter 41 Joseph as Joseph, as the Jacob-Joseph, the full original meaning of Joseph, the beast Joseph claiming a divine visage. Adversity now will force Jacob to stop being Joseph and by force take the aspect of the servant. The reversal highlights the predicament of Jacob. He must learn the lesson from the victim side/seat. A divorce has been effected between Jacob and

Joseph, but not the expected one. Adversity will now usher in the full lesson, and as Jacob has to eat the bitter bread, the major character "adversity" will make Joseph start to mellow and start regaining his remembrance, moved by the developing Jacob-Servant character. The elements of the lesson are assembling now, while the reversal of roles propels the story forward.

Jacob must be prevailed upon to let go of what he is holding back in order to get out of the situation he is in. The reversal of roles involves also the land. Joseph is in Egypt. Egypt is the land of plenty, while Jacob resides in the land of famine. Adversity and force of circumstance collude to force the hand of Jacob to let go. Simeon is sequestered by Joseph, placing the ascendency in the hand of Joseph, signaling the changed power constellation (cf. section 2.1.2 above on the semantic weight of Simeon). Simeon is wryly said to be the first to be accorded "rest" in Egypt by Joseph (42:33). Joseph administers the law now. But what is required still is much more difficult. Jacob must let go of Benjamin. As indicated above (section 2.1.1), this refers to the warrior clan. Having lost wealth and progeny and ascendency Jacob holds on to armed resistance. The hotheaded warriors will not let go. Reuben representing Samaria and consequently Israel, and offering the death of his two sons, cannot entice nor prevail on Jacob to let go. The adversity must become greater to force the hand of Jacob. Judah together with all Israel is now in mortal danger. The redactor must pull all the redactional plugs to force the hand of Jacob. For the first time since chapter 37 and the loss of Joseph the name Israel again is invoked in Gen 42–43. More importantly, the appellation *'l šddy* (God Almighty) is employed again for the first time after 35:11, where Jacob was reminded of the name-giving of Israel at Bethel. It had also been the occasion for setting out to Ephrath, the birth of Benjamin and the death of Rachel in Bethlehem (House of Bread). Now Jacob must lose Benjamin in order to access bread again and get back on the road to Ephrath (fruitful land). Collateral must go beyond the two sons of Reuben. God Almighty, the only strongman of Israel, must be invoked. Bereft of Joseph, Simeon and now Benjamin, Jacob must look on as all his sons and all his goods leave to the land of plenty, Egypt, while he remains denuded of all, alone in the land of famine (43:14). The last time he was in this situation was in 32:25, when God jumped him, before entering the land to meet his brother Esau, and gave him the name Israel. As mentioned above (section 2.1.1), on that occasion he reenacted on his own the servant profile, to enter the land.[28] What he did there in God's wishful thinking willingly he does now under extreme duress. At that time Benjamin was not born yet, here he must lose Benjamin to enter the land of plenty. This corresponds totally to the teaching of Isa 40–55, where God alone is the strongman, *ăbîr*, of Jacob, as we saw in chapter 1, (cf. sections 2.2.1 and 2.2.2), and the port of entry to his pleasure is the servant of Isa 40–55 (cf. chapter 1, section 2.2.2).

In this section Joseph continues playing God and devil. His actions are ambivalent. The motif of the order to return the silver, the purchase price for the grain, to the sacks of his brothers is one such action. It appears like planting incriminating evidence to do someone in, but is not used as such. The motif comes to a head when Joseph's silver cup[29] is placed in the sack of Benjamin. This time the trap is sprung, "foul play," everyone must say! Both Joseph (44:15) and his steward (v. 5) point out that the high and mighty practice divination, that is have eyes to see! The verbal root used for divination, *nḥš*, is the same triliteral as the word for snake, viper. Joseph is at this point in full measure devil/Pharaoh. He is also at the same time God of the servant; he reveals the true nature of the high and mighty. The redactor makes clear to the reader that the true visage of Pharaoh is not the one which will eventually unfold in the story. The actions of Joseph as viceroy of Pharaoh read like the list of malfeasance attributed to kingship with which God replies through Samuel to Israel

---

28 Cf. chapter1, section 3.
29 Cf. the excursus in section 2.3.6 below.

clamoring for a king (1 Sam 8). At the same time, the actions of Joseph as God's executor replicate those of the servant and the teaching of Isa 40–55. Joseph returns the silver, just as the God of Isa 40–55 says through His prophet that Jacob will be redeemed without silver.

The resume of the teaching in 45:1–8 and repeated in 50:19–21 is the teaching of Isa 40–55. Compare Gen 45:5, 7, "And now do not be distressed, or angry with yourselves, because you sold me here; for God sent me before you to preserve life . . . And God sent me before you to preserve for you a remnant on earth, and to keep alive for you many survivors" (RSV), with the resume in Isa 53:10–12. The plot of the story of Joseph reenacts Isa 40–55, together with the ambiguity of the paradox therein. Joseph stands between the treachery of his brothers and the malfeasance of Pharaoh and yet must carry forward the design of the God of the servant.

At the outset of chapter 45 we are told, "Then Joseph could not control himself (*lĕhit'apēq*) . . . Joseph made himself known to his brothers. And he wept aloud, so that the Egyptians heard it, and the household of Pharaoh heard it," (45:1–2, RSV). The verb used for "could not control himself" is the *hitpa'el* of *'pq*. The same form of this verb is used in Isa 42:14 to announce the intention of God to initiate the action which he had withheld so long, the news of which would be addressed to Israel and reach the nations, "For a long time I have held my peace, I have kept still and restrained myself (*'et'apāq*), now I will cry out like a woman in travail, I will gasp and pant," (RSV). The remnant mentioned in 45:7 picks up on Isa 46:3. This is the only use of the word in the Pentateuch. The motif will be expanded on in the book of Jeremiah. The remnant will be saved not by the warriors of Benjamin as the foolish Jacob imagines but by the servant of Isa 40–55. At the end of the resume in Gen 45:8 we are told that God has made Joseph a father to Pharaoh! The story of Joseph tells that Pharaoh made Joseph lord over his house. It is Isa 40–55 that tells us that God is over above Cyrus and has appointed him as his shepherd. Nothing in the Joseph story makes of Joseph the "father" of Pharaoh, but after all Joseph has become the lord of his own father, Jacob!

2.3.6 Excursus: Joseph's silver cup in Gen 44:2–5

Before we move on to the next section, an extended note on the preceding section is in order regarding Joseph's silver cup in Gen 44:2–5.

The innuendo implicit here in Gen 44:2–5 in the crafting of the wordplay is very pointed. A silver cup/goblet/chalice is a regal implement. The word used for cup in Hebrew is *gābîaʿ*. The "Hill/Gibeah of Saul" the Benjaminite first king in Israel is portrayed in 1 Sam as where he made his headquarters as king. Gibeah, which means "hill" in Hebrew, is written as *gibʿâh*, basically with the same three root consonants (*gbʿ*) as *gābîaʿ* (cup/goblet). The redactor regards Benjamin as found wrongly with the kingship, the kingship as misplaced with Benjamin. Kingship in Isa 40–55 belongs only to God, and all hills must be levelled (v. 40:4). This is reflected in the Deuteronomic History in the polemic against kingship and the hills "high places" as well as in the portrayal of the assignment of kingship to Saul as a mistake. On the other hand, the regal cup in the hands of Joseph reflects the kingship of God. The amazing thing is that in the blessings of Jacob in Gen 49:26 we hear "The blessings of your father are stronger than the blessings of the eternal mountains, the bounties of the everlasting hills; may they be on the head of Joseph . . ." (so the NRSV, but cf. footnote 33 in section 2.3.9 below). This is similarly echoed in the blessing of Moses in Deut 33:15 at the end of the Pentateuch. Joseph does not reign on the hills, rather God, his f/F-ather,[30] reigns

---

[30] With "f/F-ather" I render the apparent ambivalence in the text of Gen 49:25–26. Most translations render the subject of 49:25 as "God of your father." This makes of the "blessings of your father" in verse 26 the blessings of Jacob. In verse 25 we have the short form for God, "el" with "your father." This is often read as in the construct/genitive formulation as "God of your father." However, if we read "your

over and above all and pours on Joseph as the *rahām* His bounties. From the end of the book of Genesis to the end of the book of Deuteronomy Joseph functions as the *rahām* (more on this further below). At the current stage of the story, however, the character of Joseph is still ambivalent. He seems to practice divination in the service of Pharaoh, though we have been told (Gen 40:8; 41:16) that the source is God. Unlike Pharaoh, he does not have a cupbearer, in Hebrew *mašqēh*. The cupbearer (Gen 40:1, 2, 5, 9, 13, 20, 21, 23; 41:9) of Pharaoh was "one-upped" in "divination" by Joseph when they were together in prison. His (Joseph's) cup, we are told here in v. 44:5, is the source of his "divination." God is the one who fills up his cup! The regal implement is qualified by God's kingship. God is the *mašqēh*. The word used in Hebrew for Pharaoh's cupbearer is the *hip'îl* participle of *šqh* (give one something to drink/supply land or animal with water). The repetitive use (ten times, twice in v. 21) of the participle for the cupbearer/cup-bearing in the prison pericope in Gen 40–41 in conjunction with the assignment here (Gen 44:2-5) of Joseph's cup as his source of divine inspiration functions here as an invocation of the role of water and God as source of water as found in Isa 40–55, where these function as the basic terminological matrix (chapter 1, section 2.1). We find the *hip'îl* infinitive construct of the triliteral root *šqh* programmatically used in Isa 43:20, "I give water in the wilderness, rivers in the desert, to give drink (*lĕhašqôt*) to my chosen people," (NRSV). The pendant to this is the use of the verb root *ṣm'* (thirst) in Isa 55:1, "Ho, everyone who thirsts, come to the waters; and you that have no money, come, buy and eat! Come, buy wine and milk without money and without price." (NRSV). Compare with this the proleptic statement in 43:34 when Joseph receives his brothers: "Portions were taken

---

father" as appositive to "God," the statement becomes: "God, your Father . . ." This would make of "blessings of your father" in v. 26 the blessings of God rather than Jacob. This ambivalence in the text seems to be intentional. Jacob intrudes here between God and Joseph and encroaches on the relation between God and the servant-*rahām*; this is characteristic of Jacob in that passage (i.e. the blessings of Jacob, Gen 49).

to them from Joseph's table, but Benjamin's portion was five times as much as any of theirs. So they drank and were merry with him." (NRSV).

2.3.7 Chapters 46–47 Joseph as the rahām vs. Pharaoh as Joseph

Chapters 46–47 are an extended lesson on the implications of Pharaoh's land. At the beginning God confronts Jacob at Beer-sheba and orders him to go to Egypt. This stands in contradiction to what Isaac was instructed in Gen 26:1–6. The invocation of the promise to Abraham is the same on both occasions, but the appearance to Jacob is at Beer-sheba. Beer-sheba brackets (Gen 21:33; 22:19) the testing of Abraham with the request that he sacrifice Isaac, and the resulting reiteration of the covenant. Again the reason is to be found in the differentiation between Isaac and the *rahām*. The gates of Egypt open only if the convocation comes through the *rahām*. Egypt is the land of the beast/Pharaoh, just as the house of Jacob proved to enclose within it the beast. The land of plenty opens up, even if the beast is resident, only if the *rahām* is in office. This image is used in the story of Samson also (Judg 14:8). In the book of Numbers the promised land cannot be accessed unless the Servant-Joshua together with Caleb lead the way, all other attempts are doomed. In Gen 45:13ff the convocation has come from Joseph to Jacob to come to Egypt. In Gen 46:1–6 the God of the promise to Abraham, at Beer-sheba, confirms that the convocation is from him. Joseph is confirmed as the *rahām* who opens the land. In the land of death, Egypt, Jacob will still be in the domain of the God of Abraham, as long as Joseph is in office. Had Isaac gone there he would have been eliminated. His profile does not correspond to that of the requisite *rahām*, after all he had been decommissioned in the vicinity of Beer-sheba. In an amazing passage (Gen 46:31–47:10) Joseph meticulously instructs his brothers and father what they must recite in the presence of Pharaoh. It is to be inferred that anything else will lead to their destruction by Pharaoh! The following description of the exercise of office by Joseph towards the Egyptians in terms of his other mask in this passage, that of executor of the beast/Pharaoh is unequivocal (cf. Gen 47:14–26; 1 Sam 8). The tirade against kingship is unmistakable. Do not go to Egypt if your port of entry is not the servant-Joseph, because the Pharaoh-Joseph will eat you up and enslave you. Joseph in chapter 47 is Dr. Jekyll and Mr. Hyde! We have already seen that in Isa 40–55 it is only the servant in the shape of the *rahām* who is the port of entry to God's unbreakable covenant. He resides in the land of the beast, making the beast/Cyrus docile, just like Joseph does to Pharaoh in this whole passage, "story-graphically," at length.

While the Egyptians become slaves of Pharaoh (Gen 47:14–26), Joseph prepares a place for Jacob in Goshen, a backcountry/hinterland where they could rest securely, peaceably, at ease and undisturbed (Gen 47:11–12, 27). I derive Goshen from *gw* "back of," or, similarly, *gy'* "valley," and the verb *š'n* "to rest securely, be at peace, at ease, undisturbed." An alternative would be vale of sleep, with the verbal root *šnh* "to sleep." In other passages this last could be the intention. At the beginning of the book of Exodus, for example, Moses will have to nudge the Hebrews to get a move on it. The last passage before the fourth song in Isa 40–55 is a succession of appeals "to arise" and "awake." As with all other statements in Gen 47, this name also could be an intended ironical doublespeak. With rest comes sleep and negligence.

2.3.8 The Redactional Use of the Words for Grain br *and* šbr

When the linguistic matrices of Isa 40–55 were discussed above in chapter 1, section 2.1, one very important and characteristic verb of Isa 40–55 was singled out. It was said that,

> It can be construed as pertaining to all three matrices described. It is the verbal root *br'* (usually translated as "to create"). It is basically used in Isa 40–55 (40:26, 28; 41:20; 42:5; 43:1, 7, 15;

45:7, 8, 12, 18 twice; 48:7; 54:16 twice) and the creation narrative in Genesis (Gen 1:1, 21, 27 thrice; 2:3, 4; 5:1, 2 twice; 6:7). Otherwise, its use is sporadic. Its characteristic use in these two compositions (together with the word *tōhû* "chaos, vanity" in Gen 1:2; Isa 40:17, 23; 41:29; 44:9; 45:18, 19; 49:4) is one of the reasons often taken to infer an influence of Isa 40–55 on the creation narrative in Genesis. The meaning of the root in both Hebrew and Arabic appears diverse, but can be summed up as the taking something out of an obstructing shell/covering, free someone/something from dirt, sickness, guilt. As such it has a relation to the function of cleansing waters, to that of redemption, and to that of victorious/judicial acquittal. What issues out of the verb has the connotation of clean, out of the box, pristine, healthy, innocent, without any wart or shortcoming, free, filial. The closely related root *brr* (employed in Isa 49:2; 52:11, otherwise sporadically) shares practically the same domain of meaning. Among the related words from this domain, in this case from *brr*, is the Aramaic word for son, *br* (vocalized *bār*); (this is employed in Arabic also to denote an upright person, *bār*, and uprightness, *bir*). That the redactor of Isa 40–55 intentionally chose this root and made it characteristic of the weave of his composition is underscored by its amazing scarcity and casual use elsewhere in Scripture except for the creation narrative.

It is domestic, judicial, and cosmic. The verbal form is not found in the Joseph cycle. The derivatives are equally sparse in Scripture, except in the Joseph cycle. The adjective *bārî'* (full, pristine) from *br'* is used to designate the full and pristine cows and ears of grain in Gen 41:2, 4, 5, 7, 18, 20. This is the only use of this adjective in the book of Genesis. Otherwise, its use is rare and sporadic. A telling conjoint employment of the noun and verb of this root in Num 16:30 demonstrates the use of this root as emblematic for what proceeds from God. The term for grain that has been threshed, *br (bār)*, most likely from the closely related root *brr*, is used in Gen 41:35, 49; 42:3, 25; 45:23.

This last term for grain, rarely used elsewhere, is used with another term for the same grain, also used rarely, *šbr (šeber)*, from the triliteral root *šbr* (to break). The latter term looks at the grain from the point of view of the process by which one gets the grain, which, effectively, is by threshing, essentially breaking. The first term, *br* (*bār*), looks directly at the final product ready for baking bread. The term *šbr* is also used widely to mean breach or destruction as in Isa 51:19. The verb *šbr* (to break) is also widely used in this sense in scriptures, not least in Isa 42:3. It is said about the servant that "a bruised reed he will not break" (RSV). The image is that even a reed already bruised in threshing will not be broken by him. There is no violence in him. But this verb is also used in the sense of "to buy grain." This last use is basically found once in Isa 55:1 ". . .and he who has no money, come buy and eat!" (RSV) and repeatedly in the Joseph cycle (Gen 41:56, 57; 42: 2, 3, 5, 6, 7, 10; 43:2, 4, 20, 22; 44:25; 47:14). The only other instances are Deut 2:6, 28; Amos 8:5, 6; Prov 11:26.

The two key statements using the two differing meanings of šbr in Isa 42:3 and 55:1 are expanded upon in the Joseph story in an amazing interplay in the use of the two terms for grain, *br* and *šbr*, and the use of the verb *šbr* in the rare meaning of "to buy grain." The use of the term *šbr* for grain comes with the connotation that it is acquired by violence, or bought at the cost of being broken and subjected to violence and servitude. It is a "bread of violence." The term *br* in this story implies bread without violence, pristine "freely given innocent bread, *gratia dei*." Initially in Gen 41:35, 49 Joseph suggests to Pharaoh, God driven, to store grain, *br*, for the lean years. In 42:25 he orders that *br* be given to his brothers with the intention "freely," while the same is given in 45:23 to his father. A very telling pun occurs in 42:3, the only instance where *br* is not subject to an action by Joseph but by his brothers. The English translation is "So ten of Joseph's brothers went down to buy grain in Egypt" (RSV). The Hebrew text has for "to buy grain" *lšbr br*, which equally sounds in Hebrew as "to break a pristine item/innocent bread." If Aramaic is also in the back of the mind as regards *br* (cf. Ps 2:12; Prov 31:2, for the use of this Aramaic sense of the word in Hebrew passages), it could equally sound as a description of what they had done to Joseph and as a prolepsis of what Jacob is about to do again as we shall see, "break a son." On the other hand, when Jacob speaks of the grain, or Joseph acts to reflect the visage of the beast Pharaoh, the term used is *šbr*, "grain of violence." An interesting example of this is in 44:2. Joseph gives the instructions "and put my cup, the silver cup, in the mouth of the sack of the youngest, with his money for the grain" (RSV). The grain, *šbr*, is qualified by "his money for," indicating the intention of Benjamin, while the action of Joseph replicates the visage of the malevolent Pharaoh. The teaching of Isa 40–55 is reproduced by this deliberate use of these terms. While Jacob acts violently against others, and subjects himself to violence to get bread, the servant supplies bread freely, without violence. On the other hand, when Joseph represents and acts out the diabolical visage of Pharaoh, two summary reports in 41:56–57 and 47:14, bracketing Pharaoh's campaign, reflect this through the use of the verb *šbr* in the first instance and the noun and the verb *šbr* in the second. Indeed we hear in 47:14 "And Joseph gathered up all the money that was found in the land of Egypt and in the land of Canaan, for the grain (the noun *šeber*) which they bought (participle of the verb, *šōbĕrîm*); Joseph brought the money into Pharaoh's house (RSV)." At this point it is incumbent to point out the statement in Isa 49:26 which is developed by this motif in the Joseph story: "I will make your oppressors eat their own flesh, and they shall be drunk with their own blood as with wine. Then all flesh shall know that I am the Lord your Savior, and your Redeemer, the Mighty One of Jacob (RSV)." Iniquity eats itself up, Pharaoh ends up eating his own flesh, the Egyptians.

2.3.9 The Denouement (Gen 48:1–50:13): Jacob remains Jacob

It is time now for the denouement. The story of Joseph was a parable addressed to Jacob. The lesson has been delivered, but the characters are all out of sync. Jacob is masquerading as the servant, this is certainly not how Isa 40–55 sees the matter, and

Joseph is functioning as a two-headed Hydra. We have a case of misplaced personalities. But all is not lost! Just as the God of the redactor can depend on Adam to destroy his own house, he can depend on Jacob to scheme and act compulsively to grab at whatever he can get his hands on.

The ruse by Jacob starts in Gen 48:1. He sends a report that he is ill. Joseph immediately goes to him with his two sons, whereupon Jacob suddenly puts on his strength, preparing to prance on his prey. (The *hitpaʿel* form of *ḥzq* "to be strong" is used, implying a preparedness for war.) In the following he invokes God's promise to him, which was supposed to be a reminder of the promise to Abraham, "Behold, I will make you fruitful, and multiply you" (v. 4, RSV). Jacob thereupon draws the totally incoherent and fortuitous conclusion based on the meaning of the names Ephraim (fruitful acres) and Manasseh (progeny), "And now your two sons, who were born to you in the land of Egypt before I came to you in Egypt, are mine: Ephraim and Manasseh shall be mine" (v. 5, RSV). As we saw above, Ephraim derives from *prh* (to be fruitful), and Manasseh implies progeny. Jacob interprets God's promise as a title to grab Ephraim and Manasseh. Like Pharaoh, like Jacob, Jacob eats up his sons. The same incoherent logic continues in the explanation of v. 7 with a continuation of the wordplay on the verb *prh*. Jacob's journey to Ephrath had been interrupted with the death of Rachel (Gen 35:19), and her burial at Bethlehem. Now he wishes to resume the journey to Ephrath, to wealth and fortune and plenty, at the cost of Joseph. The nearly blind Jacob asks who is with Joseph, and Joseph pointedly replies that they are the sons given to him by God. But at this point Jacob has no sight of God, nor of the blessings brought through Joseph on his house, he will issue his own set of blessings. The wily Jacob repeats the same trick he did at the beginning of his career, he switches the blessings of Manasseh and Ephraim, just as he stole the blessing of Esau, in consequence of which he had to leave the land. He wants greater wealth (Ephraim) and it seems does not care about progeny (Manasseh). The first justification for his actions that he had employed (Gen 48:4), reminiscent of the promise to Abraham, still had both included. By the second justification (v. 7), reminiscent of Rachel, he had only wealth (Ephrath) in mind. He was after all in the process of eating up Joseph. As was the case with Adam, going after the forbidden fruit meant condemnation to toil and hardship and exile from the garden. Jacob will have more wealth and less progeny. Isaiah 40–49 described this process of the collapse of Jacob as resulting from his own treachery and the consequent divine judgment. The great sin of Jacob in the book of the Former Prophets was that of adopting the worst of the Canaanite sins, passing their children through the fire, testing/consuming their own children (2 Kgs 16:3; 17:17, 31; 21:6; 23:10). In the episode of the golden calf in the book of Exodus Jacob is depicted as formally adopting the Canaanite practices. This is indicated as the ultimate cause for the divorce between God and Jacob. With the switching of the blessings, wealth becomes greater than progeny. We can hear in the background the anguished cry of Rachel in the book of Jeremiah, "Thus says the Lord: 'A voice is heard in Ramah, lamentation and bitter weeping. Rachel is weeping for her children; she refuses to be comforted for her children, because they are not'" (Jer 31:15, RSV). As a purported prophecy about the future, Jacob's "blessing" certainly backfired. Jacob completes his "blessings" to Joseph by giving him a place to bury himself in Shechem, the same place that was acquired by violence (Gen 34), and for which Simeon and Levi will be condemned by selfsame Jacob in the immediately following passage (Gen 49:5–7). He "graciously" gives Joseph this "choice" burial piece over and above what is given to his brothers! The irony cannot be greater. At the beginning of the Joseph story in Gen 37 the brothers of Joseph took his kingly coat and threw him into the pit before selling him off. Now Jacob takes Manasseh and Ephraim and gives Joseph in return a place to bury himself, a place acquired by violence.

Unlike the law of the levirate, where there is assumption of duties on behalf of the deceased, as we saw in chapter 38 with Judah, adoption implies assumption of all the prerogatives incumbent. Jacob knows that, because he goes on to state, "And the offspring born to you after them shall be yours; they shall be called by the name of their brothers in their inheritance" (v. 6, RSV). The term "inheritance" is a legal term. Jacob finishes off on the ravishment of Joseph begun by Joseph's brothers in chapter 37. Now Jacob is back to being Jacob-Joseph.

Our redactor is aware of what the implications are. Jacob has just taken over the semantic filling of the name Joseph, Ephraim and Manasseh, wealthy estates and progeny. What about the empty Joseph now? In the story of Abraham, after the main cycles of Ishmael and Isaac have been dealt with, the redactor goes on to have Abraham get more progeny from another wife (Gen 25:1–4). As long as he does not establish his own domain, that is, get a storyline of his own, *tôlēdôt*, this constitutes no problem. God after all has promised to make him a father of many nations. Building on such a possible scenario Jacob has already suggested a lame duck solution for Joseph, he can get other children. Of course getting other children would involve a change of content to the name Joseph. The redactor opts for no content, no more children for Joseph. He will be the denuded servant of Isa 40–55 with no progeny. Abraham can be the father of many nations after all, but the *rahām* can only be one, the son who gives the name that makes of Abram an Ab-rahām. Instead of the two-headed Hydra we have now two Josephs: Joseph of Jacob, increase as a factor of wealth and progeny, and the empty Joseph, the servant-Joseph, who is given by God as a covenant according to Isa 40–55 (42:6; 49:8; 54:10; 55:3), and in whose presence salvation is effected to the benefit of others. The Jacob-Joseph is in Jacob's tent, the servant-Joseph will be in God's tent. But more on that further below.

Jacob has won the day; the book of Genesis has become his book. God has been forced to wait for another day. He will have to wait till the book of Exodus to make his visitation and to resume his interrupted track. Jacob, as the class valedictorian of the book of Genesis will have to recite the "blessings" on behalf of his class. Like Adam he has usurped the office from God. What we have in fact is a redactional commentary/resume of the events of the Jacob-Joseph cycle. The "future" blessings of Reuben, Simeon and Levi are in fact a description of the episodes that preceded, and a condemnation thereof. We must assume that the two other blessings which are not just a play of words on the name, that is, the blessings of Judah and Joseph, must be of the same nature.

The question that poses itself concerning the blessing of Judah is the following: We have had too little involvement of Judah in the unfolding drama, other than the episode in chapter 38 concerning the levirate. But this episode, as we saw above, prepares for the episode about Jacob and the adoption of Ephraim and Manasseh. Judah stands in for Jacob. What is incredible is that the blessing of Judah is in major part an incorporation of the blessing of/to Jacob by Balaam in Num 24:9, 17 (cf. Gen 49: 9–10). How can this be? We need only look at Isa 48:1, "Hear this, O house of Jacob, who are called by the name of Israel, and who came forth from the loins of Judah; who swear by the name of the Lord, and confess the God of Israel, but not in truth or right." (RSV). It is the thesis of this paper that this is the point of view of the redactor of the Joseph cycle. Judah is addressed, Jacob is named. Here Judah refers to the Jacob of the story, who in effect is Judah. The second point to be made about the blessing of Judah is that Gen 49:11–12, the last part of the blessing, has Judah wrapped up in the fruit of the vine. Judah (the tribe) is intoxicated with itself. (To understand this motif cf. Isa 49:26; 51:17, 21. It is an image of violence, wrath and judgment.) The function of this would elude us, were it not for the description of Joseph in the last part of his blessing by Jacob as "Nazirite among his brothers." (49: 26). A

Nazirite may not in function of his vow approach wine (Num 6:1–4). The blessing of Judah-Jacob describes Judah as separate/disjunct from Joseph the Nazirite, in another camp, much as the servant of Isa 40–55 is separate from Judah-Jacob.

The discussion[31] about what appears to be the word "Shiloh" in Gen 49:10 in the course of the blessing of Judah and whether it should read "to whom it belongs" (that is the scepter) can be answered very simply if the point of view of this paper is accepted. Names play symbolic roles in literary texts. Shiloh is the encampment of the Ark of the Covenant, that is the place "which pertains to Him," "Him" being Yahweh. Shechem, on the other hand, is the place "which pertains to you," "you" being the addressed Jacob/Israel (cf. Gen 37:12–14).[32] This replicates the two camp setup, that was referred to above, in the wilderness. As such, Gen 49:10 is a *vaticinium ex eventu*. In Isa 40–49 God alone is King in Jacob/Israel, and He takes pleasure in the servant, Isa 50–55. Judah/Jacob can have chieftains and kings only as long as it rejects the kingship of God, and the covenant of His servant presented in Isa 40–55, that is, until it enters Shiloh, His place, and the obedience of the peoples is to Him. This is exactly the teaching of the First book of Samuel and DH as a whole. Judah/Jacob will remain "in function as class valedictorian/in rebellion/in usurpation of the kingship" until addressed by the God of Moses. (Understood like this it becomes analogous to the blessing of Judah by Moses in Deut 33:7. The prayer/hope is expressed there that Judah will return/repent to the assembly of Moses/to the assembly of His people.) In 2 Kgs Judah will continue to have kings until the book of the Law of Moses is discovered under Josiah. With the discovery comes the death knell of the monarchy. In Isa 55:3 it is the covenant of the servant which assumes the aspect of the fast and sure love of God attached to the Davidic throne.

---

31 Cf. Westermann, *Genesis* 37–50, 230–1. Von Rad, *Genesis*, 424–6.
32 The apparent location, Shiloh, as well as its pendent, Shechem, are parsed here as relative clauses: "*še*" is read as the short form of the relative pronoun attached to the corresponding possessive pronoun, "*lô*" and "*kem*."

Indeed, in the final redaction of the book of Isaiah as it stands, Judah has kings throughout Isa 1–39, while in rebellion. With the onset of Isa 40–55 all kingship ceases with the announcement of God as King, and the advent of the servant. This will bring about, according to Isa 40–55, the obedience of the nations as well. This situation continues till the end of the book through Isa 56–66 where this is pictured in realization. Illustrative of the position of the book of Isaiah and the book of the Latter Prophets are the statements in Isa 1:10; 16:5; 33:22; 49:7; 52:5; Hos 8:4; 13:11; Zech 14:16–17.

The blessing of Joseph becomes a replication not only of the Joseph character as we have it in the Joseph cycle, but also of the servant of Isa 40–55. In fact Gen 49:24 uses the same expression incorporating the word *ăbîr* (strongman), "by the hands of the Mighty One of Jacob, by the name of the Shepherd, the Rock of Israel," (NRSV) which is found in Isa 49:26, at the end of the Jacob part of the composition, ". . . the Lord your Savior, and your Redeemer, the Mighty One of Jacob" (NRSV). This expression "the Mighty One of Jacob" is found only in these two locations and in Isa 1:24; 60:16; Ps 132:2, 5. The word *ăbîr* is found only here in the whole of the Pentateuch. The summation of the blessing with the description of Joseph as the Nazirite among his brothers reflects not only his position in the story of Genesis, but also the estrangement of the servant of Isa 40–55. If the reading of Joseph here as the servant is correct, then I would read the opening words of Gen 49:25 as "from God, your Father" rather than "from the God of your father." This would make a smoother reading of verse 26, where "your Father" would stand in contrast to "my progenitors" (cf. KJV)[33] in the sense of Isa

---

[33] Cf. the footnote to section 2.3.6 above. The relevant word in Hebrew, as vocalized in the MT, is *hôray* (my progenitors); this is what the KJV reads. The NRSV vocalizes the consonantal text differently as the plural construct of "mountain" and translates with the following particle as "eternal mountains." The blessing of Joseph in Gen 49:24–26 poses several problems for translators. The Septuagint, seemingly as

63:16, "For thou art our Father, though Abraham does not know us and Israel does not acknowledge us; thou, O Lord, art our Father, our Redeemer from of old is thy name." (RSV). This fits perfectly with the end of the previous v. 24, where we are expressly told that the shepherd, the stone/rock of Israel, who is none other than the "Mighty One of Jacob," God, comes from Joseph. That God alone is the shepherd, king and strongman of Jacob is the teaching of Isa 40–55. His salvation comes in the presence of the servant. This confirms what was said above on the words addressed to Judah. Not only does the shepherd of Israel come from Joseph and not from Judah, the shepherd/king is not a scion of anyone, but God Himself. He comes from the story of Joseph we have just heard, the Servant-Joseph.[34]

Jacob still has to make arrangement for his burial. In death as in life he wants to snuggle up to Abraham. He mentions that all the family is buried in the poor man's grave at Machpelah, including Leah the mother of Judah. He plans his own return to the land on his own timetable, which proves to be a "dead" end, similar to the failed attempt to enter the land in the book

---

perplexed as modern translators, only makes matters worse. This leads translators to attempt to parse the consonantal text differently or to propose conjectural emendations. Even if we were to dispute the translation "my progenitors" here, the contents of the blessing in terms of the passage flow cannot have as author other than God (a comparison with the parallel blessing of Joseph in Deut 33:13–16, delivered there by Moses, reinforces this conclusion). The ambivalence seems to be due to the intentional portrayal of Jacob as encroaching on God and Joseph and "playing" God here. The translators of the Septuagint seem to have shrunk back from describing God in vernacular Hellenistic Greek as "father" of Joseph. This would be equivalent to declaring Joseph as king/Pharaoh! (The "blessings" are actually described as "the blessings of your father and your mother"!) Similarly, modern translations have difficulty in rendering the blessings of Joseph here and in Deut 33:13–16 as forcefully expressing the intimate relationship between Joseph and God comparable to the relationship of God and the servant in Isa 40–55. Even the KJV in v. 25 renders the text as "Even by the God of thy father . . ." and thus makes of the expression "blessings of thy father" in v. 26 coordinate, grammatically, with Jacob.
34 Compare this with the blessings of Moses in Deut 33:13–16, particularly v. 16, ". . . and for the good will of him that dwelt in the bush: let the blessings come upon the head of Joseph, and upon the top of the head of him that was separated from his brethren." (KJV).

of Numbers (Num 14:40–45) without Joshua and Caleb and the Ark of the Covenant. He is given an "Egyptian" burial, with an Egyptian Pharaonic accolade/entourage,[35] at Machpelah. This is unlike the "Hittite" (a wordplay on the verbal root htt "to be broken, brought down low") burial of Abraham in the field of Ephron (derived from 'pr, the dust of the earth). In fact Jacob is embalmed, he will not return to the dust of the earth, even when returned to Machpelah. Joseph has already been left to God, outside the family grave, to be buried in Shechem, with the violent and rich, just like the servant in Isa 40–55. Jacob-Joseph has arranged for the promised land to function like Pharaoh's Egypt. He (Jacob) dies holding the tribal scepter and the benedictions in his grasp, both of which should have been with God. Unlike Gen 32 where God's wish was expressed, where Jacob had dispensed with all that appertains to him and God had the upper hand over Jacob, Jacob has "beaten" God in the book of Genesis in the same way that Adam had beaten Him in the garden of Eden. They both jump to grab at what they were given freely and end up outside the domain of God. The result will be four hundred years in the barren "wilderness of Egypt" under servitude.

2.3.10 The Servant-Joseph Comforts Jacob

The brothers of Joseph are worried after the death of Jacob that Joseph will take revenge. Joseph takes the occasion to repeat the teaching of Isa 40–55. Echoing Gen 45:5, 7 and Isa 53:10–12 Joseph says in Gen 50:20, "As for you, you meant evil against me; but God meant it for good, to bring it about that many people should be kept alive, as they are today," (RSV). Here, what befell Joseph is interpreted in terms of the suffering of the servant in Isa 53. God will turn to good the evil they have done. The conversion of Joseph into the role of the servant/scapegoat, which started in the last passage of chapter

---

[35] The motif of the nations coming to honor the God of Jacob/Israel is ironically superposed here on the motif of the aggressor coming to bury Jacob under the rubble.

37 (cf.section 2.3.1 above), is consummated here. Joseph dismisses the memory of what they had done to him, "So do not fear, I will provide for you and your little ones" (Gen 50:21a RSV). The text goes on to say, "Thus he reassured them and comforted them" (21b RSV). The word used in Hebrew for "comforted" is the *nip'al* form of the verb *nḥm*. This is the theme of Isa 40–55. This is the opening verse "Comfort, comfort my people, says your God" (Isa 40:1 RSV). It is repeated in Isa 49:13; 51:3, 12, 19; 52:9; 54:11. It brackets the work of the servant in part two of Isa 40–55, who is presented as the means by which God can work to comfort Jacob. In Gen 50:21 the Servant-Joseph is described in this last summary of his work as bringing comfort to his brothers. At the news of the loss of Joseph in Gen 37:35 we had heard concerning Jacob, "All his sons and all his daughters rose up to comfort him; but he refused to be comforted, and said, 'No, I shall go down to Sheol to my son, mourning.' Thus his father wept for him" (RSV).

2.3.11 Joseph and the 'ārôn

As he is about to die Joseph assures his brothers about the promise God gave to Abraham (Gen 50:24–25). He enjoins them telling them that when the time of God's visitation to bring them to the land comes, that then they should take his bones with them. Joseph's return to the land will take the way prepared by God, according to His promise, unlike the Jacob way we saw above. The last verse of the book (v. 26) prepares for the subsequent journey. He is embalmed and placed in an *ărôn*. His remains will not return to the dust of Egypt, they will be kept in waiting till the time of God's visitation.

The bare and denuded bones of Joseph can now fit into the *ărôn*, the ark (of the covenant) (Gen 50:26). This is the only place where this term, *ărôn*, is used in the Pentateuch other than for the yet to be constructed Ark of the Covenant. Translations are misleading because they translate it here as "coffin." The bones in the ark will be carried for four hundred years in Egypt and then in the peregrination in the wilderness, until the ark is constructed in the book of Exodus. The ark will be in the tent of the tabernacle, outside the camp of Jacob. The bones of the servant-Joseph will rejoin Joshua in the tent of the tabernacle, and give way to the tablets of the Ten Commandments. They will pertain to the tent of the God of Abraham.[36] When laid to rest after many years of peregrination in the wilderness (Josh 24:32), they will be a witness and a surety in Shechem to the people of the promise to Abraham, just as the bones of Abraham function in the cave of Machpelah. (Machpelah is to be derived from the triliteral *kpl*, meaning "to double over" in Hebrew, and "to provide surety" in Arabic.) The bones of Joseph, rather than being in the same place as the bones of Abraham, will function in the same way. Joshua will write all the words of the covenant he made with the people at Shechem "in the book of the law of God" (Josh 24:26 RSV), and set a stone in Shechem as witness thereof, effectively together with the bones of Joseph. The two tracks are established, the one, the track of Jacob/Adam, is addressed by the second track of Abraham and the *Rahām*-Servant-Joseph and Joshua with the book of the law of God. All three (Abraham, Joseph, and Joshua) will not have *tôlēdôt* ascribed to them; their story/narrative/paradigm is subsumed to that of God and His words of salvation. This is the design and teaching of Isa 40–55 about Jacob and the Servant.

2.4 Epilogue: The Blessing of Joseph by Moses in Deut 33:13–17

The blessing of Joseph by Moses at the end of the Pentateuch in Deut 33:13–17 is interesting for this discussion. Verses 13–16 parallel the blessing by Jacob in Gen 49:22–26, but instead of the motif of his being assailed, which reflects the events within the Joseph story in Genesis, we have a significant variation. The

---

36 This motif, introduced schematically in this paragraph, will be recapitulated in section 3.2 below in this chapter and further expanded in chapter 3, section 1.2.1. It is regarded by the present writer as the basic leitmotif of the redaction of the Pentateuch.

variation fits the theme "Sinai" running through the Pentateuch. In v. 16 we have ". . . and the favor of him that dwelt in the bush . . ." (RSV). This reflects the manifestation of God to Moses in the burning bush. The word in Hebrew for bush is *snh*. It is similar to the word for Sinai, *sny*, which is the translation preferred here by the NRSV. It is also phonetically similar to *śn'*, "the one who hates" (parsed as the *qal* participle of *śn'*). The pun would be a reference to the fact that the God of Joseph was operative in the land of "the one who hates," that is, in the land of the enemy (Egypt). At the same time this reflects the situation of both the redactor of Isa 40–55 and of the servant, both exercising their work in the land of the enemy (Babylon). As to v. 17, it appears to be out of context when read as introducing Ephraim and Manasseh. Gerhard von Rad in his commentary on the book of Deuteronomy[37] comments, "The mention of Ephraim and Manasseh in v. 17b might be understood as a later amplification, identifying the more ancient 'house of Joseph' with these two tribes." In fact, the verbal syntax of the verse is still speaking about Joseph. The superlatives spoken about Joseph in the preceding verses continue here. He appears to be the divine heir (cf. lengthy footnotes to sections 2.3.6 and 2.3.9 above), and, in continuation of the metaphor of the bull, reference is made to the two horns of Joseph. They function to "push the peoples all together to the ends of the earth." The following phrase mentioning Ephraim and Manasseh should be understood epexegetically. The apparently "military" metaphor used preceding their mention calls forth the "redefinition" of the military attributes "the myriads of Ephraim and the thousands of Manasseh." They are mentioned appositively, and introduced with epexegetic demonstratives. This brings to mind the whole armory of descriptions that appear to be militaristic in connection with Joshua and Caleb. It is postulated here that the "starting" complements to the notion of increase in the type

---

[37] Gerhard von Rad, *Deuteronomy* (trans. Dorothea Barton; OTL; London: SCM, 1966), 207.

"Joseph," Ephraim and Manasseh, are themselves redefined here together with the redefinition of the "militaristic" terminology. In Num 13:8 we are told that Hoshea/Joshua is the representative of Ephraim. Further below, we will see that Joseph continues in Joshua. Joshua-Ephraim is the new complement of the "transformed" type "Joseph." Just as "Joseph" is transformed, the defining complements of Joseph, Ephraim and Manasseh, are transformed. It is suggested here that the appositive demonstrative introducing Ephraim and Manasseh is in fact an oppositive interjection. I would paraphrase it in terms of the thesis being presented here as: "the true 'myriads of Ephraim' and the true 'thousands of Manasseh' are rather the attributes of the 'transformed Joseph,' (defined in this blessing in essentially divine terms), and the characteristics of his continuation in Joshua-Ephraim." The following section will present an intermediate summation expanding, synthetically and retrospectively to chapter 1, the proposed reading regarding the transformation of the Joseph type, and elucidating, prospectively to chapter 3, what up till now appears enigmatic at this point regarding the blessings of Moses in Deut 33.

3. An Intermediate Summation: Retrospective and Prospective

In the foregoing, an analysis of the dramatic flow of the Joseph story has attempted to highlight the impact of Isa 40–55 on the redaction of Gen 37–50. The alternating peripeteias of the characters have illustrated the contrast and interplay between the Jacob/Adam track and the narrative track of the God of the servant-*rahām*. Joseph's peripeteias have alternated his profile between the two tracks, landing him in Gen 48 squarely on the track of the servant-*rahām*. In the course of these alternations the profile has often been ambivalent. In section 2.3.8 we have seen him accomplishing a/the major work of the God of the servant, supplying bread to both Jacob and the Egyptians. He also brings water to the thirsty. The function of water in Isa 40–55 proves to be highly figurative. In Isa 55:11, we hear that it is God's word that waters the earth like rain, accomplishing its task and bearing fruit. The question that arises is: to what extent is this true for the language used in the Joseph story? In Deut 8:4 we hear that "one does not live by bread alone, but by every word that comes from the mouth of the Lord." According to the redactor of Deuteronomy, this is the resume of the lesson to be learned from all that transpired in the wilderness since the exodus from Egypt. Does this use of pedagogical language apply to the Joseph story and Joseph type in the book of Genesis? Only by answering this question will we be able to fathom the full nature and extent of the transformation of the Joseph type as effected by Isa 40–55, and ultimately of the impact of Isa 40–55 on the redaction of the Pentateuch.

3.1 Revisiting the Major Work of the God of the Servant in Isa 40–55

In chapter 1, commenting on Isa 45:14–19, the following was said:

> We have here the most succinct description/announcement of scriptural monotheism: a god with no image, whose representation is solely in scriptures enunciating truth and equity. This passage points to a body of "words" that will reveal the hidden deity, effectively the announcement of scriptural monotheism. The chapter ends with a call to the nations to turn to this deity. The teaching of the conditional covenant applies to the nations as it applies to Jacob. This chapter is the chiastic hub of the subsection dealing with the teaching incumbent on the prospective servant (43:1–48:22).

Further commenting on Isa 48, the following was said:

> The "new action" (already heralded in 41:15, 25; 42:9–17; 43:18–19) about which Jacob had not been informed before (48:6) is about to be announced.

And further commenting on Isa 49:7–13, the following was said:

The passage 49:7–13 is an extended commentary on the second song of the servant. It is also a signature of the author/redactor of Isa 40–55. The servant is a despised and abhorred servant of rulers, and yet the recipient of adulation by selfsame. His day is one of salvation. . . . At this point it is difficult not to see in vv. 7–13 a description of Joseph in the court of Pharaoh. Just as significantly, rather more significantly, the work described here is in fact a description of the implicit design and task guiding the work of the redactor/redactors of the Pentateuch and the books of the Former and Latter Prophets. This is a blueprint for the redaction of those books. These will be the new action and words that God has withheld in the past and is about to blurt out in the latter/current day of our author.

In section 2.3.4 above, the name given by Pharaoh to Joseph was analyzed in terms of Isa 41:25 and Isa 42:14. The following was said:

> The two verses (Isa 41:25; 42:14) indicated above come practically bracketing the first song of the servant, and describe the disposition of God as he embarks on His new plan.

Let us revisit here these verses in the context of Isa 41–43. In Isa 41:25, the God of the redactor says: "I have raised up (someone) from the North and he will come from the rising of the sun and call in My name." (My own very literal rendition of the Hebrew). This is usually understood as referring to Cyrus. The problem is that before Cyrus is mentioned in 44:8, it is the mysterious servant who is introduced in chapter 42. The person is raised up "from the North" (*mṣpn* in Hebrew, vocalized *miṣāpôn*). From the same triliteral root we have the verb *ṣāpan* (to hide/treasure up). The noun *maṣāpôn*, found only in Obad 6 in our literature, is commonly translated as "hidden thing (KJV)/hidden treasure (NJB)." The ambivalence in Isa 41:25 and generally in Isa 40–55 regarding the "servant" is well known. The description of the servant as being hidden in God's hiddenness has been highlighted in chapter 1. The name of the prophet Zephaniah, *ṣĕpanyāh*, is derived from the same verbal root and commonly translated as "Yah has treasured." In section 2.3.4 above it was suggested that the name given to Joseph by Pharaoh should be seen as an invocation of Isa 41:25 and Isa 42:14 and translated as "(from) the north came a cry of travail for release to rest." If Isa 41:25 is an intended wordplay by the redactor, meaning alternately "from the North I roused up (someone) and he came" and "I roused up a hidden treasure and he/it came as the rising sun," it would be an intentional introduction to the first song of the servant and invocation of the intended program to bring forth a previously hidden body of literature that we found rounding up the first half of Isa 40–55, both introducing the second song of the servant and embedded in it. The task and the one charged with it are reciprocally defining of one another (Cf. Isa 49:2). The alternate translation of Joseph's name as given by Pharaoh would become: "(from the) hidden treasury came a cry of travail for release to rest."[38]

Nomen est Omen. If the solution proposed in section 2.3.4 and in the preceding paragraph above to the analysis of the name Joseph as given by Pharaoh is correct, it becomes very relevant to see how the task (of Joseph) is defined in Isa 41–43, the centerpiece of which is the first song of the servant—practically bounded by the two verses invoked by the Pharaoh-given name of Joseph. The task is typically embedded in the first song of the servant, Isa 42:1–9. Particularly relevant are verses 3c–4 and 6. In v. 3c–4 we hear: "he will faithfully bring forth justice. He will not grow faint or be crushed until he has established justice in the earth; and the coastlands wait for his teaching." (NRSV). The word "justice" is repeated twice here, invoking a jurisprudential topology. In Hebrew, it is the singular of what is translated in English as "judgements." This is a rhythmically repeated word in the book of Deuteronomy. What the NRSV translates here as "his teaching," in Hebrew is actually "his

---

[38] The crisp rendition of a phrase as a programmatic personal name is in fact a method employed characteristically in Isa 1–39 (cf. Isa 7:3, 14; 8:1–4), a work, as suggested in chapter 1, written by the school of the redactor/author of Isa 40–55 as an introduction and expansion of his work.

torah." The teaching/torah he will bring forth is modified by the possessive pronoun "his." This is equivalent to saying that he will bring a new torah. This is a very polemical statement against the existing priestly body of laws/torah. In v. 6 we hear: "I am the Lord, I have called you in righteousness, I have taken you by the hand and kept you, I have given you as a covenant to the people, a light to the nations." (NRSV). In the further reflection on the first song of the servant, we hear in Isa 43:18–19: "Do not remember the former things, or consider the things of old. I am about to do a new thing; now it springs forth, do you not perceive it? I will make a way in the wilderness and rivers in the desert." (NRSV). As has been elaborated in chapter 1, this is a blueprint for the Pentateuch as we know it. The question that poses itself here is: what does this have to do with Joseph? Obviously, what was said in section 2.3.8 above about the word use regarding the supply of pristine grain as opposed to violent grain, if understood figuratively, is relevant. But how does this work out practically with regard to Joseph? The answer is introduced enigmatically in section 2.3.11 above, entitled "Joseph and the *ārôn*." Just as we are to bid farewell to Joseph, his story is given a prolongation into the remaining books of the Pentateuch. It is in the Joseph story "part two" as continued by Joshua that we will have the full spelling out of the transformation of the Joseph type that we set out to decipher.

3.2 A prospective revisiting of "Joseph and the 'ārôn"

The word used in Hebrew for the "coffin" of Joseph, *ārôn*, is the same as that used for the Ark of the Covenant. Joseph, in his *ārôn*, will accompany the rest of the story of the Pentateuch until the promised land is reached. Giving narrative and semantic weight to the identity of designation of such an important word (the Ark of the Covenant will contain the tablets of the ten commandments and be placed in the tent of meeting), we would have to co-localize the two, and regard them, for the purposes of the narrative, as coextensive. If this is the case, then the "bones" of Joseph will be in the company of Joshua, who also resides in the tent of meeting, and not in the company of Jacob/Israel, who reside in a separate encampment following the incident with the golden calf. Through this semantic "trick," the track of Joseph intersects with the track of Joshua. Joshua will be indicated as the continuer of the Torah of Moses, as the person who completes what we know as the "Pentateuch." It is postulated here that the semantic trick employed through the word *ărôn*, bringing about the conjunction of the tablets and the bones of Joseph, designates, in fact, the Pentateuch as the posthumously published work of the redactor of Isa 40–55, completed by his disciples, his school, according to his instructions, and that this group is given collectively the name Joshua Son of Noun. While Moses remains in the encampment of Israel, and only briefly communicates with the tent of meeting, standing in front of it and not within it, Joshua and the bones of Joseph reside within it. Moses is the literary name of the project, the Joseph story is written as a "literary" transposed/dissimulated biography, as tribute to the teacher of the school and author of the blueprint for the project. In terms of the question posed at the beginning of this chapter and expressed in its title, we are still in the middle of the road. The transformation of the Joseph type continues in Joshua-Joseph, and will accompany us till the end of the Pentateuch. Joshua, as the "representative" of the tribe of Ephraim, will replace the sons of Joseph taken by Jacob. The narrative of Joseph will continue in the narrative of Joshua the "Ephraimite," while the original Ephraim and Manasseh will be part of the continuing narrative of Jacob/Adam! The next intermediate summation will come at the end of the Pentateuch, in the commentary on the blessings of Moses in Deut 33. Chapter 3 of this work will elaborate the continuation in Joshua-Joseph and the "Joshua school." The teaching of the book of Deuteronomy will fill out the contours that we have seen so far of Joseph, of the new definition of "increase."

Chapter 3
Joshua Son of Nun as the Continuation of the Transformed Joseph and Further Elements of the Redaction of the Books of the Law and the Prophets

Preamble

This part/chapter in the presentation of the main thesis continues elucidating the transformation of the Joseph type that we saw in chapter 2, but here is seen as continuing in the person/character of Joshua Son of Nun. At the same time, the central thesis explicated in chapter 1 will be further fleshed out with the highlighting of further salient redactional elements of the Pentateuch and the Deuteronomic History (DH) and the book of the Latter Prophets undergirding the thesis.

1. Joshua Son of Nun as the Continuation of the Transformed Joseph

Joshua Son of Nun is perhaps the most enigmatic figure we encounter in the second to fifth books of the Pentateuch and then at the beginning of the book of the Former Prophets. He is both astoundingly dominant and uncannily recessive. He is totally subjunct to the Moses character, I would say to the Moses "project." Whenever he appears, it is done unannounced and without introduction, and then he disappears again. When information is given about him, it is done so in a peremptory manner, as it were, for granted. He is the "body"-loyal of Moses, and yet apparently higher positioned, residing within the tent of meeting, while Moses remains outside. He seems to be more consistently faithful to the Moses "charge" than Moses, even when the latter is punished by the God of Sinai! It is almost as if he is the puppeteer behind the scene, who "faithfully" "one-ups" Moses and all the other characters; the master puppeteer of the whole narrative—were it not for the God of Moses. In this he takes on the role that Joseph takes on in Gen 37–50, where at times he is the son of Jacob, at others the lord of Jacob, at times the face of Pharaoh, at others the slave, and in all of that, both Joseph and Joshua appear to be the passive instrument rather than the actors of the God of the Pentateuch, uncannily in all of this similar to the servant of Isaiah 40–55.

1.1 The Name of Joshua Son of Nun

The name of Joshua son of Nun in Hebrew is *yĕhôšûaʿ*. It is derived from the root *šwʿ*. As we have seen in chapter 2 (section 2.3.2), this can be translated as "to raise a plaint/a plaint." The name would mean "Yahweh is our cry for help/Yahweh will adjudicate our plaint." This fits well with the fact that after the divorce that occurred in Exodus 33 between the tent of Yahweh and the encampment of Israel in the wilderness, Joshua is said to stay in God's tent continuously as we saw above. He abides in the tent which judges Israel, to which Israel brings its plaints and which adjudicates in Israel. In fact, we hear in Exod 2:23 that God decides to intervene for the sake of Jacob after "their cry (*šwʿtm*) for help rose up to God" (NRSV). What is amazing in the Pentateuch is that after we hear of Joshua several times (Exod 17:9, 10, 13, 14; 24:13; 32:17; 33:11; Num 11:28) the redactor intervenes in Num 13:16 to report to us that, "Moses called Hoshea the son of Nun Joshua" (RSV). In Deut 32:44 Joshua is called Hoshea outright. (This last is reflected in the KJV but not in the RSV nor in the NRSV translations). In Num 13:8 we had heard that the representative from Ephraim for the task at hand was "Hoshea the son of Nun." In effect, we are told by the redactor that after we have understood the office of the son of Nun, it was time to tell us the pedigree concomitant with that office. Translators, it would seem, have a predilection for obfuscating names for the reader. This is one of those instances.

Although Hoshea is written in Hebrew exactly the same as the name of the prophet Hosea is written in the book of Hosea, our translations (KJV, RSV, NRSV, TOB etc.) prefer to spell the name in each case differently. This name means, for whomever it is used, "may God save" or "God has saved." It is derived from the root *yš'*, "to save." This root might be closely related originally to the root *šw'*, but each has its own functional topic. Whereas *šw'* seems to function as a judicial topic, originally also one of the functions of a king, the root *yš'* functions as a military function, the king as victorious warrior. By giving us the information in Num 13:16 that he does, the redactor is telling us that the visage of the servant of Moses the lawgiver, Joshua son of Nun, functions in the judiciary office of Yahweh, because initially he functions as the visage of selfsame Yahweh as savior, who saved in the Exodus the oppressed people subsequent to their raising their plaint to the heavens, and who will save. This is important at this juncture because Joshua assumes here a new office as one of those chosen to survey and eye out the land. There is in view a military office, preparing for the entry into the promised land. Although there are other surveyors, Joshua is the only one residing in the tent of the tabernacle of God. He is presented at this juncture as in the same seat as the redactor of Isa 40–55 and the servant. On one hand, he is functioning on God's behalf as lawgiver, and consequently later on in the book of Joshua as the one who adjudicates the division of the land together with Eleazar. Compare this with Isa 49:8–9, "Thus says the Lord: In a time of favor I have answered you, on a day of salvation I have helped you; I have kept you and given you as a covenant to the people, to establish the land, to apportion the desolate heritages; saying to the prisoners, 'Come out,' to those who are in darkness, 'Show yourselves.' . . ." (NRSV). On the other hand, he is functioning in consequence of/under the aegis of the day of salvation of the same God. This motif is equally reflected in this same quote from Isa 49:8–9. The name Joshua, *yĕhôšûa'*, also resembles uncannily the noun *yĕšû'â* (salvation), from the root *yš'*, both in terms of consonance and assonance. This phonetically suggestive aspect reinforces the literary correlation of the name with the notion of salvation in this text.

1.2 Joshua and the Tent of the Tabernacle

In the early chapters of the book of Genesis, God creates the garden of Eden, and Adam and Eve rebel. As a result, God throws them out, allowing them to create their own version of the creation, their own narrative based on rebellion. God becomes a recluse, looking for a way to tell his narrative to a rebellious human reality, to Adam and Eve. From the point of view of Adam and Eve, this narrative is a fantasy; it does not conform to the inexorable and violent rebellious reality that is the status quo. The redactor/redactors of the Pentateuch work this out as a contest of narratives. The dynasties proceeding from Adam and Eve repeat in multifarious forms the rebellious "reality," and this, in the composition of the redactors, is presented as a monotonous series of endless genealogies, producing hapless actions, meaningless "achievements," and most importantly, bereft of justice. God's "imaginary" narrative, versus this ever duller, violently imposed reality, breaks into this status quo of violence as pedagogy. In the Noah narrative, God is his own "first" model student, "learning" that total destruction/violence was not such a good idea. This first model lesson sets the tone for the further pedagogy. God's narrative itself becomes the pedagogy contesting Adam's violent injustice and destructive senselessness.

Abram is cut off from his father's house in order to create another narrative line, contesting Adam's narrative. On the dynastic line this leads to Jacob repeating (and according to Isa 40–55 outdoing) the rebellion of Adam and Eve. Narrative "circumstances" lead to the cutting off of Joseph from his father's house. As we saw in chapter 2, Joseph, through a series of peripeteias, goes from being equivalent to the summation of Jacob's achievements to taking on the form of the servant-*rahām*; from being violently separated to becoming a *nazir* from his brothers through God's actions in the narrative. Both Abraham and Joseph are separated not only from their respective progenitors (house/community of father/ forefathers), they are separated also from their progeny (in the case of Abraham, he is tested in order for this to be verified). Not only do both no longer belong to the "narrative" as postulated by Adam and Eve, they no longer produce their own versions of this rebellious narrative. This is expressed by the redactors of the Pentateuch by a compositional structuring element/ gimmick. While every other character in the Pentateuch produces a genealogy (as explained earlier, to be understood as a narrative of achievement), in Hebrew, *tōlĕdôt*, Abraham and Joseph, as well as Joshua, are denied this (in the case of Joseph, it is cut off by Jacob's adoption of Ephraim and Manasseh, while all that remains to him are his bare bones). They will only function for our redactors as part of God's narrative/pedagogy.

Following the Exodus, the giving of the ten commandments to Moses, together with the Covenant Code and the instructions for the building of the ark, the tabernacle, and all that pertains to the sanctuary (Exod 1–31), there is the incident of the golden calf. This epitomizes the fullness of the sin of Jacob-Israel. The "fullness" of the sin of Jacob, reflected in the rebellion against God's salvific actions and lessons, repeats the sin of Adam and Eve and outdoes it. Again, God must take the same action that was taken at the time of the rebellion of Adam and Eve. He must again become a recluse, this time vis-à-vis Jacob (and Aaron as the leader of the rebellion). God separates between the encampment of Jacob and His tent, the Tent of Meeting with the Ark of the Covenant. A new character in God's narrative must be cut off to service this chapter, Joshua Son of Nun. Although introduced earlier, he is now peremptorily introduced as residing in the tent of meeting, almost as an afterthought. The procedure has become ingrained in the storyline. Moses becomes a go-between between the tent of meeting and the encampment of Jacob, effectively, between Joshua, his servant/acolyte, and Jacob. Joshua, like Joseph (Gen 49:26), becomes a virtual Nazirite, cut off from his brothers, the rest of the children of Jacob; like Abraham and Joseph, he will not have his own narrative/achievements, *tōlĕdôt*, his story is part of God's narrative confronting Adam's and Jacob's narratives of "achievements." The Pentateuch and the books of the Former and Latter Prophets are constructed redactionally as an interplay between these two narrative sequences/ tracks/ encampments. This is the structure that was discerned and highlighted as the redactional framework of Isa 40–55.

1.2.1 Joshua, Joseph, and the 'ārôn (Ark)

As we saw, the bones of Joseph (Gen 50:26) are placed in a chest, in Hebrew, *ărôn* (in the Masoretic text, this is vocalized as introduced by the definite article, i.e. "in the chest, *bā'ărôn*"). The word *ărôn* is subsequently used approximately 130 times from the book of Exodus, through the Pentateuch and the book of the Former Prophets for the "Ark of the Covenant/Ark of the Lord." It provides practically the central narrative thread for the stories in all these books. It is also present in the parallel passages of the work of the Chronicler (some 45 times). It is also used once in Ps 132:8 and once in Jer 3:16. In all these instances it refers to the Ark of the Covenant except for one instance, this being the passage 2 Kgs 12:10–11 and its parallel in 2 Chr 24:8–11. This passage is part of the attempt to simulate a partial reform under the "good" King Jehoash of Judah. The priest Jehoiada sets up "a chest, *ărôn 'eḥād*." It is for a money collect for the temple, and it is set up "beside the altar on the right side as one entered the House of the Lord." (NRSV). Even this deficient reform fails with the rejection of ("conspiracy against") the reign of Joash. This is the last instance we hear of (an/the) *ărôn* (a chest/the Ark) in DH. From here on we have an inexorable descent into self-destruction of Jerusalem, interrupted briefly under King Josiah with the discovery of "the Book of the Law." In other words, the mention of "the *ărôn*" in conjunction with the bones of Joseph in the last phrase of the book of Genesis is followed in Exod 25:10 with the instructions to build the "Ark of the Lord," in which "You shall put . . . the testimony which I shall give you" (Exod 25:16, NASV). In the scriptural writings, the Hebrew word *ārôn* is given the semantic weight of the "chest" containing the "testimony" of the God of Exodus, the place of which is the sanctuary, the tent of meeting. It is introduced, apparently with the definite article (according to the Masoretic vocalization), for the chest containing the bones of Joseph as the final dispatch from the book of Genesis to the book of Exodus, where on Sinai it takes its full semantic significance as the central thread of the narrative. The only exception being the chest for the collect in 2 Kgs 12:10–11, which, although part of a well-meant but deficient reform, belongs also within the sanctuary. The bones of Joseph kept in a/the *ārôn*, chest, though mentioned only at the beginning of the wilderness trek, will also be remembered at the end of the work of Joshua in the penultimate phrase in the book of Joshua. Thus, like the ark of testimony, it functions as a necessary accoutrement at the center of the wilderness trek and the work of Joshua. The semantic weight given in our literature to the word *ārôn* collocates the bones of Joseph with the tent of meeting and the testimony therein and consequently with Joshua, both being "separate" from, while in the midst of, the descendants of Jacob. Inherent to all this is the polemic against Aaron and the sons of Aaron. While Joshua and the bones of Joseph are collocated with the ark of testimony, Aaron and the sons of Aaron may enter once only into the tent of meeting on the Day of Atonement to offer sacrifice for the sins of the people and themselves. In Hebrew, Aaron is written as *'ahărōn*. Phonetically, spoken quickly, it approximates the sound of *'aḥ ārôn*, brother of the *ārôn*, in spite of the difference between the *hê* and *ḥêt* sounds. In "carnivalesque" wordplay, Aaron, the "brother" of Moses, is only "proximate" to the testimony and not co-locative with it as Joshua and the transformed Joseph are!

1.2.2 Cyrus and the Tent of the Tabernacle

In the description of the construction of the tent of the tabernacle in the book of Exodus, also called the tent of Meeting, *ʾōhel môʿēd*, (of the appointed time), we find two terms in Hebrew used for two elements used in its construction, *qrš* (boards), and *qrs* (clasps). Both terms are used repeatedly in the instructions for the setting up of the tabernacle. The first, *qrš* (boards), is used in Exod 26:15, 16, 17, 18, 19, 20, 21, 22, 23, 25, 26, 27, 27, 28, 29; 35:11; 36:20, 21, 22, 23, 24, 25, 26, 27, 28, 30, 31, 32, 33, 34; 39:33; 40:18; Num 3:36; 4:31, (in many of these verses it is used twice). In all of these instances it is used exclusively for the tabernacle. In the whole of the OT it is used only one other time in Ezek 27:6, in the course of the description of the riches of the king of Tyre. The second, *qrs* (clasps), is used in Exod 26:6, 11, 33; 35:11; 36: 13, 18; 39:33, again exclusively for the tabernacle. The only other occurrence in the OT of the verbal root corresponding to this noun is in Isa 46:1, 2. In Isa 46:1, 2 the verb is used as a pun on the name of Cyrus, *krš*. Bel and Nebo are said to stoop, bow down, implicitly to Cyrus (*krš*) who had been invoked in Isa 44:28 and 45:1. In the book of Exodus the pun intended through the use of the aforementioned terms on the name of Cyrus becomes evident by the exclusive use of these terms for the tabernacle of God in the wilderness. Just as the redactor of Isa 40–55, together with the servant, functions on grounds symbolically provided by Cyrus, Joshua son of Nun functions in the tent of the tabernacle in the wilderness on materials, planks and clasps, suggestive of the name Cyrus. It should be stressed that the same tent is called the tent of meeting, that is, of the appointed time, *môʿēd*. This is the same term used in the promise to Abraham for the time set by God for the realization of the promise as regards the birth of Isaac, in conjunction with the covenant (Gen 17:21; 18:14; 21:2). It points to a time of realization. The tent is both an abode and a time of realization. Regardless of when Isa 40–55 was actually written, whether in the Persian or the Hellenistic period, the literary cross reference implicit in the use of the two terms, *qrš* and *qrs*, to Isa 40–55 and the situation of the redactor/servant therein is unmistakable. Indeed, the wordplay would be weightier in Hellenistic times. As has been suggested in chapter 1, the reference to Cyrus would appear to appeal rather to past events and not to the new envisaged action, which appeared to point to a body of writings that would reveal the otherwise hidden, reclusive deity. In Hellenistic times the mythical stature of Cyrus the Persian had developed and grown. This was linguistically facilitated in that in Greek, the name of Cyrus was written exactly the same as the Greek word κυρος, meaning "supreme power/authority/validation." It would be an invocation of supreme authority and surety, the highest possible seal of validation. The highest regal authority in Isa 40–55 is the God of the redactor. The expression of this, the insinuation in Hebrew, is that He wields the κυρος / "Cyrus."

1.3 Joshua Takes on New Roles and Appellations in the Book of Numbers

In the first chapter of the book of Numbers stock is taken of the tribes of Jacob. For each of the sons of Jacob, except for Levi (The sons of Levi had already been "awarded" the term *tōlĕdôtām* in Exod 6:16), we find the expression: "As for the sons of so and so, their genealogies/narratives (*tōlĕdôtām*)" followed by the census numbers. This is the standard collocation of the name of the individual tribe with the term *tōlĕdôt* that we have in this chapter of the book of Numbers. The term (together with the plural of the attached possessive pronoun referring to "the sons") follows immediately on the name of the relevant tribe. This is the formulistic usage. However, in Num 1:32–34 we find an exception to this. Although mention is made of the sons of Joseph, the word *tōlĕdôt* does not follow directly on the name. The phrase "sons of Ephraim" intervenes before the term *tōlĕdôt* is introduced, and then "the sons of Manasseh" are mentioned and the term follows. Compare with this Noah and his sons. The *tōlĕdôt* of Noah are referred to in Gen 6:9, introducing his story. In Gen 10:1 we have "These are the descendants of

Noah's sons, Shem, Ham, and Japheth . . . (NRSV). The "sons of Noah" have their *tōlĕdôt* referenced to them, distinct from the *tōlĕdôt* of Noah in 6:9. In the book of Numbers chapter one, Ephraim and Manasseh are mentioned as sons of Joseph, they are after all his "natural sons." But formally, and consequently legally, they are sons of Jacob, and must be mentioned individually as the other sons of Jacob in the census. The word "Joseph" remains, even as a tribal designation, twice-removed, apart, without the term *tōlĕdôt* directly conjoined to it. Joseph's story was subsumed to God's salvific narrative. Ephraim and Manasseh will have their own tales/versions of the sins of Adam and Eve. They will have an abundance of such, related in the DH, as well as in the books of the prophets Hosea, Amos, and already, before all, Ezekiel. The transformed Joseph will remain like the servant of Isa 40–55 cut-off from all except from God. His remembrance is in God's narrative.

What is astonishing is that Joshua is presented in Num 13:8 as the representative of Ephraim—under the appellation "Hoshea son of Nun." And immediately after that we hear in Num 13:16 that "Moses changed the name of Hoshea son of Nun to Joshua" (NRSV).[1] He is the third major figure in the Pentateuch who will not have a formulistic *tōlĕdôt* attached to his name. The lengthy narrative revolving around him is ascribed to God's narrative not to achievements for him or others to boast of.[2] At this point we have two Ephraims: One on the track of Abraham–Joseph reflecting the narrative of the God of Abraham, and one on the line of the narratives of Adam and Jacob. The story of Gideon in the book of Judges chs. 6–8 offers

---

[1] Cf. section 1.1 above.
[2] Technically for students of antiquity, these are known as "aretologies," in English best translated as "listings of outstanding deeds and/or virtues." These are lists of achievements, whether of a deity, a king, or a personage. The redactors of the biblical literature take a derogatory stance regarding these. For them, the monotheistic deity is the author of all of creation. The aretology of anyone can only be either a deterministic succession of monotonous events or a catalogue of sinful actions. No human being can boast except of vanities. This is most pointedly given expression to in the book of Ecclesiastes.

a pedagogical illustration of this point. The narratives of the "major" judges in the book of Judges continue the narrative of the God of Sinai while counterpointing the narrative/sins of the descendants of Jacob and Adam. The story of Gideon, who comes from a "lesser" clan of the tribe of Manasseh, must reflect the narrative/lesson regarding the God of the redactors. God calls him to throw back the threat of the Midianites. Initially, Gideon calls his tribesmen and other tribes to muster against the Midianites. God rejects this "army" and asks Gideon to whittle down this host. In the final step he asks Gideon to test who of the remaining men lap water like dogs; they are to be chosen. In Hebrew the word for dog is *keleb*. In Arabic it is *kalb*. The insinuation is that they are Calebites. Just as the opening of the promised land would be allowed only to Joshua and Caleb from among the first generation in the book of Numbers, here again it is Calebites who will be allowed to join Gideon in facing off the Midianites. The important thing for the storyteller and his God is that the action should be understood unilaterally as God's (cf. Judg 7:2). The pedagogy is the point. In Judg 8:1–3, the tribe of Ephraim comes angrily to Gideon, castigating him for having overlooked calling them to the confrontation. His answer is effectively, neither you in your rich vineyards nor I in my poorer vineyards could do anything; it is God who delivered the Midianite kings to us.[3]

Joshua/Hoshea son of Nun, while an Ephraimite, is alone with Caleb to paradigmatically open the promised land in the book of Joshua in a narrative/lesson whose only effective actor is the God of Sinai, of Abraham. Joshua the Ephraimite becomes the "son" of Joseph in God's storytelling through the

---

[3] The "virtue" of Gideon is illustrated in that he refuses the offer of kingship presented to him by the tribes of Jacob, Judg 8:22–23. On the other hand, the presumption of his son to assume kingship provokes the ban of God to be imposed on Gideon's progeny (cf. ch. 9). The action of Gideon's son Abimelech leads through fratricide and God's ban to a cut in God's storyline, giving way to the sins of the descendants of Jacob and the undoing of God's salvific actions. When God resumes his narrative, it is again not through dynastic continuity; it is through a new narrative lesson.

agency of Moses, replacing the Ephraim taken away from him by Jacob. The transformed Joseph is now defined/ "filled in" by the transformed Joshua-Ephraim. The increase implicit in the name "Joseph" will now be redefined and complemented by the Joshua-Ephraim. The Jacob-Ephraim will continue to define increase in terms of rich vineyards, wealth, and economic prosperity. We saw in chapter 1 that "increase" of this sort is rejected by the God of the servant in Isa 40–55. Effectively, closing the Jacob part in Isa 40–55, we hear "no more increase of this sort," no more of the increase that Jacob revels in, no more the boast of Joseph, no more the Ephraimitic boast of wealth. The increase planned by this deity is otherwise.

Already before the report about the re-naming of Joshua/Hoshea in Num 13:16, we are introduced to Joshua in a new role. When the sons of Jacob murmur in the wilderness against the God of Exodus, God responds by asking Moses to go out of the camp with seventy elders (this number being symbolic of the nations) and pours of the spirit given to Moses on them and they prophesy. Two men were left in the camp, and the spirit came on them and they too prophesied. Thereupon, Joshua son of Nun objected and asked Moses to stop them. Moses responds: "Are you jealous for my sake? Would that all the Lord's people were prophets, and that the Lord would put his spirit on them!" (NRSV). Joshua appears here as the more zealot/jealous servant of Moses, again outside the encampment and juxtaposed against it (which is God's position also at this point of the narrative) just as the whole passage in Num 11–12 posits the camp of Jacob's sons as opposed to the God of Moses. Just as in Exod 33 God breaks with the encampment of Jacob/Israel, Joshua, who since Exod 33 has been resident outside of the encampment in the tent of meeting, articulates this break but is enjoined by Moses to understand that God had not changed his "wish" regarding Adam and consequently Jacob, even in the midst of utter apostasy. It is noteworthy here to bring to mind Isa 44:2–3, where the God of the servant expresses his desire vis-à-vis a wished for "upright, 'Jeshurun'" Jacob: "Thus says the Lord who made you, who formed you in the womb, and will help you: Do not fear, O Jacob my servant, Jeshurun[4] whom I have chosen. For I will pour water on the thirsty land, and streams on the dry ground; I will pour my spirit upon your descendants, and my blessing on your offspring." (NRSV). Joshua is being taught here to view matters from the perspective of the God of Abraham.

In Num 13:16, Joshua is named as representing the tribe of Ephraim in the company chosen to "check out" the land and bring back report. While all the other members of the company report back that whereas the country they checked out was rich and fruitful, it would be impossible to take, Joshua and Caleb protest against their report, saying that if God wills it, then He would give them the land, a land "flowing with milk and honey" (Num 14:8). Joshua separates here again from the rest of the sons of Jacob, this time in company with Caleb. The mutiny of the sons of Jacob having reached its apogee, God addresses Moses and Aaron and in Num 14:30–31 He concludes: "not one of you shall come into the land in which I swore to settle you, except Caleb son of Jephunneh and Joshua son of Nun. But your little ones, who you said would become booty, I will bring in, and they shall know the land that you have despised." (NRSV). The cast has been set. From here on, Joshua with Caleb become the bearers of God's narrative, preparing the ground for the next generation. Joshua becomes the transformed and transforming Ephraim, defining the term "Joseph/increase" differently from the Ephraim of Jacob. The Joshua-Moses will lead into the "promised land," while the Moses of Aaron and the other leaders of the sons of Jacob are condemned not to enter it. Moses in conjunction with Aaron is adjoined to the production of a distinct narrative, *tōlĕdôt*, in Num 3:1, and, as we saw, both are punished in Num 14; they will not

---

[4] Cf. chapter 1, section 2.2.1 for the reading of "Jeshurun" as a conditional clause incumbent on Jacob in order to meet the requirements of the God of the servant.

enter the land of the promise. Further below, we will see what happens with the Joshua-Moses, who will not have a narrative distinct from that of the God of Abraham.

1.4 Joshua and Moses in the Book of Deuteronomy

While the book of Numbers is a series of parochial problems and adjudications, the book of Deuteronomy is a book of discourses framing the Deuteronomic Code. Its name in Hebrew is very fitting, "words, *děbārîm*." In Hebrew, the books of the Pentateuch are named by the word commencing each of the books. Indeed, the emphasis on the "words" of the God of Exodus pervades the whole book of Deuteronomy and provides for the distinctive cadence of the discourses we encounter in it. We have already seen in chapter 2, section 3, that the metaphor of bread for "word" is prominently underscored as a leitmotiv in Deut 8:4: "one does not live by bread alone, but by every word that comes from the mouth of the Lord." Already the book opens with "These are the words that Moses spoke to all Israel beyond the Jordan." (NRSV). This phrase or variants thereof is repeated throughout the book. Moses in the book of Deuteronomy becomes "words," pedagogical discourses. When he dies beyond the Jordan, he is buried in an unmarked grave, at what appears to be the foothill of a Mount Nebo. A most unpretentious, lowly burial, or is it? Before his death, Moses goes up the mount, and God shows him all the promised land from North to South. We are told the following:

> Then Moses went up from the plains of Moab to Mount Nebo, to the top of Pisgah, which is opposite Jericho, and the Lord showed him the whole land: Gilead as far as Dan, all Naphtali, the land of Ephraim and Manasseh, all the land of Judah as far as the Western Sea, the Negeb, and the Plain . . .The Lord said to him, "This is the land of which I swore to Abraham, to Isaac, and to Jacob, saying, 'I will give it to your descendants'; I have let you see it with your eyes, but you shall not cross over there." (Deut 34:1–4 NRSV).

The terminology used mimics that of mystery religions. Pisgah, from the Hebrew triliteral *psg*, would seem to indicate a slit from which one would be shown a vision in a mystery religion. Indeed it would be impossible to get a view of the whole land as described, unless understood as a divine vision. The God of the Exodus, after having allowed Moses to "see" God on Sinai, here allows Moses to "see" the spread of the promise. But, nevertheless, Moses is not buried on the mount but in an unmarked grave in the valley. To understand what the text is saying here, we should take note of the fact that the Mesopotamian god of wisdom and scribal activity is Nabu (from the same Semitic triliteral root from which we have the Hebrew word for Prophet, *nābî'*). The location of the remains of Moses will be outside the land, in fact, in Moab, in enemy land. But where would one find him? The answer is, in the "Book." Moses has become a book. It will be completed by Joshua. In Deut 34:9 we read: "Joshua son of Nun was full of the spirit of wisdom, because Moses had laid his hands on him, and the Israelites obeyed him, doing as the Lord had commanded Moses." (NRSV). Moses, in the hands of the scribal redactional group, like Joshua, resides now outside the encampment of the sons of Jacob. He is not on a high place, but in a valley. He can be found in the redactional work of the Joshua "group." He will have no other narrative or listing of works/progeny of his own, he "achieves" finally becoming subsumed totally to the narrative of the God of Exodus/Sinai. He will not be put on a pedestal or encountered anywhere else other than in the scribal work brought to conclusion! He cannot have any boast of his own. Though mentioned several times in the Pentateuch as the servant of Yahweh, this designation competed up till now with the gravitational pull of Aaron, Miriam, and the sons of Jacob. At this point at the end of Deuteronomy he is "freed" from this pull into the narrative, *tōlĕdôt*, of Aaron and the sons of Jacob. The Moses of Aaron will continue to have in the hands of the sons of Aaron a track continually attempting to assimilate him to the track of Adam and Eve. The redactional group producing this "work" wins its confrontation against the clerical group by producing this scribal work; not by winning in wealth or military prowess, but by losing through "outing" itself, spilling its guts out, in this book. This is now a witness against all the sons of Jacob, and all sons and daughters of Adam and Eve. In conclusion, let us take a step ahead to the end of the first book of DH, the book of Joshua, to this group's own understanding of its legacy:

> So Joshua made a covenant with the people that day, and made statutes and ordinances for them at Shechem. Joshua wrote these words in the book of the law of God; and he took a large stone, and set it up there under the oak in the sanctuary of the Lord. Joshua said to all the people, "See, this stone shall be a witness against us; for it has heard all the words of the Lord that he spoke to us; therefore it shall be a witness against you, if you deal falsely with your God." So Joshua sent the people away to their inheritances. (Josh 24:25–28 NRSV).

The increase planned by the deity of Isa 40–55 is a body of writings that reveal the mind of this deity, effecting through this body of writings justice and salvation in Jacob and the nations. Compare the above quoted passage with the opening phrases of the first song of the servant:

> Here is my servant, whom I uphold, my chosen, in whom my soul delights; I have put my spirit upon him; he will bring forth justice to the nations. He will not cry or lift up his voice, or make it heard in the street; a bruised reed he will not break, and a dimly burning wick he will not quench; he will faithfully bring forth justice. He will not grow faint or be crushed until he has established justice in the earth; and the coastlands wait for his teaching. . . . I am the Lord, I have called you in righteousness, I have taken you by the hand and kept you; I have given you as a covenant to the people, a light to the nations, to open the eyes that are blind, to bring out the prisoners from the dungeon, from the prison those who sit in darkness. I am the Lord, that is my name; my glory I give to no other, nor my praise to idols. See, the former things have come to pass, and new things I now declare; before they spring forth, I tell you of them. (Isa 42:1–9 NRSV).

1.5 Summation re the Couple Joseph–Joshua

Joshua cohabits in the tent of meeting with the bones of Joseph. The bones of Joseph share not only cohabitation with Joshua but also co-localization with the tablets of the law in a chest called in Hebrew *ărôn*. This term seems to have cultic signification, has its natural habitat in a sanctuary, and phonetically invites wordplay with Aaron in Hebrew (cf. section 1.2.1 above). It appears to pertain to a mobile sanctuary, as might be expected to be found among a nomadic community. The tablets of the law are a *pars pro toto*. They stand for the whole law, the Pentateuch. The bones of Joseph point to a posthumous publication of the work. The "young" Joshua at the service of Moses appears to be the school of "Joseph," charged with carrying out the project. The name Joseph (add/increase) indicates a proposal of an alternative trajectory/ perspective/ track towards dealing with a dire predicament and opening up the future. The name Moses would appear to be the name given to the project of producing this literature.

Excursus: The beginnings, before this project was started, must have seen a widespread collaborative effort of various parties on a wide scale in the face of extreme adversity; a "national" reform movement, joining the clerical, the militant warrior, and the political leadership, each party, clan or tribe pulling its own way. A "younger" group we see reflected in the book of Jeremiah seems to have developed around the personality behind Isa 40–55, distancing itself from both the clerical and the military parties. This again we can see reflected in the book of Jeremiah. In the course of the resistance reform movement legal codes would have been proposed by the various component parties. The group formed by the author of Isa 40–55 set itself to producing the body of literature we are studying as its counterproposal to the other parties and this may have been the group that came up with the name "Moses." In the book of the Latter Prophets, we find this designation in the work of the first generation of the disciples of this school in Isa

63:11–12. The reason for this designation may best be discerned in the writing ascribed here to the second generation of disciples and postulated as Isa 1–39, written to frame the work of the founding teacher and the first generation and reflective of the full project. There are passages in the book of Isaiah chapters 8 and 30–31 that can help in clarifying the factors that were in play for the choice of the appellative "Moses." In chapter 8 we hear:

> Because this people has refused the waters of Shiloah that flow gently, and melt in fear before Rezin and the son of Remaliah; therefore, the Lord is bringing up against it the mighty flood waters of the River, the king of Assyria and all his glory; it will rise above all its channels and overflow all its banks; it will sweep on into Judah as a flood, and, pouring over, it will reach up to the neck; and its outspread wings will fill the breadth of your land, O Immanuel. . . . Bind up the testimony, seal the teaching among my disciples. I will wait for the Lord, who is hiding his face from the house of Jacob, and I will hope in him. See, I and the children whom the Lord has given me are signs and portents in Israel from the Lord of hosts, who dwells on Mount Zion. (Isa 8:6–8; 16–18 NRSV).

Similarly in chapter 30 we find:

> Go now, write it before them on a tablet, and inscribe it in a book, so that it may be for the time to come as a witness forever. For they are a rebellious people, faithless children, children who will not hear the instruction of the Lord; . . . For thus said the Lord God, the Holy One of Israel: In returning and rest you shall be saved; in quietness and in trust shall be your strength. But you refused and said, "No! We will flee upon horses" — therefore you shall flee! and, "We will ride upon swift steeds" — therefore your pursuers shall be swift! . . . Alas for those who go down to Egypt for help and who rely on horses, who trust in chariots because they are many and in horsemen because they are very strong, but do not look to the Holy One of Israel or consult the Lord! . . . The Egyptians are human, and not God; their horses are flesh, and not spirit. When the Lord stretches out his hand, the helper

will stumble, and the one helped will fall, and they will all perish together. (Isa 30:8–9, 15–16; 31:1, 3 NRSV).

In both these passages, the decision to write down the teaching is directly linked to a description of opponents as trusting in military strength. The choice of the term Moses may be an attempt to describe this project as a "pedestrian" (derived from the Semitic triliteral *mšy/mšh*), or scribal pedagogical approach (derived from the Semitic root *wšy/wšh*) opposite groups cowered by and looking to armed "horsemen" for salvation. A similar portrayal of the "pedestrian" man of God being more powerful than horsemen/chariots is found in the Elijah cycle in DH (1 Kgs 18:45–46; 2 Kgs 2:12).

1.6 Revisiting the Blessings of Moses (Deut 33)

While the Song of Moses in Deut 32 is a harsh indictment of Jacob, the mood changes to the opposite in Deut 33. In Deut 32:15 the actual Jacob is juxtaposed to the divinely wished for Jacob, called to uprightness. The called-for Jacob is named Jeshurun, a jussive form that can be translated as "may he/they be upright" or as suggested for the use of the appellative in Isa 44:2 (in chapter 1, section 2.2.1) as a conditional clause "when they/should they deign to function uprightly." We find this appellative in biblical literature only in Isa 44:2 and three times here in Deut 32–33 (Deut 32:15; 33:5, 26). It expresses an unrealized wish on the part of the deity. The mood in the Song of Moses (Deut 32) expresses the reality of Jacob. The mood in Deut 33 (the Blessings of Moses) portrays the wish of the deity in the "imaginary" realization time of the God of Jacob (similar to what we saw in chapter 1, section 3.4, regarding the story of Jacob in Gen 32. After the Moses associated with Aaron is upbraided and his punishment is pronounced in Deut 32:50–52, in Deut 33 we have the Moses associated with Joshua, expressing in the blessings the wished for Jacob. It is the time when the God of Abraham, the God of the Exodus, would be King in Jeshurun, in Jacob, with all the tribes united (Deut 33:5). God is asked to bring back Judah to his people. Judah is no longer addressed as holding the scepter as in Jacob's blessings in Gen 49:10. In God's time as king, there is no place for Judah's pretensions to kingship. Judah instead is seen as in rebellion against God's kingship, and the wish is expressed that God will return him to his people. The reality expressed in chapter 32 is seen as an anomaly in God's time. Judah here is equivalent to Jacob in Deut 32. Levi in God's time does not have the say (Simeon). Aaron, as has been made clear in Deut 32:50–52 does not have the say; he may not claim the book of Moses to reclaim obedience through the Torah of Moses! (Aaron had been reported in Num 20:28 as having been divested of his priestly robes by Moses on Mount Hor (written with *hê*) and had died there. Ḥor or Ḥorus (depicted with the Egyptian glyph corresponding to Semitic *ḥêt*) was the god of the Pharaohs, of kingship. Already at the beginning of the chapter, the people had rebelled and practically petitioned Aaron and Moses to go back to Egypt; as a result of the rebellion, both Aaron and Moses will not be allowed to enter the land of the promise. Aaron in death is effectively associated with kingship. Moses, as we saw above, will be associated with the Babylonian god of scribal activity and wisdom. The "divinely" ordained death and burial of Aaron on Mount Hor is a very pronounced jab against the priesthood: it allies itself with kingship and thereby effectively leads back to Pharaoh's Egypt!) The sons of Levi in the blessings of Deut 33 conform to the requirements and limitations placed upon them in the book of Deuteronomy. They have to instruct Jacob in the ordinances of the book of Deuteronomy, but may not have a domain of their own (Deut 33:9–10). Benjamin is no longer a ravenous hunter seeking his prey as in Gen 49:27. The "military" Benjamin is reduced to having his security provided for him by God, sheltered in his hills as in the shoulders of the deity. With the "say" belonging to God as king, there is no mention of Simeon (cf. chapter 2, section 2.1.2). The effusive praise for Joseph is unrestrained. He is practically declared the divine heir in 33:16, but this remains short of a pretension to kingship as it remains subject to the will/good will of the God of Sinai/Exodus, and his apartness from his brothers remains as a *nazir* dedicated to God. The metaphor of divine heir is expressed again in v. 17 as "firstborn" of the bull, the bull being a metaphor for kingship applied here to God. The mention of bull brings forth the metaphor of the two horns pushing peoples to the end of the earth. The concatenation of kingly power metaphors at this point brings mention here of Ephraim and Manasseh. It is not a blessing of the two tribes; it is still an illustration of the blessing of Joseph. As was suggested already in chapter 2, section 2.4, it should be understood as an epexegetic oppositive. However, the Joseph blessing in Deut 33:13–17 demands a more detailed look.

This blessing provides several difficulties for translators and interpreters. The vocabulary is unusual; equally so the formulations:

- The word *meged* is repeated five times, monotonously so. The translations usually render it in various ways, with the result that the reader remains unaware of this compositional monotony. Even more strange is the fact that the word is used only here in the Pentateuch, and in the rest of biblical literature only three times in the Song of Songs, 4:13, 16; 7:14. In Canticles it is all three times in the plural and refers to the fruits of a paradisiacal garden. In Deut 33:13, 14 (twice), 15, 16 it is all five times in the singular. In Arabic it means "glory"; it is a widely used word, both as a common noun and a proper noun. The background to where this passage was redacted was most probably an Arabic background. This can explain much of the difficulties encountered here as well as in the Balaam story in Num 22–24. The greater difficulty, however, is in deciphering the intended message in the passage. It should be clear that the monotony and rhythmic cadence in the use of an unusual word (for Hebrew) is compositionally emphatically intended by the redactor. The question is, why?

- Verse 16 makes clear that the intended addressee of the blessing is the Joseph of the preceding narrative in the Pentateuch and not as in the other blessings here the tribe of Joseph. Reference is made to Joseph as a *nazir* separate from his brothers as in Gen 49:26, and the wish is expressed that he should be granted the favor of the one who dwells in the bush, this being a reference to the God who appears to Moses in the burning bush, Exod 3. The word used for bush is used five times in Exod 3:2 (three times), 3, 4 and once here in Deut 33:16. It is not used as such any other time in biblical literature. The same triliteral is used, differently vocalized and with an "apparently" different meaning in Josh 15:49 and 1 Sam 14:4 (more on these two locations further below and their coincident usage, in fact, with the term under discussion here). Again we see a very determined choice of words.

- In verse 17 we are suddenly faced with a different matrix in the choice of words. From the divine and paradisiac we come to a series of metaphors/similes associated with *šôr* (bull, ox). The "firstling of his bull" is accounted as his splendor/honor (in Hebrew *hādār*). A very mundane metaphor is joined to a very exalted word. We have heard of first fruits of cattle in the previous passages of the Pentateuch, this "weighty" firstling must be seen as God's due, Lev 27:26; and yet, it is reckoned as splendor/honor to Joseph! We should note that the servant-rahām in Isa 53:2 is said to have no *hādār* (honor/splendor/majesty). In continuation of the presumed metaphor, another strange word is encountered. His horns are likened to the horns of a *rĕ'ēm*. This again is a rare word in our literature. It is found twice in the Balaam story in Num 23:22; 24:8 and once here in Deut 33:17. All three in the singular. We do not encounter it otherwise in the Pentateuch. A plural form is found in Isa 34:7; Ps 22:22; 29: 6; 92:11, and in Job 39: 9, 10 we find it written as *rêm*. It has affinity to the verb *rā'am* (to rise) found once only in Zech 14:10. Even stranger is the fact that LXX translates it as unicorn (this in spite of the fact that it is followed by the mention of two horns). It is sometimes translated as referring to the white Arabian oryx or as wild ox. The only other usage, in Num 23:22; 24:8 offers further linguistic problems. Balaam, brought by the king of Moab to curse Jacob, instead blesses Jacob saying: "God, who brings them out of Egypt, is like the horns of a wild ox for them" (NRSV). The simile is applied to the God of Jacob! Moreover, what the NRSV translates as "horns" here renders another *crux interpretum*. The word translated as "horns" is *tô'ăpōt*. Gesenius–Buhl indicates it as *"unsicher"* (uncertain). It is found only here in Num 23:22; 24:8 and in Job 22:25; Ps 95:4, and Sir 45:7. One suggestion is to derive it from a supposed root *y'p* corresponding to the Arabic *yf'* by metathesis (cf. both Gesenius–Buhl and HALOT), to be translated as to tower above/stand above. I would suggest another derivation from Arabic *tuḥfah* by homorganic commutation.[5] The meaning of the word *tuḥfah* in Arabic was "a rare and pleasing present."[6] The usage in modern Arabic applies the word to an artifact or work of art with the connotation "exquisite." Be that as it may, the implication in the Balaam narrative seems to wish to refer to God's action towards Jacob in the Exodus and as divulged in the Pentateuch as extraordinary in grace and power to be likened to that of a practically mythical dimension. Both in Num 23:22 and 24:8 it is used in the plural as a simile and not a metaphor for God's action. The twofold exact repetition of the statement shows the weight attached to it by the redactor. The Balaam narrative comes nearly as a closure to the wilderness time and sendoff to the opening of the promised land. Although there are many chapters between them, the blessings of Moses in Deut 33 are still in the same time. We cannot but see a direct relationship intended between the Balaam narrative and the blessing of Joseph. The linguistic matrix is the same; the literary fictional time is the same.

- The second half of Deut 33:17 turns to specify the function of the metaphor of the bull and the horns. They will push the peoples all together to the extremities of the earth. This foreshadows the work of Joshua in the book of Joshua. It is at this point that we have the interjection regarding Ephraim and Manasseh. Three emphatic demonstrative pronouns come in succession to close the blessing. The first refers directly to the

---

5 Cf. GKC, paragraphs 6p, q, r.
6 Lane, p. 298.

horns as the tool with which the nations are pushed/forced/gored to the ends of the earth. We have seen in the Balaam narrative that the "horns" effecting the action are predicated of God. In Deut 33:17 they are predicated of Joseph under the aegis of the God of Abraham and Sinai, of the God of the Pentateuch. While the mysterious creature *rĕ'ēm* is the same in both passages, the word translated as "horns" is not. In the Joseph blessing it is the mundane word "*qeren*" (horn). In the Balaam narrative it is the enigmatic word *tô'ăpōt* (plural of *tô'ăpâ*). The second and third demonstratives are also directed to the same aforementioned "horns," but seem to define them as referring to Ephraim and Manasseh. As has been previously mentioned, this leads some commentators to regard them as later poorly applicable insertions into the original texts. The multiple referencing to God, Joseph, Ephraim, and Manasseh seems totally improbable. Particularly the reference to Ephraim and Manasseh would be dubious in the light of their reputation in the books of the Former and Latter Prophets. The expression "myriads" versus "thousands" makes no sense in reference to Ephraim and Manasseh. Neither of the two has been presented as displaying military skills. The expression is borrowed from the taunt of Saul in the book of Samuel. While David has the force of myriads, Saul has only thousands. Here there is no taunt, no comparison, and, again, no story or history of actions by Ephraim and Manasseh; the phrase falls flat. The case for rejecting it as a later insertion is very strong. However, as I have already indicated in chapter 2, section 2.4, it should be read not as appositive, but as oppositive. Not myriads or thousands will work the indicated actions, but God's actions through Joseph. Unlike David, unlike Saul, Joseph, in continuation of Abraham, will be the agent of God's unilateral actions.

Taking all these points into consideration, I venture to propose the following, by its very nature, conjectural reading of the blessing to Joseph: The fivefold invocation of the word *meged* is one salient point. Whether translated as "glory" or as "precious things/produce" relating to the heavens, the luminaries, and all there is on the earth, it sounds like the invocation anew of the heavens and earth. The monotony reflects the monotony inherent in consequent monotheism. Coming in the penultimate chapter of the Pentateuch, the fivefold book, it seems to be an invocation of the master work to be "rounded" up by Joshua according to Josh 24:26. It is this project that is referred to as the firstling of the bull (Joseph);[7] the "glory" in the heavens and on earth is God's, to Joseph, the initiator and master of the "Joshua" school is the honor and the splendor. Joseph as the servant-*rāhām* is rejected and despised by his brothers, but he is posthumously given honor and splendor by the God of the *rāhām*. The horns that accomplish this are the God of Exodus/Sinai, God and king of Jacob. The selfsame through Joshua will open the land of the promise and conquer the peoples. This will be achieved not by Jacob's power but by selfsame God, the God who showed His strength in the Exodus. This lesson will be repeated in the book of Joshua and the book of Judges. The victory is not a "military" victory, it is a scribal victory. The Joshua group taking refuge in Arab Calebite (Kenizite) regions completes the work on the basis of the blueprint it was entrusted with, Isa 40–55. The Pentateuch will have been the "firstling" work. Already the second part of the

---

7 Joseph seems to be confounded here once with the "firstling," with the opus, and once with the "bull" as divine heir. This is similar to what we have in the Joseph narrative in Gen 37–50, where Joseph is at times confounded with Pharaoh and/or God.

book of Numbers indicates that the second tome is being prepared. The view in Numbers and Deuteronomy is already directed to the entry in the book of Joshua and the rise and fall of David and the Davidic dynasty in DH. This also was in the blueprint of Isa 40–55. There we have in the second part the parable of Abraham and Sarah, the lesson worked out in the Pentateuch, but we also have the invocation of "an everlasting covenant, my steadfast, sure love for David." (Isa 55:3 NRSV). This is an invocation of steadfastness from God's side, already invoked for all human beings through the invocation of Noah in 54:8–10. From Jacob's side, this will involve a doubling back and the undoing of God's work. This is the pedagogical lesson of DH, moving in the reverse direction of Isa 40–55. From the narrative of Abraham and the God of Exodus and Sinai in the Pentateuch through the work of the Joshua group at the beginning of DH, we go on to the progressive regression ending in the destruction of Jerusalem at the end of DH. The scribal pedagogy required both tablets, reflecting in reverse order the diptych of Isa 40–55.

The last chapter of Deuteronomy, ch. 34, following the blessings by Moses effectively tells us that "Moses" is now a scribal book; that he is no longer accessible except as the "book." This was already explicated in ch. 30 and particularly in Deut 30:9b–14:

> For the Lord will again take delight in prospering you, just as he delighted in prospering your ancestors, when you obey the Lord your God by observing his commandments and decrees that are written in this book of the law, because you turn to the Lord your God with all your heart and with all your soul. Surely, this commandment that I am commanding you today is not too hard for you, nor is it too far away. It is not in heaven, that you should say, "Who will go up to heaven for us, and get it for us so that we may hear it and observe it?" Neither is it beyond the sea, that you should say, "Who will cross to the other side of the sea for us, and get it for us so that we may hear it and observe it?" No, the word

is very near to you; it is in your mouth and in your heart for you to observe. (NRSV).

This was the previously "unheard of" project announced in Isa 40–55 as the salvation action that God was about to do. The "transformed" Joseph is in continuation of the *rāhām*. The question posed at the end of chapter 2 as to whether the Joseph story is to be understood figuratively is to be answered in the affirmative. The "success" of Joseph and his providing grain to Jacob and to the Egyptians is in effect the providing of scribal provision, a feast of words, or as we hear in Deut 8:3 "in order to make you understand that one does not live by bread alone, but by every word that comes from the mouth of the Lord." (NRSV).

2. Further Elements of the Redaction of the Books of the Law and the Prophets

2.1 The Legislative Codes and the Structuring of the Pentateuch

The general background to the writing as conjectured here is a national reform movement as schematized in section 1.5 above. The various and competing groups will have proposed reform law codes to strengthen the internal front in the encounter with invading powers. An early collaborative effort will have produced an early form of what we have as the Covenant Code in the book of Exodus chs. 21–23. Internal liberation was paramount as we see reflected in the book of Jeremiah. The plutocratic group reneged on this when the danger from outside seemed to recede as we are informed by this book. The militant warrior groups will have wanted centralization of efforts and aligned themselves with the higher clerics in an effort to centralize administrative and clerical power. An earlier version of their proposal will have served as the major source for the Deuteronomic Code in Deut 12–26. The third major code proposal we are faced with is the Holiness

Code, Lev 17–26. In contrast with the two previous codes, this code suggests itself as a solo proposal in imaginary time. It might be best called the Jubilee year code. Jacob practically disappears here except for one mention in 26:42 reminiscent of both Isa 40–55 and the teaching of the finished Pentateuch as a whole. The whole composition shares the same sovereign compositional cadenced style as Isa 40–55, equally oblivious to real time, equally composed in fictional pedagogical time. It has often been placed in connection with the author of Isa 40–55. It fits well with the founder of a scribal school, disillusioned with the extant clergy and ritual, and equally disillusioned by the militant warrior groupings. In an "academy," one has the freedom, even in exile, even on foreign or hostile grounds, to write in "imaginary" fictional time, particularly if the intent is pedagogical, particularly if all the "real time" proposals had led to utter collapse. The view that this is a composition by the author of Isa 40–55 is shared by the present writer.

How were these codes built into the Pentateuch, and how was the Pentateuch structured around them? This will be schematically proposed in the following brief exposition:

The book of Genesis leads us from Abraham to Joseph, from Ab-raham to the *rāhām*, seen here as the author of Isa 40–55. In the book of Exodus, the creation of the literary composite figure "Moses" begins. Moses is initially assimilated to an exile in a foreign court. He must call his brothers, the sons of Jacob, to the wilderness, outside Pharaoh's domain and outside the promised land. He is portrayed here as marshaling all the various groups in a collaborative effort. This has a resemblance to Plato's Socrates taking his disciples outside the city of Athens to teach them. Once they reach the Mount Olympus of the redactor's deity, Mount Sinai, in the middle of the wilderness, the confrontation with the other groups begins to heat up. Initially, the collaborative covenant code is presented as mediated by Moses, Exod 21–23, and adapted to the view reflected in the book of Jeremiah by the prophet Jeremiah. The charta of the ten "words" of the monotheistic deity is introduced ahead of it, making it the basic tonality of all what follows, anticipating the book of Deuteronomy and bracketing with the second edition of the "ten words" in Deut 5 all that lies in-between. Once they have turned the corner out of sight of Pharaoh, the recidivist plutocracy in alliance with the clerical leadership is portrayed in rebellion, Exod 32–34, similarly to what we have in the book of Jeremiah. This apostasy is placed in the middle of the prescriptions for the wilderness sanctuary, highlighting thus that the apostasy of the leadership is directly against the "divine" sanctuary outside the gates of Pharaoh and Jerusalem, against the mountain of God. The "original" tablets written by the hand of the deity are broken and new copies are made by human hands. The scribal school commences its work in the face of this apostasy.

The third book, Leviticus, is positioned timelessly in the divine sanctuary in the wilderness. It is structured like Isa 40–55 in two parts. The first part is Lev 1–15, the Aaron part. Much of the legislation will have been collections in the hands of the upper clergy. Aaron's sons, Nadab and Abihu, are punished in Lev 10:1. They represent the rich (Nadab) and hereditary (Abihu) priests. The adaptation of these "priestly" laws is made such as to make the Aaronide priesthood subject to "Moses." The central chapter of Leviticus and consequently of the Pentateuch is Lev 16. It is also the interstitial chapter between the two parts of the book. In chapter 16, Aaron on the most solemn Day of Atonement presents offerings for his sins and for those of the community. He is then superseded by the "scapegoat," who does the work for the sins of the community and the "greatness of God" (cf. chapter 2, section 2.3.1, footnote 16). The scapegoat functions by being sent outside the community into the wilderness. He stands for the servant-*rāhām* of Isa 53 and for Joseph as portrayed in the book of Genesis. Immediately following this central chapter we have the Holiness Code, or, as I suggested, the Jubilee Code. As suggested above, this appears to be the work of the author of Isa 40–55. Towards the end in

26:42 Jacob is mentioned only to be warned in the style of Isa 40–55. The code is a call to the people to become assimilated to the servant-*rāhām*, through whom alone the perspective of Jubilee time, of entry into the land of the promise, is offered. Jubilee time is formulated as a re-consecration of all the land, as a time of "rest" for the land. The Jubilee period is an exponentially "turbocharged" sacral time, it is seven times seven years; the sacral time is raised to a new plane: it thus becomes "divine time"; it is a restoration of the land as it was initially given by the divinity. The sacral time of Aaron's sons in chs. 1–15 is declassed. The time initiated by the "scapegoat" in ch. 16 is on a different order of sacralization. The offering of the scapegoat on the Day of Atonement initiates the second half of the book, that is, of the Holiness Code; so also the offering on the Day of Atonement after seven weeks of years initiates the Jubilee year, Lev 25:8–10. This reflects the extreme critique of Isa 40–55 of the Jerusalem priesthood organized around the temple.[8] The Holiness Code "one-ups" also the Covenant Code, which was based on a seven-year cycle, The initial entry into the land is itself stylized as a re-consecration of the land, Lev 19:23–25; 25:2–5, and thus is, effectively, an initial "Jubilee year." Every Jubilee year thereafter must reset back to the initial situation as given initially by God, Lev 25:8–13.

The book of Numbers brings us back to real time, down from the mountain. Both Aaron and Jacob are back at work. Aaron gravitates to Jacob, and Moses gravitates to Aaron, and we have the Aaron-Moses. Moses is overwhelmed by the sons of Jacob and by Miriam and Aaron. This is expressed in literary terms at the beginning of the book by "awarding" Moses in conjunction with Aaron a joint "*tōlĕdôt* (aretology/narrative of achievements)" in Num 3:1, and, as a result of which, in Num 20:12–13 Moses is punished in conjunction with the sin of Aaron and the sons of Jacob. The book "Moses" in the hands of Aaron and Jacob is shown not to work. After the death of

---

8 Cf. chapter1, section 2.2.2.

Aaron in Num 20:22–29 events start to turn around. The Moses as communicated by Joshua starts to become effective. In Num 27:12–23 Joshua is formally appointed to succeed Moses. Caleb had already been singled out in Num 14:24 as not pertaining to the rebellious people. In Num 26:65 and 32:12 Caleb and Joshua are named together as the only two of the generation entered in the census at the beginning of the book of Numbers who will be allowed to enter the land of the promise. The Joshua group apparently resides with Caleb the Kenizite (cf. Num 32:12). Caleb, it appears, does double duty, representing both Judah and the Arab Kenizites.[9] Ephraim is represented by Joshua. The Moses of Joshua is the only "legitimate" continuation of "Moses."

In Deuteronomy it is the Joshua-Moses at work. He is portrayed as a "lecturer" delivering pedagogical discourses. The school is at work. As it would seem to be resident outside the urban centers, hosted by Caleb, it must have come into confrontation with the militant groups offering a different view to liberation/salvation. The legal code proposed by this militant group is taken up and redacted in the sense of its own teaching, and framed within the Joshuan-Moses discourses. In lieu of the centralization requested by the opposing group, it proposes a unitary but ambulant form thereof, coherent with its own view of itself and its role. It shared the critique directed against the poorer levites, but provided a framework for their sustenance,

---

[9] The "banu Kalb" was a designation for a group of northwestern Arab tribes. At times the designation would be extended generically to designate the northwestern Arab tribes bordering on the Levant. In biblical literature we see Abraham, Moses, and David having extensive relations, including marital relations, with the various clans. Joshua grants them a part of the domain of Judah under the designation of Caleb, equivalent to "banu Kalb." What appears extended diachronically over nearly a millennium in the biblical narrative is actually synchronic, narrated in a variety of different forms and settings. For the designation "banu Kalb" and the northwestern Arab tribes, cf. J. Spencer Trimingham, *Christianity among the Arabs in Pre-Islamic Times* (Beirut: Longman and Librairie du Liban, 1979), passim. Though this book is written about a somewhat later period, the nomenclature therein is likely to reflect older usage.

again coherent with its own views and corresponding to its own taking refuge among the Calebites. The structure of the completed work, the Pentateuch, will be reflected in various ways again in the redaction of its other literary production, the books of the Former and Latter Prophets.

2.2 Elements of Style that Span the Pentateuch and the Books of the Prophets

As has been repeatedly stated, the basic concern of the redactors is to highlight God's actions as in contradistinction to Jacob's and Adam's (and Eve's) actions, a paramount concern of the author of Isa 40–55. To this end stylistic elements are brought into play. The most prominent in the Pentateuch is the use of the term *tōlĕdôt* (aretology/narrative of achievements) in counterpoint to God's "narrative." This has been repeatedly highlighted in this presentation. The reason this is employed only in the patriarchal timespan is that aretologies in the ancient world were listings of virtues/achievements of individual gods or apotheosized heroic individuals, thus they belong to "mythological" time. Only at a later time do they begin to be created for very prominent individuals. After Adam and Eve venture to play God at the behest of the serpent, our redactors use this stylistic element to make sport of this human pretension. The one other time outside the Pentateuch that this stylizing term is used, illustrative of this use, is in the book of Ruth. It is used in conjunction with Perez, the son of Judah. Perez is the pendant to Ephraim in the Pentateuch and is thus at the epochal limit for applying this element for the redactors. The intent is to put down human boasting in terms of private domains, dynastic lists, wealth and numbers of progeny. These are displayed as a monotonous succession of deterministic sinful nonsense and as a chain of barren vanities. Already the coining of the word in Hebrew displays this bias. That translators choose to translate it as genealogies is not accidental. It is built from the verbal root *yld* (to give birth, bring forth). It is used as exact counterpart to the Greek aretology, which is a compound of αρετη (virtue, merit) and λογος (word, discourse). The contrast in derivation displays the intended sarcasm. The deity of our redactors already in Gen 1:20–28 ordained for all living creatures that they multiply and fill the earth. The tool that our redactors' God wields is His word, *dābār* in Hebrew, *děbārîm* in the plural. This has been shown to be the quintessential proposition of the author of Isa 40–55 and thus adopted by his disciples both in the creation narrative and in the book of Deuteronomy where it is the keynote word from the beginning of the book. As opposed to barren human boasts and dynasties, this is presented as the "mono"-creative and all-creative tool, the only one that always brings forth fruit. An example of the opposite "principle" was hinted at above. While God's action in the Joseph narrative and through Moses in the book of Exodus brings forth a huge multitude departing from the Mount of God, as is shown in the census at the beginning of the book of Numbers, barely by the middle of the same book, as a result of the actions of selfsame multitude, only two are left useful for God's purposes in order to enter the land of promise, the others perish in the empty wilderness. Neither the progeny of Jacob and their dependents nor the closed succession lines of Aaron are of any use. The two "wild cards," Joshua and Caleb, will continue God's narrative. The contrast between discourses/*děbārîm* versus accumulation of numbers, wealth, progeny, dynasties does not stop with the patriarchal "mythical" times. Thus, although *tōlědôt*/aretology as a literary structuring element is no longer applicable after the mythological time of the founding forefathers, other structuring elements are ushered in to continue this basic "carrier" theme underlying the whole work and forming its articular sinews. These are simply the intended components of the put-down mentioned above employed as caricatures of human "stately," highbrow foibles.

The lists of cities defining domains in the book of Joshua caricature the lists we have from ancient times and specifically Hellenistic times. In the book of Judges we find sardonic resumes of the "lesser" judges such as:

After him Ibzan of Bethlehem judged Israel. He had thirty sons. He gave his thirty daughters in marriage outside his clan and brought in thirty young women from outside for his sons. He judged Israel seven years. Then Ibzan died, and was buried at Bethlehem. After him Elon the Zebulunite judged Israel; and he judged Israel ten years. Then Elon the Zebulunite died, and was buried at Aijalon in the land of Zebulun. After him Abdon son of Hillel the Pirathonite judged Israel. He had forty sons and thirty grandsons, who rode on seventy donkeys; he judged Israel eight years. Then Abdon son of Hillel the Pirathonite died, and was buried at Pirathon in the land of Ephraim, in the hill country of the Amalekites. (Judg 8–15 NRSV).

Interspersed between the narratives about the judges, greater and lesser, there is the formulistic report: "The Israelites again did what was evil in the sight of the Lord, and the Lord gave them into the hand of . . ." (Judg 13:1). In contradistinction, as we saw in the narrative about Gideon in section 1.3 above, God's action of salvation is translated as a pedagogical discourse in the form of a narrative, mimicking reports of heroic deeds in the ancient world. The most explicitly indicated literary element employed is in the books of Kings. Starting with Solomon and continuing with the reports about the kings of Israel and the kings of Judah, we are presented with a mock-up of official kingly annals. The formulation in the case of Solomon is the following: "Now the rest of the acts of Solomon, all that he did as well as his wisdom, are they not written in the Book of the Acts of Solomon?" (1 Kgs 11:41 NRSV). Starting with Jeroboam, first king of the northern kingdom, this becomes: "Now the rest of the acts of Jeroboam, how he warred and how he reigned, are written in the Book of the Annals of the Kings of Israel." (1 Kgs 14:19 NRSV); for the southern kingdom, starting with Rehoboam, the formulary is similarly modelled: "Now the rest of the acts of Rehoboam, and all that he did, are they not written in the Book of the Annals of the Kings of Judah?" (1 Kgs 14:29 NRSV). Interesting in this is that we do not have such a formulation for David. David, in spite of his sins, remains in God's time. Because of his sin, God announces that he will cut his line; the continuation cannot reside in Solomon or the kings of the northern and southern kingdoms, it can only come from God. It must come as proof of God's "steadfast . . . love for David," as we hear in Isa 55:3. This is understood in the school of this master as:

> A shoot shall come out from the stump of Jesse, and a branch shall grow out of his roots. The spirit of the Lord shall rest on him, the spirit of wisdom and understanding, the spirit of counsel and might, the spirit of knowledge and the fear of the Lord. His delight shall be in the fear of the Lord. He shall not judge by what his eyes see, or decide by what his ears hear; but with righteousness he shall judge the poor, and decide with equity for the meek of the earth; he shall strike the earth with the rod of his mouth, and with the breath of his lips he shall kill the wicked. Righteousness shall be the belt around his waist, and faithfulness the belt around his loins. The wolf shall live with the lamb, the leopard shall lie down with the kid, the calf and the lion and the fatling together, and a little child shall lead them. The cow and the bear shall graze, their young shall lie down together; and the lion shall eat straw like the ox. The nursing child shall play over the hole of the asp, and the weaned child shall put its hand on the adder's den. They will not hurt or destroy on all my holy mountain; for the earth will be full of the knowledge of the Lord as the waters cover the sea. On that day the root of Jesse shall stand as a signal to the peoples; the nations shall inquire of him, and his dwelling shall be glorious. (Isa 11:1–10 NRSV).

The continuation of David's narrative is God's to write. The cutoff of David is because of his sin, but the result is the same as with Joseph, the continuation can only come from God. David functions not as a dynast (when he does, he is punished and his dynastic claim is denied): in his sin he functions as Jacob/Adam, in the cutoff he functions as Abraham and Joseph, as parables in God's domain. Most indicative of the view of the redactors is the passage in 2 Sam describing the reception of the ark by David in Jerusalem:

> David danced before the Lord with all his might; David was girded with a linen ephod. So David and all the house of Israel

brought up the ark of the Lord with shouting, and with the sound of the trumpet. As the ark of the Lord came into the city of David, Michal daughter of Saul looked out of the window, and saw King David leaping and dancing before the Lord; and she despised him in her heart. (2 Sam 6:14–16 NRSV).

David is acceptable and allowed to host the ark only because he acts self-depreciatively as a dancing dervish; for the same reason that he is acceptable to God he is despised by Saul's daughter. It is this David—who concedes kingship to God, represented by the Ark of the Covenant, of the book—who is the recipient of God's "everlasting covenant" and who is a token of God's "everlasting . . . sure love" (Isa 55:3). He thus joins Abraham, Joseph, Joshua as a parable of God's action. He becomes a "virtual" servant and the continuation can only be in God's time, in Jubilee time! The redactors of the books of the Former and Latter Prophets cannot display more clearly their dependence on the two works: Isa 40–55 and the Holiness Code. Denying David the formulistic ending referral to kingly annals awarded to all the kings starting with Solomon and including both the houses of Samaria and Judah functions exactly as the denial of a *tōlĕdôt* (aretology) to Abraham, Joseph, and Joshua. As with the names of Abraham, Joseph, and Joshua, *nomen est omen*, in this case, in the name is the parable. "David" is derived from *dwd* (beloved, love).[10]

2.3 The Structural Framework of the Books of the Former and Latter Prophets

It is difficult not to see continuity between the book of Deuteronomy and the book of Joshua. Proposals to either adjoin Joshua to the Pentateuchal books to produce a Hexateuch, or to detach Deuteronomy and adjoin it to the historical books leaving a truncated Tetrateuch, fourfold book,

---

10 A beautiful variation on this root is in the opening line of the song of the vineyard in Isa 5:1–7. The short poem functions as a beautifully succinct resume of the plaint expressed in Isa 40–55 against Jacob.

have variously been put forward. The designation of the historical books from Joshua to 2 Kings as the Deuteronomic History (DH) has had wider reception as a neutral indication of the intimate relationship between the book of Deuteronomy and the books Joshua to 2 Kings. While the designations Hexateuch and Tetrateuch were important for source-critics, the designation DH underlines the observation that the program of Deuteronomy seems to be carried out in DH. For the redaction-critical presentation being attempted here, the tripartite division of the Hebrew Bible is taken as a basis for the analysis. The book of the Torah is what has been referred to as the Pentateuch, the fivefold book. The second part of the Hebrew canon is named *nĕbî'îm* (Prophets). The New Testament uses this terminology referring to "the Law and the Prophets" to refer to the scripture we call the Old Testament. The book of the Prophets is seen as bipartite in the Jewish tradition: the "Former Prophets" is equivalent to what we have referred to as "Deuteronomic History"; the second part is called the "Latter Prophets," comprising the books of Isaiah, Jeremiah, Ezekiel, and the book of the twelve 'smaller' prophets. The thesis being presented here is that the project was a deliberate project by a school of disciples of the author of Isa 40–55 and this is indicated as such in the main header title of this presentation. An attempt will be made here to delineate schematically, however briefly, the structural design of the book of the prophets displaying the redactional intent of this work if approached as a unitary work. The term "Deuteronomic History" (DH) coined by Martin Noth will be employed in the analysis. The insistence of Noth on prioritizing the literary approach in dealing with the biblical books (as opposed to a historicizing or archeological approach) is shared by the present writer.[11] The concern here, however, is to decipher the redactional intent from the perspective of the wider work of the

---

11 This is so, in spite of the fact that, in my current situation, I have been unable to access his major works on DH and on the book of Joshua directly. However, his work is a major premise to the approach taken by this presentation.

Law and the Prophets seen as a unitary and deliberately produced canon. In a final section[12], the third part of the Hebrew Bible, the *kĕtûbîm*, the (other) books, will be analyzed in continuation of this same thesis.

Firstly, I will give a description of how the redaction of the book of the Prophets can be read if the hypothesis presented here were to prove applicable to the data. In other works, taking the thesis as a working hypothesis, what can be deciphered regarding the guidelines followed by the, thus far hypothetical, redactional activity that can be seen reflected in the completed work. The shape of the book of the Prophets as found in the Hebrew Jewish tradition is assumed for the working hypothesis to be the original shape. This will prove surprising for Christians used to the shape given to the material based on the Septuagint translation and transmission, but it should be remembered that all too many editorial concerns came into play in the translation and transmission that are foreign to the concerns of the presumed original redactional group, however such a group might be construed.

On the basis of this premise the following can be said: We are faced with two tetrateuchs; the first is the book of the Former Prophets, the second is the book of the Latter Prophets. In the Jewish tradition, the two books of Samuel are one book, and the two books of Kings are one book; thus the first tetrateuch consists of the books of Joshua, Judges, Samuel, and Kings. The second tetrateuch consists of the book of Isaiah, the book of Jeremiah, the book of Ezekiel, and the book of the Twelve Prophets. In contradistinction to the Pentateuch, which seems to be organized as a full punch, a full fist, of the deity, and thus seen as his full panoply against any (military) power, the two tetrateuchs of the book of the Prophets are seen as the four gates of the temple facing the four directions. This is viewed as clearly intended to reflect the organization of the temple in the book of Ezekiel and in the organization of the marching plan in the

---

12 Cf. chapter 4 below.

wilderness in the book of Numbers around the tent of the tabernacle. Thus their tasks, the prophets, would seem to be to address the instruction of the God of the Pentateuch to the four corners of the earth, but passing through, initially, the twelve tribes. As we see throughout this work, they are the paradigm, in Hebrew, the *māšāl* to be given to the peoples of the pedagogy of this deity. (Similarly in the NT the twelve disciples become, as addressees of the pedagogy, pedagogical paradigms for any would-be disciple).

The book of the Former Prophets describes the collapse resulting from the introduction of kingship together with the building of the temple. These are seen in the book of Samuel as a mutiny against the God of Sinai/Exodus. This corresponds to the Jacob part of Isa 40–55 as well as to Genesis 1–11, where the culprit is Adam and Eve's attempt at self-apotheosis. The literary tool used to achieve this is similar to the one we saw in the book of Numbers to contrast God's work as against Jacob's efforts to undo it. In Numbers, the book starts with a census showing the extent of the multitude that had evolved as a result of God's work, and ends with only two people left through which to work out a path out of the predicament, out of the wilderness. In the Former Prophets, we begin in the book of Joshua with a sweep of the promised land, accomplished by God working alone. The walls of Jericho fall with no assist from human hands; it is accomplished by the Ark of the Covenant paraded around the walls. The pedagogy is that it is God's work and God's victory through the ark in which are the tablets; the God of the Book achieves the victory, the people must keep their hands off any booty, they must follow the prescriptions of Joshua. Already in crossing the Jordan to enter the land, it is the Ark that leads the way. Witness stones are placed to remind of the lesson, and at the end of the book again a stone as a witness of the book of Moses is placed under the oak in God's sanctuary. The warning not to rebuild the city of Jericho, Josh 6:26, is effectively a warning not to undo God's work: this is precisely what is accomplished in the rest of the books of the Former

Prophets, leading to the destruction of Jerusalem. Joshua is only figuratively a military leader here, he is effectively an instructor and a judge giving forewarning witness; he is a "savior" precisely by "wielding" God's word. The pedagogy functions through figurative language. In chapter ten, this continues to be expressed through literary inversion of properties, but more on this later. The book of Joshua functions as a pendant to the book of Genesis in the Pentateuch. The primordial time is described, and the primordial work of the deity is described, in order to contrast in the ensuing pedagogy the actions of Adam and Eve and then of Jacob. In the book of judges, the cacophonic counterpoint between the actions/narrative of the deity and those of Jacob, represented by the twelve tribes, is brought to the fore. This book is a pendant to the book of Exodus. The book of Samuel presents the request for kingship and then temple, setting into motion the full reversal of the work of the deity. This is a pendant to the book of Numbers, where the people together with Aaron effectively request a return to Egypt, to Pharaoh's domain. In the book of Samuel as in the book of Numbers, the deity forebodingly plays along; his pedagogy comes as an alternative narrative, becoming now an occasional interjection into Jacob's narrative. The fourth book of this tetrateuch, the book of kings, brings both narratives to their conclusion, vindicating God's narrative. The hard reality of the present contrasting with the mythical time of the beginning brings God's narrative in full focus to the addressees. This is where Isa 40–55 starts, with the contrast between the present reality of the addressees and the actions, past, present, and future of the deity. The book of Kings graphically translates the curses of the book of Deuteronomy counterpointed by the interjection of the warnings and teaching of Deuteronomy. Much of the literary inversions we see in the narrative are governed by this scheme of presenting a paradigm and then applying it. The direction of the inversion is determined by the starting point, whether it is in mythical beginnings or the present reality of the addressees. As we saw, Isa 40–55 starts with the reality of the addressees and then goes on to the parables expressing the pedagogy and the future salvation. This is continued in Isa 56–66 into the equivalent of the Jubilee time, the myth transposed into the future time.

The book of the Latter Prophets covers the same pedagogy as that of the book of the Former Prophets. This second prophetic tetrateuch, however, covers it from the throne room of the deity. Materially it is dominated by God's words not by Jacob's actions. God in the first prophetic tetrateuch, (other than the book of Joshua, which presents the mythical premise), reacts to Jacob's actions, which, materially, predominate. In the second tetrateuch, it is God's words through the prophets that take the initiative and predominate; thus it parallels, as tetrateuch, the predominance of God's words in the book of Deuteronomy. The sequence: Jacob's actions followed by God's actions that we have in the two tetrateuchs parallels the sequence we have in Isa 40–55 as well as the sequence in the Pentateuch. In the first tetrateuch, God grudgingly concedes Jacob kingship and temple. In the second tetrateuch, God contests kingship and temple and unequivocally reclaims sole Kingship. We are back here where Isa 40–55 starts. The first book, according to the thesis being presented here—seen as a working hypothesis—mandates how and where the book of the Latter Prophets starts. Following the lengthy "historical" introduction, Isa 1–39, effectively a midrash on the Jacob part of Isa 40–55, we go on to Isa 40–55 followed by an extended midrash on the second part of Isa 40–55, Isa 56–66. The book of Isaiah corresponds functionally to the book of Genesis in the Pentateuch. It is the keynote book. Isa 40–66 corresponds in its position in Isaiah and the book of the Latter Prophets to the placement of the Joseph narrative in the book of Genesis and the Pentateuch; both narratives are in a seemingly anonymous "timeless" time (we have already mentioned that, most often, the Joseph narrative is assimilated by critical exegetes to wisdom literature, which is timeless and general human experiential). They both gravitate from two completely differing literary genres and supposedly distinct starting points to the same indistinct anacoluthon vanishing point. The book of Jeremiah corresponds to the Moses of the book of Exodus in the Pentateuch.[13] The prophet stands in an extended altercation against Jacob and the leadership in Jerusalem in a manner similar to the situation of Moses vis-à-vis Jacob in the book of Exodus. The parallelism between the concerns of the Covenant Code in Exodus and the situation reflected in the book of Jeremiah was already pointed to above. The third book of the second prophetic tetrateuch, Ezekiel, rather than being parallel to the book of Numbers, counterpoints the Aaron we are faced with in the book of Numbers with the prophetic discourse of the prophet Ezekiel. The people and their leaders keep on referring to the prophet, but unlike Aaron, Ezekiel keeps on rebuffing them. As already mentioned in chapter 1, the book of Ezekiel is postulated here as anterior to Isa 40–55 and the Pentateuchal redaction. As argued in Tarazi, "Jeremiah and the Pentateuchal Torah,"[14] Ezekiel seems to have been the bone of contention between the Jeremiah group and its opponents. The book of Ezekiel is placed after the book of Jeremiah in the book of the Latter Prophets within the coordinates of the redactional group presumed here for the mega-project.[15] Like Isa 40–55, it precedes the redactional work postulated here and admits interjection of redactional passages but very limited alteration to carryover passages. It will thus remain until late in the first century A.D. problematical for the rabbinic tradition because of its variance with prescriptions of the Torah. For the redactional group envisaged here, it is seen as a basic source for its work. However, as stated in chapter 1, "the blueprint" for its

---

13 Cf. Paul Nadim Tarazi, "The Book of Jeremiah and the Pentateuchal Torah," in *Sacred Text and Interpretation: Perspectives in Orthodox Biblical Studies* (ed. Theodore G. Stylianopoulos; Brookline, Mass.: Holy Cross Orthodox Press, 2006).
14 Ibid.
15 One glaring example of this is chapter 20. It is manifestly a resume of the Pentateuchal account written in straightforward prose and inserted into the text of Ezekiel. Basically, I agree here with the analysis of Gustav Hölscher, *Hesekiel: Der Dichter und das Buch* (BZAW 39; Giessen: Alfred Töpelmann, 1924), 108–110.

redactional work is postulated here to be the work of its "master," Isa 40–55. The fourth book of the Latter Prophets is the book of the Twelve Prophets, rounding up the work. The words, *děbārîm*, of God have now been addressed to Jacob as God's response to the misdeeds of Jacob/Adam. The number twelve refers to the twelve tribes of Jacob. Their pedagogy is fully spelt out and functions now as paradigmatic for all sons and daughters of Adam and Eve. The Pentateuch and the two prophetic tetrateuchs all end at the same point: the destruction of Jerusalem and Judah. This is the point at which Isa 40–55 starts in order to bring comfort and salvation to Jacob and thereon to the nations. Regardless of which starting point each of the three collections has, they all have a synchronous ending, they are all addressed to the same addressees. All three collections end looking prospectively to God's work of salvation beyond the total apocopation of the present reality. The book of Leviticus remains without a pendant in the two prophetic tetrateuchs, it represents, after all, the central tabernacle of which the two tetrateuchs function as the four gates. The juxtaposition of the words, *děbārîm*, of the deity vis-à-vis the dynasties, war parties, numbers of Jacob/Adam is all-pervasive and characteristic of all the books. If we take the Hebrew titles of the five books of the Pentateuch, these being the first word in each of the five books, we have the resulting phrase: "In the beginning (were) names, and then, in the wilderness, (came about) words." This is the program that was announced in Isa 40–55. The first tetrateuch (the Former Prophets) corresponds to the "names/dynasties"; the second tetrateuch (the Latter Prophets) corresponds to the "words."

In spite of all that has been said above in this section regarding the characterization of the two prophetic tetrateuchs, the basic all-defining characterization has yet to be expounded. Just as the Pentateuch elaborates the "parable of Abraham" of Isa 40–55 as expanded in chapter 1 of the present work, the two prophetic tetrateuchs elaborate the parable of the "everlasting covenant, my steadfast, sure love for David (Isa 55:3 NRSV)," as elaborated in Isa 55:4–13: it is not David, but God's "steadfast, sure love" for David as pedagogical lesson for all sons and daughters of Adam and Eve. Already in Isaiah ch. 54, Noah is mentioned before David is referred to in ch. 55, similarly to his mention before Abraham in the book of Genesis; and this is portrayed as the lesson God had "to learn," determining his further actions vis-à-vis all humans. From the starting point of Isa 40–55 and end point of the three multifold works, God's severe judgement is counterpointed by the description of his "everlasting covenant," His "steadfast, sure love." This is exemplified in his dealing with David. David accepts to play "second-fiddle" to the God of Abraham, God accepts to display His commitment at the example of David, not Aaron! David is cut off from his progeny, from a dynastic listing; his sins are an occasion for God to tell his narrative, to show His pedagogy. A "natural" continuation of David is made impossible by God in response to David's sins, reflective of Jacob's and Adam and Eve's progeny's sins, he is in the same situation as Abram was before God promulgated with him His Covenant. The only continuation possible, as for all addressees of the Pentateuch and the two tetrateuchs, can come only from God. This is reflected aptly by this redactional school in Isa 11:1–10. God's expected action will not come from a "son of David," but from a "parallel" David from the root of Jesse. Just as David did not come from a dynasty, the expected David will not be a dynastic continuation.[16] God's words must be at work again against the

---

[16] The name of king Josiah, *yōšīyāhû*, is most likely from a root cognate with the Arabic triliteral root, *'sw/'y*, meaning to dress a wound/heal/console. (This derivation is ascribed in Halot to Noth). The name would mean, "God (Yahu) will heal/console." King Josiah (son of Amon) is the only king endorsed by DH. He takes the throne as an infant, cut off from his father's work, and educated as per the "rediscovered book of the law," initiating a religious reform on its basis. He dies standing up to the Egyptian Pharaoh, in continuation of the position of the book of Jeremiah. This loss is left uncommented by the redactors of DH, inserting it after the closing formula referencing the list of his acts in the kingly annals (2 Kgs 23:28–30). The blame for it is placed by DH institutionally and ascribed to the history of the kingship (2 Kgs 23:25–27). In contradistinction to DH, the Chronicler version of

dynastic lines in order to "activate" the "everlasting covenant," the "everlasting love." The parable of the everlasting love of God to David, standing in for all mankind, is what is expounded and elaborated in the two prophetic tetrateuchs. The face of God as judge is brought into the sharpest relief as being expressive of God's everlasting love. This is the pedagogy of the two tetrateuchs, such is the scroll which is sweet in the mouth of Ezekiel but proves to provoke bitterness and rage in his spirit once digested, Ezek 2:9–3:14.[17]

2.4 Redactional Elements Specific to Individual Books of the First Prophetic Tetrateuch, the Former Prophets

2.4.1 Redactional Methods in the Book of Joshua

We saw above the redactional role of the book of Joshua in the book of the Former Prophets. It sets the measure for the contrast between God's actions vis-a-vis those of Jacob. The announced victory is achieved through the fivefold book of Moses. By virtue of its role, a basic literary tool employed in the book is that of inversion. We pointed out above that the warning against rebuilding Jericho is in fact a warning not to undo God's work. The two tetrateuchs go on to expansively detail how the tribes of Jacob proceeded to undo all of God's work in every

---

events seems to be critical of Josiah's "last stand" (cf. 2 Chr 35:21–22) and possibly also of Jeremiah (2 Chr 35:25). Gesenius–Buhl, *Handwörterbuch*, says of the conjectured Hebrew root *yšh* that it is related to the Arabic root *'y*. This is taken to be the root of the Hebrew predicative particle *yēš*, (there is/exists), and the noun *tûšîyâ*, (applied practical wisdom/insight/skill). If this were to be taken as the root for the name Jesse, *yišay*, it would attribute to it a derivation from a root cognate with the Semitic root conjectured for Josiah. Both names could be a paronomasia on the name of Moses. Another derivation for Jesse is imputed from its use in what appears to be a put-down for David as "son of Jesse." It would then be practically equivalent to *'š*, (a man), and in this construction imply "a commoner, subject (of the king)." (Cf. Gesenius, *Thesaurus*, 638).

17 It is noteworthy that all four instances of the mention of David in the book of Ezekiel, Ezek 34:23, 24; 37:24, 25) refer the name David (and not "son of David") to a future figure, not to a past personage.

aspect of their actions. One could say, the book of Joshua is a book of inversions. What Jacob does, proving inimical to God's will, is attributed to the opposing peoples. The threats and warnings directed to Jacob in the book of Deuteronomy and overall in the Pentateuch are acted out by God sweepingly against the opposing nations. The methods employed by Jacob and the nations are attributed to God as he displays in literary figurative language his power. The storyteller's use of the grotesque and the comic are employed.[18] It is the language of political caricature. It caricatures the exploits of human beings in general, but also the narrative "achievements" of would-be heroes and pretentious military campaigns of all times, from ancient to contemporary. One need think only of Julius Caesar's *Gallic War*. An inattentive reading of the book leads by neglect of the inbuilt inversions to substitute the actions of man in general with those of the biblical deity and vice-versa. In the book of Job, this deity takes on the challenge and adopts the inversion, in what can only be described as a masterfully adept literary coup by the redactor/storyteller.

Keeping in mind the master coordinates of the mega work governing the individual narratives and discourses, coordinates that I have attempted to delineate in the preceding sections and parts, let us go on to some of the details illustrative thereof. If what was said above regarding the "weapon" employed by the God of our redactors is correct, this means that the number five of the fivefold word, the Pentateuch, becomes representative of God's full "punch"/fist of power. In chapter ten of the book of Joshua, the number five in the narrative is "commuted" to the "five opposing kings." That by which victory is achieved leaves its imprint on the defeated; in consequence of the "victory," Joshua "hangs" the "five" kings" on "five" trees. The Hellenistic rulers utilized crucifying defeated opponents no less than the Romans. The inverse communication of characteristics, a literary inversion, appears to be at work in the literary rendition

---

18 This is particularly true of the immediately following book of Judges.

of events. This is inherent to the work of the servant-*rāhām* in Isa 40–55. What people see is the inverse of what God sees in the servant! All too frequently in history, the consequent antimilitary stance of the redaction is repeatedly bypassed because this literary inversion is overlooked and bypassed. In consequence, an inversion of the inversion occurs thereby destroying the message. This same process often is at work when a literary work of fiction is translated into a motion picture bypassing the literary coordinates defining the topology of the figurative language of the written work, thus bringing to naught the efforts of the author. This happens as much if not more with texts of the New Testament. The attempt to do away with the problem through allegorical interpretation fails to come to grips with the utensils of literary crafting. In Josh 10:1 we are told that Adoni-Zedek, *ădōnî-ṣedeq*, the king of Jerusalem, musters the "five" kings to destroy the "Joshua troop." This already sounds suspicious. This title would best apply to the high-priestly group in Jerusalem. In the book of Ezekiel, the prophet projects the high priests of the utopian "divine" Jerusalem to be "sons of Zadok," Ezek 40:46; 43:19; 44:15; 48:11, meaning righteousness, *ṣedeq*, will be the defining trait (cf. Ezek 45:10). The priestly "party" in Jerusalem will define itself by this name as we see in NT times, the Sadducees. The name Adoni-Zedek translates as "my lord is righteousness." This king of Jerusalem sounds awfully like the priestly party allied to the palace opposing the prophet Jeremiah. Further on in the narrative, the five kings after being defeated by Joshua flee to the cave at Makkedah. That the five kings after being defeated in their plot against Joshua flee to hide in a cave replicates the charge made by the prophet Jeremiah against his contemporaries in Jerusalem, i.e. that they have turned the temple of God into a hideout for their thievery, Jer 7:11 (cf. the whole passage Jer 7:9–16, illustrating the teaching implicitly guiding the narrators in the book of Joshua). The same word for "cave" in Hebrew is used in both locations. Furthermore, the purported proper name "Makkedah" (written with the emphatic palatal *qôp*, *mqdh)*, with the Masoretic pointing *maqqedâ*, in the LXX μακηδα, is in fact a common noun taken from Arabic and used in the narrative as a name for a locale. We should remember that in the book of Joshua, Joshua is hosted by the Arab/Kenizite Caleb. We should expect considerable borrowing from Arabic. In Arabic the noun *makīdah* (written with the middle-hard palatal *kāf*) denotes a "treacherous plot/ambush." In the riposte of Joshua to the attack, after "crucifying" the five kings, Joshua goes on to execute the ban on seven cities. While the action of the five kings was a display of full power, the riposte takes the shape of a "holy action/war." The reversal of epithets is bidirectional. The five kings take the number of the "weapon" used against them, the Pentateuch, the "Joshua troop's" action takes on the number of the Jerusalem sanctuary, the number seven. Moreover, while the king of Jerusalem was mentioned, as ringleader, first among the five kings, Jerusalem is not one of the cities targeted by Joshua's riposte, or is it? The first "town" that Joshua executed the ban on was not even involved in the original plot, Makkedah. It was simply the town near the cave where the five kings fled to; yet it was the first town that Joshua executed the ban against. It is a stand-in for the Jerusalem leadership opposing Jeremiah. Three towns added to the list of towns subjected to the ban by Joshua are Libnah, Gezer, and Debir. (One locality other than Jerusalem whose king was mentioned as one of the five kings, (and whose name means "their mule, wild ass"), but was not named in the sevenfold riposte, is the apparently small and insignificant "locality" of Jarmuth; possibly listed among the five in their chiastic center because its name means "he will see death," making the central phrase equivalent to "their throne (mule) will see death"). Libnah and Debir, as well as Hebron, are named in Josiah ch. 21 as cities assigned to the leading clan among the sons of Kohath son of Levi, that is, Aaron's sons. Gezer is among the towns assigned to the other clans of the sons of Kohath. Two further localities named both in the list of five and the account of the seven targets of Joshua's riposte are Lachish and Eglon.

Lachish is underscored in DH and the DH passages in Isaiah, as well as in Jeremiah and Micah, as a fortified town, to which the king could take military refuge or alternately the besieging army could use as a command center in its siege of Jerusalem (2 Kgs 14:19; 18:14, 17; 19:8; Isa 36:2; 37:8; Jer 34:7; Mic 1:13). The last mentioned, Mic 1:13, indicates its significance for the redactors as symbolic of the sins of Jerusalem, "the daughter of Zion." Basically, what the redactors are saying is that Jerusalem, together with the fortified fallback town(s) of its kings, and the cities/towns for the sons of Aaron, the leading clan of the sons of Levi (who were in charge of the sanctuary including the Ark) were subjected to the ban. This encapsulates the diatribe of Jeremiah against the king, the king's men, and the leading priests of the temple in Jerusalem opposing him: that they would be wiped out and have no refuge! Even more so, this reflects the diatribes of the book of Isaiah against selfsame in Isaiah chs. 1–39, and the end result of the total destruction of Jacob as described in Isa 40–55. What initially appeared as a book relating to the mythical foundational time proves in fact to be no less than the books of Samuel and Kings descriptive of the misdeeds of Jacob in the synchrony of the redactional group's situation (cf. Hos 8:14; Amos 5:11; Mic 1:13). If we accept consequently the inversion of roles, epithets, and actions in this passage, then we must assume that the Joshua "troop" was subjected to treachery on the part of the Jerusalem leadership and that, in consequence, leaders and/or members of the Joshuan group were "crucified" in the process. We confront developments of this type not only in DH but more specifically in reports from the so-called Maccabean and sub-Maccabean period[19].[20]

---

19 Cf. Dan 9:25–27. For Josephus, such developments become run-of-the-mill elements in his version of events.
20 An analogous narrative constructed on the basis of literary dissimulation and inversion of perceived outcome is in Acts 28:1–10. Malta would appear to be a stand-in for the Roman world and Rome in particular. The carrier of the Pauline message

Chapter 3

Following the paradigmatic narratives regarding Jericho and the war with the five kings, the first half of the book of Joshua is rounded up with a listing of kings defeated by Joshua. These are specified as thirty-one in number; through the literary reversal of attributes, Joshua is effectively described as having achieved the work of the messianic David in a broad sweep in one year after investiture (the number thirty-one). In the second half of the book, the division and apportionment of the domains is carried out in fulfilment of the program of Isa 40–55 for the servant. What formally appears to be a monotonous official listing of domains dissimulates in its folds the instrument employed for this "victory" as per Isa 40–55.

In chapter 15 of the book of Joshua we have a very heavyweight use of wordplay on two semantically central terms of the redactional school we saw in the book of Deuteronomy. In Josh 15:49 we read: "Dannah, Kiriath-sannah (that is, Debir)," (NRSV). This seems at first sight to be an innocuous part of the listing of cities in the domain assigned to Judah. Let us take a closer look at the name "Debir." In the story about the war of the five kings it was employed twice: once as the name of one of the five kings, the king of Eglon; once as the name of one of the seven cities subjected to the ban in Joshua's riposte. Eglon itself, while indicating the name of a town in the book of Joshua, is used as the name of the king of Moab in the book of Judges. Otherwise, "debir" is the name of the inner sanctum of the/a temple, the so-called Holy of Holies. From the same triliteral

---

is bitten by a viper emerging out of the fire and the Pauline figure appears to be mortally struck down. The beast would appear most probably to be a stand-in for the emperor Nero. Nero had called for the extermination of the early Christian community, claiming that they were behind the burning of Rome. After the dust had settled, the initial perception of the criminality and perdition of this community by the Roman public was reversed, probably in the wake of the death of Nero. The leading man on the "island" was named in Greek as ποπλιος, in translations Publius, a stand-in for the *populus romanus*, the Roman public. The initial "defeat" was perceived, after all the "ballots"/elements of the situation were in, as "victory." The pericope reflects the basic credo of the Lucan double-work. A similar literary toolkit, with similar inversion of roles and reversal of perceptions of the outcome, seems to be at work in the passage discussed above.

root we have the word for a bee or wasp, *dĕbôrâ*, and the personal name Debora, as well as the word *dâbâr*, meaning "word." "Eglon" is possibly intended as a pun, construing it as a diminutive of *ʿegel*, (*ʿegel* refers to "calf"). In the list of the five kings we discussed above, the mention of "King Debir of Eglon" can be understood as a putdown in the sense of "king of the Sanctum of the little calf," consequently a putdown of the Aaronic priesthood of Jerusalem: such a reference would remind that that priesthood serviced the cult of the golden calf and that it continues in selfsame in its treacherous plotting.

The noun "Debir" is used as a "common" noun to refer to the Sanctum (Holy of Holies) in the design of the temple of Solomon in Jerusalem in 1Kgs 6:5, 16, 19, 20, 21, 22, 23, 31; 7:49; 8:6, 8; 2 Chr 3:16; 4:20; 5:7, 9; Ps 28:2. In Ps 28:2, the prayer of the supplicant is actually directed to the "Sanctum of your (Yahweh's) Holiness." It remains noncommittal as to where that is to be conceived. In the OT the word is otherwise used as a "proper" noun in Josh 10:3, 38, 39; 11:21; 12:13; 15:15 (twice), 49; 21:15; Judg 1:11 (twice); and 1 Chr 6:43. The mention in 1 Chr 6:43 is parallel to the mention in Josh 21:15; it is in the list of cities assigned to the sons of Aaron. We have already seen it as the name of the king of Eglon in Josh 10:3. Other than the mention of the word in 1 Kings in connection with the temple of Solomon, the redactors of DH display a great interest in highlighting the name of the town in the book of Joshua and the first chapter of the book of Judges. Elsewhere, we do not encounter the word or the town. The mention in the first half of the book of Joshua describing the conquest references the city as subjected to the ban by Joshua in Josh 10:38, 39 and as a conquest of Joshua in 11:21 and 12:13. The references to the town that interest us most are in the listings of the second half of Joshua and in the first chapter of Judges. In Josh 15:7 it is mentioned simply as a town defining the border of the tribe of Judah. In 15:15 it turns out that it was a conquest by Caleb and that it was in the portion of Judah awarded to Caleb. For the first time since it was first mentioned in the book, we are told that previously it had been called Kiriath-sepher; translated this means "town of the book." The added info regarding its name comes on the heels of our being told that the exploits of Caleb in defeating the Anakim, the race of longnecks that had possessed Hebron and frightened the sons of Jacob in the book of Numbers, opened the way for his conquest of Debir. In the process we are told that Hebron had previously been called Kiriath-arba, but more on that further down. Then in Josh 15:49 we have the information cited above in the listing of the towns of Judah: "Dannah, Kiriath-Sannah, that is, Debir." Suddenly, it seems we are being flooded with names for Debir. Our redactors do not do this idly, just to give archaeologists a run for their money and linguists headaches. This information, appearing as "bumps" in a mundane listing, would not be here were it not essential for the redactors in their narrative. Linear logic does not help here; the redactors were neither archaeologists nor academicians. They are pedagogical storytellers. Regarding Hebron, we will see later its centrality for the David narratives, where David is effectively wedded to the town. In fact, Hebron brings about an intersection between the Abraham narratives in Genesis and the David narratives in DH. Before that, the question here is: what is the significance of the three appellations of Debir: Kiriath-sepher, Kiriath-sannah, and Debir? The first, Kiriath-sepher, is so important for the redactors of this narrative that they repeat this remark regarding the "previous" name again at the head of the narrative in the first chapter of the immediately following book of Judges. They are not giving historical data, they are superposing semantic layers to highlight their teaching narrative. Firstly, let us remember that we are in the center of the Calebite domain within Judah, just as we are in a central section in the narrative presenting us how Joshua and Caleb opened the land of promise. This town, together with Hebron, is subjected to the double actions of Joshua and Caleb, related as two distinct narratives, the first, in the first half of the book, destructive, the second, in the second half of the book, making it a paradisiac habitat. One could surmise that Debir was a center for the production of the Pentateuch, the book par excellence for our redactors. By being the town of the book, Kiriath-sepher, it becomes the "debir" of the Joshuan school, the Holy of Holies challenging the temple in Jerusalem; the ambulant debir corresponding to the prescript of Deuteronomy and containing the entire book, not just the "pars pro toto" tablets in the Ark placed in the Debir of the Jerusalem temple. What about the appellation "Kiriath-sannah"? The word vocalized in translation as "sannah" is written, in the unvocalized Hebrew text, exactly as the Hebrew of the word rendered as "bush" in Exod 3:1–4 and Deut 33:16. Moses encountered God for the first time in the burning bush. In Exod 3:1–2 we read: "Moses was keeping the flock of his father-in-law Jethro, the priest of Midian; he led his flock beyond the wilderness, and came to Horeb, the mountain of God. There the angel of the Lord appeared to him in a flame of fire out of a bush; he looked, and the bush was blazing, yet it was not consumed." (NRSV). In Num 10:29 we hear: "Moses said to Hobab son of Reuel the Midianite, Moses' father-in-law, 'We are setting out for the place . . .; come with us, and we will treat you well; . . .'" (NRSV). In Judg 4:11 we read: "Now Heber the Kenite had separated from the other Kenites, that is, the descendants of Hobab the father-in-law of Moses . . ." (NRSV). Then we go on to hear about Jael the wife of Heber, who made the victory against Sisera perfect for Barak, and we hear in the song of Deborah and Barak following this: "Most blessed of women be Jael, the wife of Heber the Kenite, of tent-dwelling women most blessed." (Judg 5:24 NRSV). We can see that these reports all indicate a special relationship between Moses and at least both the Midianites and the Kenites, and that these relate to both the first encounter of Moses with God in the "burning bush" and the exploits of "saviors" in the book of Judges. A third group or clan is present in all this in the person of Caleb the Kenizite. The Kenites, Midianites, and Kenizites are all Arab tribes related to the general area of southern Palestine. There even seems to be an intersection between Kenites and Kenizites in the person of the Kenite Heber, who carries the name of the Calebite/Kenizite city of Hebron in his name. That the redactors of the passage under discussion, after already having given us two names for the town of Debir (and who will repeat this double designation at the outset of the book of Judges) should go on here to supply us with a third name for the locality, this time Kiriath-sannah, cannot but be of essential importance for them. Remember that the climax to the blessing of Joseph in Deut 33:16 is: "that he (Joseph) should be granted the favor of the one who dwells in the bush." The redactors are telling us that this town is where "Moses" encountered God in the "bush." We have previously pointed out that there is an affinity in the consonantal sound of the word for "bush" and the word for "enemy" in Hebrew. Among the tribes previously perceived as inimical, God was encountered and the enemies became companions, so that a kinship, marital alliance, was established with Moses (and later on also with David). There is yet further wordplay here. The vocalization by the Masoretes, if reflecting the original intent of the redactors, would be a non-plus-ultra of literary artifice. In Arabic, "*sanā'* and *sannā*" refer to brightness of high flames or lightening.[21] It would, in effect, be superposing through the vocalization the notion of burning on the triliteral of "bush," in one word![22] If the Masoretic vocalization is not original, we should remember that their work was under the dynasties of the early Islamic empire. They will have been well informed that after the less significant city of Yathrib had given refuge and aid to the prophet Mohammad against his own city of Mecca, thereby becoming the first city to accept his message, it was renamed the "Enlightened City (*Al-Madīnah Al-Munawwarah*)." This may have influenced the Masoretes. However, from whichever direction the influence came in these two analogous situations (though greatly distanced from each

---

21 Lane, 1448–1450.
22 The Masoretes employed this method with the tetragram of "Yahweh," superposing on it the vocalization of "*adonay*" (Lord).

other in time), the original design of the redactors would have been well served.

The major city in the region was Hebron. It seems to have been the major center of influence of the Calebites. We are told that Caleb himself captured it from the Anakim. It is the military and political center for the Joshua Calebites. For the redactional group, it is central for their exposition of the second doctrinal theme based on Isa 40–55. As we saw above, they unfold this second theme in a diptych of two tetrateuchs. The central character, David, will have Hebron as his basic seat of power and will throne there for seven years before he succeeds in moving the seat of his reign to Jerusalem. This explains the insistence in the book of Joshua on Hebron. Its name "Hebron" seems to derive from "*ḥeber*" (associate/companion). It is a place of association between distinct groups/tribes; it thus facilitated alliances and cooperation between them. It seems to have been the most important city of refuge, and thus it was assigned to the preeminent priestly clan, the sons of Aaron. We are told that its previous name was "Kiriath-arba." In the mythical register that these passages are written in, "Arba" is said to be the ancestral father of the Anakim, that is, the "arch-longneck" of the Anakim. In fact, "arba" as written in Hebrew is the equivalent of the number four in Hebrew and Arabic, and its rendering would best be as "Capital city of the tetrarchy." We meet with this Hellenistic designation for smaller administrative districts in the NT. In the Arabian Peninsula we still meet with this use of "quarter" as a designation for a part of a larger area in the designation "empty quarter" for the arid southern part of the peninsula. The Anakim (the long-necked) were very possibly Macedonians. The designation "Kiriath-arba" may have been a translation of the Hellenistic Greek administrative designation. The area could not have been taken without the Calebites is what this narrative stretching from the second half of the book of Joshua to the first half of the book of Judges is telling us. This is insisted upon in the twice repeated story about Caleb's brother, Othniel, and the conquest of Debir (Josh

15:16–19; Judg 1:12–15). Othniel will then have his own narrative as first judge and savior in the book of Judges, Judg 3:7–11.

This double "double-billing" for Othniel the brother of Caleb must have been as a result of the profound impact of this group on the fate of the redactional group. Their center of operation, Hebron, and the center for the production of their scribal school and mega-work, Debir, were made possible through their alliance with this group. They had to face their opponents in the Jerusalem leadership and at the same time their opponents from the surrounding peoples and empires: without this hideout from their internal and external opponents, this would not have been possible. A short excursus is in order here to explain nomenclature and attributes in Semitic and Arabic in particular. The expression "son of so and so" and "father of so and so" or "mother/ daughter / sister / brother / uncle / father-in-law of so and so" is a way to highlight attributes, with nuances depending on which is used and in what context. It is a way to build attributes and portray characteristics. This manner of telling stories has found its way into Eastern Church ascetic literature in Europe, which had as a major source the Christian churches in the Levant and western Mesopotamia. The literature of Aramaic-Syriac Christianity was primarily a storyteller literature. Pedagogy was by way of storytelling. In ascetic literature, the relation between vices and between virtues is often expressed as which vice or virtue engenders which vice or virtue. A tree of family relations expresses like a diagram the interrelationships. Names in biblical literature should not be the business of archeologists, they are a narrative tool and the coordinates for understanding them are intertextual. The tools for studying them are narrative criticism and redactional criticism. The Othniel narrative is a good example. The name of Othniel is obscure as far as the specialist lexicons are concerned. Let us try to piece the narrative together from the perspective just presented. The name of Othniel's father, and consequently of Caleb and the "kenizites," is Kenaz. This word means "treasure" in Arabic. For our redactors, the Kenizites were a treasure found. They hosted the group and helped them against their opponents. This is expressed by Othniel's promised bride, Achsah, the daughter of Caleb. It is from the triliteral Arabic root ʿks meaning to be opposite/to reverse. Being both the daughter of Caleb and wife of Othniel, she defines the group. They stood opposite the redactional group's opponents and reversed the tide for them. This group seems to have been all-pervasive, accessing both the high and the low of society, making them thus acquire tremendous advantage and strength. This is reflected in the narrative about Aksah. She receives from her father Caleb access to both the higher source of water and the lower source of water, she could both mount a donkey and dismount (or approach) from it; she had access to both high and low. All this helps us to solve the enigma of Othniel's name. It can be derived from the triliteral Arabic root ʿthn (similar to Hebrew ʿšn), from which we have rising smoke/fumigation/perfume/odour and the related verbal actions.[23] Othniel's name would mean God is my all-pervasive smoke, fumigator, perfume. The Kenizites were everywhere in the area and on all levels and helped the redactional group in "cleaning up" the area. This now makes it possible to understand the name of Caleb's "immediate father," or better "professional name." Ever since he was introduced in Num 13:6, he has been introduced to us ceremonially as "Caleb son of Jephunneh." This encapsulates in Hebrew the meanings of both Othniel's and Aksah's names (as derived from the Arabic). Jephunneh is to be derived from the *pi'el* verbal stem of the Hebrew root *pnh*. The examples given in BDB for the translation of this stem are: "turn away; put out of the way"; "make clear . . . i.e. clear away things scattered about, make orderly, Germ. 'aufräumen'"; "empty"; "make clear, free from obstacles"; "clear away (ground) . . . to plant it."[24] These were the characteristics delineated in the "professional" card of

---

23 Lane, 1954–1955.
24 BDB, 815–816.

Caleb ever since he appeared in Num 13:6, when he stood and opposed the other members of the group sent out by Moses to "spy out" the land. This is why only he and Joshua would be allowed to enter the land of promise of that generation. Caleb and the Calebites proved to be the turning point in the fortunes of the Joshua group. Once we are on this subject, didn't Joshua have a "professional card" when introduced *in officio* in Exod 33:11 that could help us understand his role in the narrative? We are nearing the end of his mission, what might it tell us about selfsame? Contemporaneously with his instatement at the tent of meeting in Exod 33:11, we are told that he is Joshua "the son of Nun." "Nun" in Hebrew derives from the hollow triliteral *nûn* and its cognate *nîn*. These, according to BDB, can mean "propagate, increase, have increase," and, alternately, "fish." In Aramaic the word indicates "fish." Other suggestions for Hebrew are "shoot" or "scion" or "progeny." Fish may have inspired the notion of increase and reproduction much as "rabbit" later on in our times will have this connotation, "to increase like a rabbit." The bottom line in all of this is that what we said up till now regarding Joshua, that he fills the term "Joseph, increase" with a different filling than that of "Ephraim" (understood as prosperity and rich harvest) was already in the designation "son of Nun"; again, *nomen est omen*. He (as representative of the Joshua group, the first generation of disciples) is the son/heir of the transformed Joseph, "he" is the alternative Ephraim. Increase and an open door to the future hinge on him. Continuity of God's narrative will be through him; this he achieves through the publication of the Pentateuch, the Torah. His disciples, second generation disciples of Isa 40–55, will continue and publish the two tetrateuchs constitutive of the book of the Prophets. This, at least, is the thesis being proposed in this work.

In Josh 19:51 we are told how and where the apportionment was completed: the place is where Joshua had begun his work in Exod 33:11, at the tent of meeting, effectively God's tent, thus at Shiloh; moreover, at the door of the tent, because Eleazer and the heads of the families were present, they were not allowed to go into the tent, just as had been stipulated in Exod 33. The apportionment is described as having been in consensus with them in Yahweh's presence. They will be held to account.

We must still deal with the closing chapters of the book of Joshua, Joshua's testament. In chapter 23 we have a resume of the book of Joshua. This is followed in chapter 24 with the assembly at Shechem, effectively Jacob's/Israel's tent. This is a formal resume of the Pentateuch and call to decide regarding the covenant implicit therein. We have already seen how this follows to the letter the described work of the servant in Isa 40–55. (Cf. again Josh 24:25–28 and Isa 49:8–9). In fact, the following is the description given in Josh 24:29, "After these things Joshua son of Nun, the servant of the Lord, died . . ." (NRSV). In the following verse we are told: "They buried him in his own inheritance at Timnath-serah, which is in the hill country of Ephraim, north of Mount Gaash." (Josh 24:30 NRSV). We had been prepared for this in 19:49–50. We are reminded that he is an Ephraimite, and like the servant will be buried among the rich. I agree with John Pairman Brown on equating *"timnâ"* in Hebrew with Greek τεμενος and Latin *templum*, meaning sacred precinct.[25] As for the second half of the name, *seraḥ*, I would see its derivation from Arabic *saraḥ* (to roam, pasture freely, walk untethered, stream). If my assumption is correct, the name of the location would be equivalent to "ambulant temple." That is, Joshua is now to be found in the *vade mecum* Torah, challenging the temple in Jerusalem and reflecting the conception of Deuteronomy and DH regarding the ambulant Ark (of the covenant). The mythical "location" of this is "in the mountain of Ephraim north of Mount Gaash." The mythical location is somewhere in the highland of Ephraim but "north" of Mount Gaash; a mysterious location north of a mysterious Mount Gaash. Psalm 18 can help

---

[25] John Pairman Brown, *Israel and Hellas* (BZAW 231; Berlin: Walter de Gruyter, 1995), 21.

us "locate" this mount: "In my distress I called upon the Lord; to my God I cried for help. From his temple he heard my voice, and my cry to him reached his ears. Then the earth reeled and rocked; the foundations also of the mountains trembled and quaked, because he was angry." (Ps 18:6–7 NRSV). The phrase "I cried for help" in Hebrew is " *ăšawwēaʿ* " from the same triliteral root as the name Joshua. It can also be rendered as "I raised my plaint." The two words rendered in NRSV as "reeled" and "quaked" are two verbal stem forms from the same triliteral verbal root "*gāʿaš*," often rendered with the same English verb "to quake." The name Gaash is a noun from this root, written and vocalized exactly as the simple verbal stem. In Joshua 24:30, what we are actually told is that the location of Joshua's burial is in fact deep into God's regions and mount. Psalm 18 is designated as a psalm of David; it could just as well be a psalm of Solomon, directed towards the temple in Jerusalem. Joshua 24:30 makes Joshua's burial site equivalent to Mount Sinai and surpassing the temple mount in Jerusalem. It is effectively a perpetual divine manifestation placed in mythical time and place, a fitting place to be at the end of the mythical age presented to us in the book of Joshua (cf. v. 31). It is equivalent to a sword of Damocles, which we will see being wielded in "real" time in the following "books" of the book of the Prophets counterpointing the sins of Jacob/Adam. The formula in v. 31 is reminiscent of Exod 1:6–8. In the book of Exodus, following the passing of Joseph and his generation there came a Pharaoh who "did not know Joseph." Here in the book of Joshua, the final inversion reintroduces us into the "real" synchrony of the addressees. Those who will follow "not knowing" Joshua and the deeds of His God will be the sons of Jacob (as explicated in Judg 2:10–11), repeating thus the wilderness experience. With the work of Joshua completed, the bones of Joseph can finally be laid to rest. Joseph's work had not finished until completed by Joshua son of Nun, until the posthumous work was published! Joseph is buried at Shechem, a place that reminds Jacob of the sins of the sons of Jacob, of the judgement incumbent on the breach of the covenant. Levi and Simeon had done grave wrong to the sons of Hamor[26] endangering the future of Jacob as Jacob had told them. "Hamor" is the word for "donkey" in Hebrew, The daughter of Caleb, Aksah, had ridden on a "donkey/*hămôr*" to ask her father to give her access to springs of water. Her husband, Othniel, Caleb's brother, had made possible the capturing of Debir and will be the first savior judge to follow Caleb in the book of Judges. What Levi and Simeon risked undoing, the future of Jacob, was secured by Joshua and Caleb. We are here at the closing of a bracket that had opened in Genesis 34 immediately following the passage in which Jacob was "awarded" the title "Israel," which was analyzed in chapter 1. This was a bracketing of the whole Joseph narrative, which came to the close only now. Joseph also is buried in a rich man's grave, in Ephraim as Joshua was. The alternate Joseph–Ephraim has been fully spelled out now. It has the shape of the servant of Isa 40–55 embossed in the text of the Pentateuch and rounded up with the book of Joshua. From here on the original Ephraim will start to show up again. Progressively in the book of Judges we will see Ephraim increasingly oppose the work of the Pentateuch deity until the bitter end in the book of Kings, setting the paradigm for the mutiny of Judah. There is still the burial of Eleazar son of Aaron, also in the mountain of Ephraim. This report in v. 33 in its banality is more ominous. He is buried on the "hill of his son Phinehas." That the burial is on a hill is bad enough. Do not let the NRSV confuse you. The only time that the Hebrew word for "hill" is used in the course of the three burials is only here in v. 33. In the course of

---

[26] The term "sons of Hamor," Josh 24:30, very likely refers to the Himyarites, an Arab tribe of southwestern Arabia, approximately modern-day Yemen. They supplanted the Sabaean dynasty (kings of Saba or Sheba) in Yemen around 115 B.C. Cf. Griffiths Wheeler Thatcher, Philip Khuri Hitti, and anonymous. "Arabia, History," page 176 in vol. 2 of *Encyclopedia Britannica* (Editor in Chief Harry S. Ashmore. 23 vols. & index vol. Chicago: William Benton, 1962) 2:176. Like other western Arab tribes, they will have been active on a trade route stretching from Africa to Asia Minor passing through the Levant, irrespective of the time of their ascendancy in Yemen.

the books of Samuel, Kings, and the Latter Prophets, Jacob/Israel is condemned in the severest terms for running to every hill to join in idolatry, what the prophets will call adultery with other deities. Worse than this is the last name we hear, Phinehas son of Eleazar. The name Phinehas while possibly used as apotropaic, in fact, can be translated as "mouth of the serpent." The bronze serpent will be done away with from the temple in the course of a reform by King Hezekiah in the book of Kings, even though it is ascribed to Moses (Num 21:9; 2 Kgs 18:4). Phinehas, although commended in Num 25:7, 11; 31:6, has been completely sidetracked in the narrative we have seen, condemned to almost total silence. In Josh 22:13, 30, 31, 32 he plays what appears to be a leading role in the negotiations with the trans-Jordan two and a half tribes. He appears leading the mediation, or possibly threatening a repeat of the massacres he was involved in in the book of Numbers. The bloodletting is averted through securing the exclusive rights of worship for the central cult. In effect, the last verse in the book of Joshua tells us that after the work of Joseph–Joshua had been completed, the mouth of the serpent encountered in Gen 3 has reappeared center stage. In the following books of the Prophets, we will hear the virulent diatribe of the prophets confronting in the severest terms the temple of Jerusalem and its priesthood conjointly with the kingship.

2.4.2 The Redaction at Work in the Narratives of the Book of Judges

Up till now, the narrative strand has portrayed a united effort, a coalescence of diverse groupings against "foreign gods" perceived as idolatry. The book of Judges describes a liminal time intercalated between the mythological epoch of the "mountain of God" and the time of Adam and Jacob outside the "Garden of Eden." The Law, together with its paradigmatic "garnishing" in the book of Joshua, has now been set. But the "garnishing" is meant as a threatening Damocles sword hovering over the time of Adam and Jacob. The coalescence starts breaking up into two groups: the scribal group of Joseph–Joshua and the centralized cultic power group prefigured in the person of Phinehas. The uniting platform of opposition to idolatry, "foreign gods," proves to be two distinct platforms. The redactional Joseph–Joshua group underlines two issues both in the preceding and subsequent narratives: solidarity with the less privileged (as in the pericope concerning the Gibeonites in Joshua 9; they are powerful warriors but not the high and mighty, nor yet is a king mentioned among them); and rapprochement with other ethnic groups as evident in the same Gibeonite narrative. This reflects their indebtedness and dependence on Isa 40–55. Opposition to "foreign gods" is repeatedly explained as opposition to those "gods" not to the foreign people. Theirs is a mono-anthropic monotheism in which social justice within Jacob and among the children of Adam and Eve in general is imperative. By following the teaching of Isa 40–55, they take an antimilitaristic and antimonarchical posture. The opposing group understands monotheism as ethnocentric and consequently as monism. They play power politics. The "promised land" becomes a land grab, expansionist and exclusivist. The opposition to idolatry becomes an occasion to centralize power, reestablish a pyramidal social order, and establish alliances with the powerful. The result is an alliance between throne and temple, no different from the foreign idolatry being opposed; thus constraining ramparts are raised apotheosizing the few and disdaining the many. Again, the Gibeonite lesson in Josh 9 displays this tension between the two outlooks. Joshua saves the agreement, and those with whom the agreement was reached, against the leaders and the populist sentiment. As we have seen, the situation of the Joshua group is embedded in an alliance with the Calebite Kenizites. Moses was presented as establishing kinship with the Kenite–Midianites, whereas in Numbers 31, Phinehas leads in the massacre against the Midianites. The occasion for that development was seen as ordained by the God of Moses, as a defense of Jacob against recidivist idolatry. The redactors relate the episode with no further comment. In hindsight they know that the opposition to idolatry can take two opposite tracks, one of which is a worse form of idolatry. This is their thesis in the book of the prophets: their "David" is not the David of the Davidic dynasty, of the alliance between the palace and the temple, which in Hebrew, (though not particular to Hebrew), is the same word, *hêykāl*. The dependence of the redactional group on Isa 40–55 will result in the following in an ever widening breach between the two groups ending up in an unbridgeable divide at the time of the redaction. The total catastrophe described in Isa 40–55 will lead to the realignment of the subgroups in the ethnocentric group and the splintering into partisan groups that is evident in what is called the intertestamental literature and the so-called NT apocrypha. The literature produced by the Joseph–Joshua group will prove to be so powerful that it becomes the measure of all things and the new bone of contention even for the opposing groups.

The book of Judges begins as we have become accustomed with a rounding up and realigning resume of the previous book and then a programmatic introduction to the book itself. These introductions help us in locating and understanding the coordinates in play in the redaction of the subsequent narratives. In this intermediate and liminal period, the redactors give themselves a free hand in setting the rules. Their skill as popular pedagogical storytellers has a free hand to address the imagination of the listener outside the mountain of God and the ramparts of kings. They present us with a carnival of stories, popular across all ages, but within a set of coordinates that is as intentionally biased as all political caricature, and as plainly illustrative as all inspired pedagogy. The judges are described as both judges and saviors, the functions we saw in the two names of Joshua–Hoshea. It is thus made clear that they will continue the same work of the same deity as Joshua. However, the coordinates have changed, and this is most clearly expressed in the "revised" edition of the burial site of Joshua.

This revision is introduced already in Judg 1:35, where we are told, "The Amorites continued to live in Har-heres . . ." In Judg 2:8–9 we find a repeat of the report about Joshua's death that we saw in Josh 24:28–30. However, there is one change—instead of Timnath-serah we have Timnath-heres as the name of the location. This question has been considerably discussed by critics with the aim being to establish the "original" name. My literary-redactional approach, which identifies these texts as catachrestic pedagogical and political caricature polemic in the style of storytellers going from town to town or travelling puppet theater, poses the question differently: what is the redactional point intended by this wordplay? The metathesis in the order of the consonants already invites the suspicion of intended wordplay. Given the extent of academic discussions that have revolved around this apparent discrepancy, I will give my response to the main literary linguistic arguments in the discussion. The main issue that is discussed is the significance of the word "heres," in Hebrew *ḥeres*. The word is described as referring to the sun, either directly or through reference to Horus, the Egyptian sun god. Soggin, who initially opted for the priority of Serah in his commentary on the book of Joshua, goes on to reverse his opinion in his commentary on the book of Judges, giving priority to heres and explaining the emendation in Joshua as an attempt to avoid the reference to Horus, a pagan divinity. But even after opting for Heres, he still expresses doubts while speaking about Har-heres in 1:35: "'Har-heres', probably the Hebrew transcription of 'Mount Horus', i.e. 'of the sun', . . . There remains, however, the problem of the final 's', a product of the 'Hellenization' of the name; in Phoenician and otherwise in West Semitic the transcription is always ḥr."[27] That a "pious" emendation would have been carried out in Josh 19:50 and 24:30 but not in Judg 2:9 is highly improbable. There is hardly any such practice evident in any of the locations in the OT where pagan deities are mentioned. There is though much

---

[27] J. Alberto Soggin, *Judges* (OTL; trans. John Bowden; London: SCM Press Ltd, 1981), 25.

caricature evident. The further historical linguistic objection voiced by Soggin to his own suggestion is very much to the point. The current presentation has seen a reference to Horus in the name of Mount Hor above in section 1.6. A dissimulation of the ḥêt through hê would seem highly probable from the point of view taken here regarding the nature of this literature. Another very questionable assumption is taking the word ḥeres as an alternate Hebrew word for sun. Two instances are usually presented for such use, Judg 14:18 and Job 9:7. This is highly improbable for two reasons: the ever present use of šemeš in Hebrew and in the Semitic languages, and the use of the word ḥeres in Deut 28:27 for scabies or some itchy skin disease. This last comes in a series of curses incumbent should the people not obey the commandments in the book.

I would propose the following explanation for the uses of Har-heres (Judg 1:35) and Timnath-heres (Judg 2:9), as well as ascent of Heres (Judg 8:13), in the book of Judges and for the use of the word ḥeres in Job 9:7 and Judg 14:18:

- In Arabic the verbal root ḥrs means to guard and the noun thereof means guard or guardhouse. In Job 9:7, God is said to order the ḥeres and (he)[28] does not rise. This can be understood in two ways. The nascent sun immediately on rising appears like a faint reddish patch, very similar to scabies on the skin. It is far from being the all-powerful šemeš of the sun at high noon in the Levant. Alternately, the sun, before rising, can be conceived as under guard. God in this passage is portrayed as the all-powerful deity alone capable among other things of ordering the sun to rise or not. The image could be of God

---

[28] The reference to the sun as "he" would be strange in Hebrew (as well as in Arabic); it is construed as a feminine noun, šemeš. If it refers to sun here, it would be by proxy of the Egyptian god Horus. As was just indicated, this would be highly improbable and would, if so, be a metaphorical use.

ordering the guard (or perhaps charioteer?) holding back sunrise to desist from allowing the sunrise to go ahead. This is a singular use of the word as reference to sunrise in our literature. It is a poetic metaphor and not a term that denotes sun.

- All the other four uses of *ḥeres* in biblical literature are specific to the book of Judges, whether in the simplex or in compounds; hence they should be understood within the coordinates of this book.

- The first mention in this book in 1:35 is very indicative of the redactional purpose. The Amorites are said to have deemed it their good pleasure to reside on Har-heres. "Amorites" is constructed from the triliteral root that is identical with the verb "to say/order" and is cognate with the known designation "emir" in Arabic designating "prince," that is, the one who has the say. In my reading it is not a reference to an ethnic group but to the highest and most powerful social class. In Joshua 10, the five kings gathered against Joshua are said to be Amorites. The extent of the challenge they pose is highlighted by the extraordinary divine intervention: first huge stones come down on them from heaven, then in a display of ultimate power, the sun and the moon stand still at the command of Joshua's deity.[29] This contrasts

---

29 Edward Noort in his article on the question of "serah" vs. "heres" points out the impact of the pericope regarding Joshua stopping the sun and moon in the history of interpretation in the Jewish, Christian, and Islamic traditions. Two very interesting instances he points out are the Genesis Rabbah midrash and Origen. In the Genesis Rabbah, Joshua is highlighted as the progeny of Joseph and his action is seen as a realization of the dream of Joseph in Genesis 37, where the sun and the moon bow

mightily with the skimpy whining of the house of Joseph, Ephraim and Manasseh, as we hear in Josh 17:16 after the apportionment of land to them: "The tribe of Joseph said, 'The hill country is not enough for us; yet all the Canaanites who live in the plain have chariots of iron, both those in Beth-shean and its villages and those in the Valley of Jezreel' (NRSV)." Joseph goes on to insist that eventually they will be able to push out the Canaanites. In Judges 1:35 we are at the same location. The Canaanites are again called Amorites. The house of Joseph has yet to gather the strength to remove them. We are told: "The Amorites continued to live in Har-heres . . ." This is the first of four times that the word "*ḥeres*" is used in this book. It is a re-invocation of the extreme contrast between the "time" of Joshua and the time of the house of Joseph. If we take seriously the use of the word in Deut 28:27, it would indicate a divine punishment against the house of Joseph and Jacob in general as is the stated thesis of DH and the book of Judges in particular. The Amorites are likened to scabies on the land. If, as usual for our redactors, a further wordplay is intended, then the Arabic connotation of guard and guardhouse is very pertinent. Just as in the Middle Ages the

---

to him; i.e. Joshua is seen as the direct heir of the Joseph of the Joseph narrative discussed in chapter 2. Origen in his homilies on Joshua sees Joshua as greater than Moses because Moses did not carry out such an action. Cf, Edward Noort, "Josua 24,28–31, Richter 2,6–9 und das Josuagrab," in *Biblishe Welten: Festschrift für Martin Metzger zu seinem 65. Geburtstag* (ed. Wolfgang Zwickel; Freiburg, Schweiz: Univ.-Verl.; Göttingen: Vandenhoeck und Ruprecht, 1993), 109–130. I agree with Noort's literary arguments in support of the priority of "serah" in Joshua; however, he bases his solution to "heres" in Judges on analysis of the archeological evidence and views it in terms of diachronic development and not in terms of intentional synchronic redactional design by DH as argued in the present work.

powerful princes and dukes built forts on high ground to control, tax, and function as garrison posts, so can the presence of the "Amorites" on the Mount of Ephraim be understood as a guard post, scabies on the land.

- In Judg 2:9, the burial site of Joshua in Ephraim is now referred to as Timnath-heres. In this second use of the word *heres* in Judges it is brought into the name of the site of Joshua's burial. Under Joshua, the site, as we saw, was a site of untethered roaming, an ambulant sanctum. In the time of the house of Joseph it becomes a sore in the land, a guard point, reflecting what will happen in Samaria and Bethel during Ephraim's epoch. Precisely the projected future "upper hand" of Ephraim will become in the book of Kings and in the Latter Prophets the sore point incurring divine punishment. What was "freed land" under Joshua, will become "enslaved land" under Ephraim's Samaria, and forced pilgrimage to Bethel. The situation is most starkly reflected in the Elijah–Elisha cycle in the book of Kings.

- We find the third use of *heres* in Judges in 8:13. It is again in conjunction with the house of Joseph. Gideon belongs to a lowly clan of the tribe of Manasseh. However, following his divine-given victory, he returns from battle "by the Ascent of Heres" (NRSV). Suddenly his affairs begin to change. He will kill the defeated kings of the Midianites, not because of divine ordinance but in revenge for those of his brothers killed by them. In fact, he said that he would have otherwise spared them. He functions in terms of clan-ethnic values and in the process endangers the relations with the peoples of the land, killing both high and low, starting with the low rather than the high. He is still one step short though of the actions of Saul later on, which will bring on God's wrath; he still rejects the offer of kingship. (In contrast, the Joseph group highlights the relations with the other peoples and insists always on the rejection of other deities and entrance into covenants understood in the sociology of the times as implicating the deities of both sides). Gideon starts to act in continuation of the actions of Levi and Simeon in Genesis 34, which brought on the severe condemnation by Jacob. The chapter closed by the assembly and covenant in Joshua 24 in Shechem begins to be questioned, the old wounds reopened. Rejecting kingship, Gideon still goes on to take first steps towards it. He gathers gold from the spoils of the battle against tent dwellers and makes out of them an ephod, a priestly garment, and places it in the "lowly" (earthen) town of Ophrah (from the same triliteral of the word *'āpār*, the dust of the earth). This effectively sets the house of Joseph on the path of the worst aspects of kingship, on the ascent to *ḥeres*, to becoming a new version of the Amorites. The comment of the redactors at the end of the Gideon narrative is very succinct: "Gideon made an ephod of it and put it in his town, in Ophrah; and all Israel prostituted themselves to it there, and it became a snare to Gideon and to his family." (Judg 8:27 NRSV). This encapsulates all the further developments of the house of Joseph, of Ephraim, in DH and the book of the Latter Prophets. Our redactors do not wait; these developments are immediately prefigured in the immediately following narrative about Abimelech, the son of Gideon, who does accept the kingship, inaugurating the fall of the house of Joseph. In chapter 8, Ephraim angrily objects to Gideon about not mustering them to the battle, apparently they wanted a piece of the cake. In that instance they still accepted the response that it was God's doing. In the case of the immediately following penultimate great savior judge, Jephthah the Gileadite, they no longer accept this response. Their tribal interests are compromised and they wage war, albeit unsuccessfully, against God's savior Jephthah who was continuing the work of Joshua the Ephraimite. The dichotomy between the ethnocentric, self-serving Ephraim and the Joshua son of Nun group has now come into full relief.

- The fourth instance of *heres* in the book of Judges is in 14:18. It is the only one of the four that is used in the simplex, and the only one that is not used in conjunction with the house of Joseph. Its use is in conjunction with Samson, who seems to be a stand-in for David and Judah. It is the locum which together with Job 9:7 has led so many exegetes to translate the term as "sun." In Job 9:7 the reference is to sunrise, in the Samson story it appears to be a reference to sundown. However, here we are in the book of Judges; it is the only book in biblical literature that uses this word in a programmatic manner for its narrative and it is here that we have four instances of the six that we find in biblical literature, Deut 28:27 and Job 9:7 being the remaining two. We must deduce its meaning here from its redactional function in the book of Judges, thus far dependent on its use in Deut 28:27. The narrative is introduced as taking place in a locale named Timnath (Judg 14:1 (twice), 2, 5 (twice). The father of the would-be bride is referred to as "the Timnite" in 15:6. Thus although not compounded with the word Timnath as in Judg 2:9, the term *ḥeres* is conjoined with the word Timnath through the narrative. As we have seen, Timnath is to be equated with Greek τεμενος and Latin *templum*, hence indicating a sacred precinct. The marriage with the would-be bride, a Philistine woman, seems not to have been consummated. The narrative of Samson courting a second woman, Delilah, apparently also under the influence of the Philistines, ends with the Philistines celebrating their victory over Samson in what appears to be a festive religious assembly devoted to their deity Dagon. The intermediate woman he "goes into" in Gaza is described as a prostitute. The combination of *templum*, harlotry, Dagon, in the domain of the Philistines indicates that from the point of view of DH, Samson was playing with fire. In spite of the fact that every divine register was brought to bear in the narrative, that all the topoi that have been employed by the redactors up till now to signify divine intervention were invoked, the resolution and "victory" will only come through Samson's death (Josh 16:30). Further down the multifold connotations of the figurative language employed in the Samson narrative will be dealt with; here, in closing this parenthesis about the use of *ḥeres* in the book of Judges as a redactional thread particular to this book, the proposed reading of Judg 14:18 is the following: The situation is one of extreme duress; the situation of the "hero" is liminal to the extreme, between two already extreme polar opposites, and the question is, to which of the poles will he gravitate and how will the situation develop for all. He is subjected to three seductions through Philistine or Philistine dominated women. Although from mother's womb ordained a Nazirite for Yahweh—the bearer of a "wondrous/ inscrutable" name (Judg 13:17–19), he is dangerously open to seduction by the opposite pole. In the first seductive instance, he is saved at the last instance by virtue of the duplicity involved in solving his riddle. He is "saved" from consummating his marriage with the Philistine woman. He will attempt anyway to go on to try to consummate his marriage in Judg 15:1, but the woman's father tells him that this was no longer an option. He is practically inviting his own catastrophe throughout the narrative. The subject of the phrase translated as "before the sun went down" is best understood as Samson; *ḥeres* is used here with the directional suffix, making it difficult to construe it as subject. The Jerusalem Bible suggests translating it as "bridal room" construing it as parallel to 15:1 (the NJB makes it simply "bedroom"). However, *ḥeres* does not denote "bridal room" even though it is used in parallel to 15:1. I understand the marriage as a metaphor of alignment with the Philistines, military and religious. I read the phrase in question as: before he entered the guard of the Philistines, the scabies lying heavy over the land, he recoiled seeing their ruse. The second seductive instance with the harlot in Gaza he escapes through a power act. The third (through Delilah) finally does him in. His Nazirite is broken as is his strength and sight. He is subsumed totally to the Philistines, carrying out what I referred to in chapter 2 as the "Isaac action," not to his own advantage, not to build his own domain, but to further the pleasure, domain, and dynastic claim of the Philistines and their deity Dagon[30] (Judg 16:23–25). In this case, he can only "vindicate" himself and "save" his people through his "suicidal" death. The only active actor in all this narrative is the God who brings forth water in arid land by splitting a dry hollow, Judg 15:19; we are squarely in Isa 40–55.

The first judge introduced in the book of Judges after the introductions is a Kenizite, the brother of Caleb, Othniel. We have already met him in the book of Joshua and in the repeat of the report in the first introductory chapter of the book. This emphasizes the fundamental role of the Calebites in conjunction with Joshua's work, and highlights the continuity of the savior judges' work with that of Joshua. It is noteworthy that we do not have a death or burial report for Caleb. In the story about Othniel in Joshua, Caleb says he has become old and Othniel, his presumably "younger" brother, continues his work. Caleb does not have progeny, at least we are not told about any, other than his daughter. He functions as part of God's narrative. Othniel continues God's narrative, not a Calebite narrative. In section 1.3 above, the implicit role of the Calebites in the Gideon narrative was pointed out. This underlines what was said above that the Calebite hosting of the Joshua group was an

---

[30] Dagon can be understood as diminutive of *dāg* (fish), meant as a putdown of the Philistine deity, the term itself being a figure for proliferation and dynastic claim. We should point out that the Philistines of the biblical texts should not be confused with modern day Palestinians. Archaeological data seems to align the ancient evidence with the "sea people." In the later time conjectured here for the redaction, the Hellenistic era, this would approximate the biblical references to their apparently Aegean origin from the perspective of the Levant. Modern day Palestinians have in common with them only the land which derives its name from the earlier group.

overwhelmingly important factor for the work of this group. Caleb functions as a clan rather than as an individual. He is not followed by a son but by a "brother." This is analogous to what we have regarding David. The follow-up to David in the book of Isaiah is a shoot from the same root, a "lateral" follow-up, not a vertical one, the connection is God's narrative.

The comic-caricature nature of the story telling comes to the fore in the story of the second judge, Ehud. He is from the tribe of Benjamin we are told, but he is left-handed. Benjamin in Hebrew and Arabic means (the tribe of) the right hand, the hand of power. Ehud does not act to achieve salvation by virtue of the power of the tribe of Benjamin but by the power of the deity.

The third "major" judge is the prophetess Deborah. Deborah means in Hebrew bee or beehive. It is also constructed with the triliteral of the word *dābār* meaning "word." She is also the only prophet or prophetess among the judges in the book of Judges. The combination of prophetess and the pun on the term for "word" immediately functions as a referral to the prophetic word and the literary project on the basis of the blueprint provided by Isa 40–55. As we have seen, the victory against Sisera is made perfect by Jael, the wife of Heber the Kenite. The powerful Sisera is felled by two women as highlighted by the narrative. Deborah still functions in Ephraim, but as noted above, in the two following narratives about Gideon and Jephthah, Ephraim is left out. The lesson that had to be learned is that Yahweh alone does salvation and He does not serve clan interests, special interests, or mete out "pieces of the cake." We have already seen this in section 1.3 above in the Gideon narrative. As for the Jephthah narrative, this is reflected in Ephraim's claims on Gilead and in Jephthah's remaining true to his oath to the point of offering his daughter to God. We can see the mounting polemic against Ephraim also in the name of the locality of Jephthah, Mizpah. We need only remember the words of the prophet Hosea (who shares the given name of

Joshua–Hoshea) against Ephraim in Hos 5:1, "Hear this, O priests! Give heed, O house of Israel! Listen, O house of the king! For the judgment pertains to you; for you have been a snare at Mizpah, and a net spread upon Tabor," (NRSV). Jephthah is introduced as the son of a prostitute who was thrown out by his clan. They then resorted to him to save them. His narrative thus has a resemblance to Joseph's as well as to the servant of Isa 40–55. It displays a resemblance also to Abraham. Salvation in the narrative is portrayed in the starkest terms as God's, and there is no sharing in the spoils.

The hardest expression of the rejection of Ephraim comes in the closing passage of the Jephthah narrative. It is the passage about smoking out the Ephraimites through their difficulty in pronouncing the "*šîn*" consonant. It is rather strange that an indigenous Semitic tribe would have difficulty with the *šîn* consonant. Semitic dialectical variations by region in the Levant are usually differences in vowel preferences. Notoriously, the Greek alphabet does not have a *šîn* sound. This is possibly a further indication that we are dealing with a Hellenized leadership and military estranged from its local roots. This is a phenomenon that we find widespread in western and central Asia under the Macedonian influence. Alexander the Great had a devastating impact on Samaria as on other cities in the Levant. His blockade and devastation of Tyre is well-documented as is his devastation of Samaria. What interests us here is that the passage about the inability to pronounce the *šîn* immediately precedes the Samson narrative. In Hebrew, Samson is written as two syllables both commencing with a *šîn*, *šimšôn*. If one *šîn* was difficult to pronounce, two consecutive *šîn* sounds would have been an impossible tongue-twister for the Ephraimites. Already before the beginning of the Samson narrative they are eliminated out of the picture, they could not even pronounce the name of the last divinely commissioned savior in the book of Judges! The satirical comedy continues, but already the consequent obedience of Jephthah is used as a total foil for Ephraim. The brutal literary frugality in his portrayal leaves no room out. Exegetes stop at the matter of child sacrifice. For the redactors, this is not the question. The question is obedience to the God of Abraham, of the *rāhām*. The grotesque is the input of the human being. The dictum, *nomen est omen*, applies to Jephthah. His name means "he will open." It does not need to be theophoric or implicitly so, this lesson can be learned from the narrative. The use of the third person singular for the "action" name is understood by the present writer as a type description in literary terms, i.e. "one such as this type will/can open the land of promise." In Arabic, the verb means both to open and to conquer. The participial epithet from the root is the equivalent of "the conqueror" in English. The narrative about Jephthah is a lesson about obedience pointedly directed against Ephraim/Samaria. From now on they will be stopped at the roadblock, they have no entry into the Samson narrative, figuratively about the peripeteias of Judah and David. The one-liner on the last "minor" judge, Abdon, effectively portrays him as a "little Pharaoh." He is named a Pirathonite (sharing the same consonants with the word "Pharaoh," and his progeny and wealth have the number "seventy" descriptive of the full number of gentile peoples. He, with his "great wealth," is buried in Ephraim among the Amalekites.

As mentioned above, the Samson narrative begins with the full arsenal of divine support. In the course of the narrative the full paraphernalia of divine intervention that has been displayed in the Pentateuch is brought to bear in support of Samson. His father's name "Manoah" means "a place of rest." It is from the same root as Noah's name and a constitutive part of Joseph's Egyptian name. His mother is barren like Sarah. The "Angel of the Lord" has to make his appearance again after the patriarchal narratives in Genesis. God ordains him a Nazirite from birth, and he comes from "Zorah," which is equivalent to the triliteral from which we have "leprous" and "struck down/prostrate." He is by divine ordinance, not by any doing on his part, "apart," and as such is a caricature of the Isaiah "servant." In the angel's appearance to his parents, God is defined as the mysterious, unnamed, worker of wondrous acts in a manner analogous to the appearance of the deity to Moses in the burning bush and on Sinai, consequently his parents are said to have seen God face to face. As we have seen above, at Lehi God makes water gush out of dry ground as he does with the sons of Jacob in the wilderness, and as highlighted as indicative of God's work in Isa 40–55. Also, Samson is humiliated by having to carry out the "Isaac action,"[31] equivalent to setting up one's own domain, for the benefit of the Philistines. It is in his death that victory is achieved.

The narrative correlates with the Deborah narrative. Wordplay and literary wit abound. Most importantly riddles are a major element as is characteristic of popular storytelling. The event occasioning the narrative riddle is, in fact, a riddle for the reader. The solution provided by the Philistines is simply a retelling of the event, the event itself remains enigmatic. Actually, it brings into play "Debora," as signifier for the written word, scripture. The beehive he finds in the carcass of the young lion he tore apart is the word "Debora" in Hebrew. He partakes of the honey and gives his parents to partake. The written word has made of the carcass a land flowing with honey. The riddle was left to be solved by the reader, not the Philistine fellows. In form, this is folk literature. The name of Samson tells us that the tale is to be understood as a riddle. In fact, whether it precedes or follows on the "open sesame" encountered in "one Thousand and One Tales" much later on, it actually implies the meaning "password." Coming on the heels of the Jephthah passage we saw above, it would have been the perfect password to stump the Ephraimites as we saw above. But also its components point in this direction: the first syllable, *šim*, is equivalent to "name"; the second syllable, *šôn*, is equivalent to "tooth." This last

---

[31] Cf. chapter 2, section 2.3.3, footnote 20. There is a deliberate reference to Isaac by the peculiar use of the verbal action in Judg 16:25 twice, each time spelled differently. More on this root (verb and name) and the variation in its spelling in Scripture further below in section 2.6.

demands the name/word which fits in like a tooth, the sharp edge/prong, to open the barrier; it invites us to look for the "pass-word"/pass-name!

The immediately following book in the Former Prophets, the book of Samuel gives us a lesson in figuring out "pass-words" on two occasions. The first instance is 1 Sam 7:12, where we are told: "Then Samuel took a stone and set *it* up between Mizpah and Shen, and called its name Ebenezer, saying, 'Thus far the Lord has helped us.'" (NKJV). This is a relatively "neutral" translation of this phrase, similarly the NASV. Most translations deal with the two apparent names as locations. However, both have the prefixed definite article and could hardly be intended as proper nouns. As common nouns, these would translate as "between the watchtower and the 'tooth.'" That is, if asked by the watchtower for the password, then the answer is literally written on the stone in front of you. "Ebenezer" is also not a proper name; it is composed of the two Hebrew words meaning "stone" and "help/support." And just to make the "password" clearer, the explanatory phrase is given, "The Lord has helped us up to this point." The password must be composed and it is a lesson, namely, the story that preceded this sentence. As we see in this passage, "*shen* (tooth)" refers to password. The second instance refers literally to a "pass" and the problem of how to go through it. The narrative in 1 Sam 14 is about Jonathan, the son of Saul, out on a solo attack against the Philistines. In the course of this undertaking, he also unwittingly goes against an oath taken by Saul, "foolishly" (as we are told with reference to Saul). Eventually he will escape punishment because the *vox populi* gives a thumps up. Jonathan is very important for the redactors, it is he who will eventually open the way for David to break the blockade against him by Saul, to escape Saul's wrath, and finally to ascend to the throne. Jonathan's name means "Yah gave," it is, in effect, the programmatic name of David's in-house prophet, Nathan. So Jonathan must succeed in our redactors' narrative, and the result must be a lesson directed at the listener/reader. In 1 Sam 14:4 we are told: "In the pass, by which Jonathan tried to go over to the Philistine garrison, there was a rocky crag on one side and a rocky crag on the other; the name of the one was Bozez, and the name of the other Seneh." His self-imposed mission will be successful, but the reason for the success must be filled in by the listener/reader. The word "bozez" means "miry swamp," the word "seneh" means "bush." (The Masoretic text differentiates the term here only by indicating a redoubling of the letter "n," otherwise the vocalization and consonants are the same.) Now what is the "password" that Jonathan used to achieve success? The two names apply to two crags, pointed rocks, effectively "two teeth." The second hint we were already given in 1 Sam 7:12, the password must be composed. If we choose "bush" it would not work; if we choose "miry swamp" it would not work. The "password" must be in the intersection between the two. It is the God of the burning bush who brought the sons of Jacob out of Egypt through the sea of reeds, the God of the Pentateuch.

Returning to the Samson narrative, the name "Samson" invites us to search for an answer to the riddle. The answer is not the locks of hair; it is the God of Debora, of the word of the prophets, the one who had made of Samson a Nazirite from the womb, the one who was invoked by the full display of the paraphernalia of the God of the Pentateuch who is the answer to the riddle. Samson does not break his Nazirite vow, he never took it, it was taken for him by God, and it was broken by the subterfuge of the Philistines. The will of the God of the Pentateuch was objectively disobeyed. This applies not to an individual element but to the whole complex of mixing with other deities and the concomitant objective implications. Various facets of these implications are illustrated in the different stories. The name of Samson applies not only to the Samson narrative, it invites us to see the whole book as a book of pedagogical fables and riddles; it is an invitation to learn the lessons through solving the riddles. The framework passages tell us what the answer is, but the pedagogical method seeks to engage the mind and imagination of the listener/reader in the learning process. Archeologists are wide off the mark. They are looking in a parallel universe they have created.[32]

Repeatedly, the methods used to counterpoint the narrative of Jacob/Adam with that of the God of Abraham have been pointed out. In no other book is this more pedantically carried out than in the book of Judges. The repeated refrain interjected between the individual stories leaves no room for interpretation. There is also a rising crescendo in the almost comic relief of the presentation of the minor judges. After all the stops were pulled in the Samson narrative to highlight divine intervention, and all the skill of the storyteller was brought to bear in the climactic presentation and rounding up of the series of twelve judges, the artifice of the storyteller seems to snap. The lengthy anticlimactic narratives that are placed after the count of the twelve judges is over are often described as appendices. It is as though someone had material and found no better place to insert it. I will suggest a different reading of the material in terms of redactional purpose. We find three times the refrain, "In those days there was no king in Israel; all the people did what was right in their own eyes." We find this at the beginning introducing this section in 17:6 and at the very end, 21:25,

---

[32] For those looking for background information, Arabic has a proverbial saying involving the word "*shann/shannun*." In Arabic it seems initially to refer to a leather-skin water container or, as verbal action, the targeted application of water from it. A derived usage is for a targeted attack. (Cf. Lane, 1002–1003). The proverbial saying is: "The container (*shannun*) has found its cover/cap (*tabaqah*). In English it would be equivalent to saying "a perfect match" regarding two objects or persons. It can be used wryly, sarcastically, vulgarly, or in earnest. In the history of interpretation of the saying, one does not find a linguistic explanation; rather a story has crystallized over the centuries to explain it. The story involves a man called *shannun* and a woman called *ṭabaqah*. The man *shannun* on a journey poses questions to a fellow traveler. These appear as foolish questions to the fellow traveler. On arrival at the destination, the fellow traveler tells his daughter *ṭabaqah* about the foolish questions. The daughter interprets the questions as intelligent riddles and tells her father the pertinent answers. When the father communicates to the man his daughter's responses, an immediate rapport between the man *Shannun* and the daughter *ṭabaqah* is established and they decide to marry. This penchant for wit, wisdom, riddles, comic situations, wordplay, and storytelling involving both the phantasmagoric and the grotesque is the type of background we have for the stories in the book of Judges.

summing it up. In 18:1 a shorter reference to it (only the first half) is invoked, maintaining in the mind of the reader/listener the circumstance and mood of the section. The question to pose is: what does this mean? Is the redactor-group saying that this will change to the better when there are kings? Certainly not; they have already offered us a different option in the preceding narratives with the savior judges. Their continuing narrative in the books of Samuel and Kings offers the exact opposite view. I will introduce my response with two concise formulations before going on to explain them: the redactional refrain sets the stage for an argumentum ad hominem; and in consequence, an argumentum ad absurdum.

The argumentum ad hominem is propounded by God to Samuel: play along with their request for a king and I (God) will know how to respond. The interplay of narrative against narrative was set into motion already in the book of Genesis. The Abraham narrative initiated God's response in continuation of Isa 40–55. The continuation of this contest of narratives in Samuel and Kings simply brings this duel of narratives to its expected resolution on the basis of the first part of Isa 40–55. In the book of Samuel we will embark on a precipitous descent to the actual and announced total catastrophe. Let us not forget that the duel of narratives in this work is being carried out by the redactional school employing all its redactional skills and narrative artifice. Thus the question is reduced back to the initial one posed above: what is the redactional intent behind the closing chapters of the book of Judges? This becomes in this presentation: how is this group proceeding on the argumentum ad absurdum? We must keep in mind that the position of the redaction expressed through its mega project is that only God can and may be King in Jacob, and by extension among the sons of Adam and Eve. This is unequivocally stated in Isa 40–55, and DH spares no effort in propounding this. The technical posing of the question becomes imperative: what literary device or element is employed here to this end? Is the absence of a pharaoh or king from the stage here the literary device? Again, hardly: This has been dealt with in the main part of the book. All the actors, characters, sets that we had in the preceding chapters remain the same; even all the extras remain and go through the same motions. In fact Judg 17:2 simply picks up on the thousand and hundred shekels paid to Delilah in the preceding narrative and uses it to initiate a totally unrelated narrative; further down, in Judg 18:2, location names are taken up from the Samson narrative in a totally unrelated context. We are once again in Dan and the town of Zorah as in Judg 13:2, and the mention of Eshtaol picks up on Judg 13:25; effectively, the mention of Dan, Zorah, and Eshtaol places the initial locale of ch. 18 in the area defined as the revere of the growing up Sampson, between Zorah and Eshtaol. In the literary figurative language that appears to be in play, this translates as "between leprosy/apartness and self-questioning." This designation reflects in the Samson narrative the polarization between the redactional group seeking to find paths for the realization of the "mission to the nations" of the servant-*rāhām* and their opponents interpreting Yahwism as an ethnocentric apartness. The to and fro of Samson between these two poles is evident throughout the narrative. But this plays no part in the narrative in chs. 17–18. The stage props and personages are all there, who or what is lacking? Simply said the answer is: the God of the redactors; the God of the servant-*rāhām*. It is as though a spell was cast on the theater stage, turning the figures and props into a lifeless nightmare of robotic motion. The absence of the divine narrative produces the argumentum ad absurdum. Not only the divine actor is absent, the redactional hand withdraws, becoming recessive. In the first composite narrative in chs.17–18, the thread becomes Micah's "idol." With pathos we hear in 18:31, "so they maintained as their own Micah's idol that he had made, as long as the house of God was at Shiloh." The work of one man, initiated in Judg 17:1–5, changes from one hand to another, going through peripeteias, and ending up in a locale and in hands having no relation to the initial circumstances; vanity of vanities! In ch. 18, the town called Laish, possibly employed to mean "no one," is found to be the ideal place to resettle by the group sent to check out the land from the extreme south to the extreme north. We are told in 18:7, "The five men went on, and when they came to Laish, they observed the people who were there living securely, after the manner of the Sidonians, quiet and unsuspecting, lacking nothing on earth, and possessing wealth. Furthermore, they were far from the Sidonians and had no dealings with Aram" (NRSV). The narrative goes on to relate to us that following the report of the scout party, the Danites of the far south went on to migrate to the far north, describing this with the following phrase: "The Danites, having taken what Micah had made, and the priest who belonged to him, came to Laish, to a people quiet and unsuspecting, put them to the sword, and burned down the city." (Josh 18:27 NRSV). Not finding a place to reside the whole length of the promised land, they went on to transform a paradisiac setting into a hell. They realize their dream of apartness. Verse 30 tells us that they maintained the "idol" of Micah until the whole land was exiled. In spite of being recessive, the redactional group manages to lob the most caustic possible remark against their opponents. Following this version of being thrown out of paradise, the next narrative, Judg 19–21, goes on to give another version of the Cain and Abel pericope in Genesis. Between the action of the Danites and exile, the picture of futile fratricidal wars is portrayed, with the sons of Jacob, applying their way of resolving problems, being on the verge of obliterating Benjamin, and consequently their own assembly. This is the argumentum ad absurdum; we already heard it in the early chapters of Genesis. It is bracketed from extreme south to extreme north by the tribe of Dan, figurative of the specter of God's judgement, ending in the exile of the whole land. Without the divine actor, it is a display of total futility, on the human and tribal level. Recessiveness is the master literary tool here! Judges 17–21 could as well be a resume of the book of Samuel and Kings. The peripeteias of the "idol" of Micah, the only thread holding together the otherwise unrelated scenes of chapters 17–18, is the most graphic portrayal of the vain futility expressed in Eccl 2:20–22: "So I turned and gave my heart up to despair concerning all the toil of my labors under the sun, because sometimes one who has toiled with wisdom and knowledge and skill must leave all to be enjoyed by another who did not toil for it. This also is vanity and a great evil. What do mortals get from all the toil and strain with which they toil under the sun?" (NRSV). Thus far, the attempt has been to trace the dependence of the Law and the Prophets on Isa 40–55. The chapters 17–21 in the book of Judges seem to be dependent on both Isa 40–55 and the book of Ecclesiastes. They can best be read as a superposition of both. Far from being tertiary addenda or dislocated or unrelated episodes, they are the *summa* of the narrative artifice of the redactor or redactors. It is the view of the present writer that Qoheleth, the convener of the assembly, is the author of both Ecclesiastes and Isaiah 40–55, as well as the Holiness Code. It is he who is the master teacher and convener of the school I have referred to as the Joshua school. But more on this further below, since it appears imperative now that we take into consideration also the third part of Scripture in the purview of the redactional design underlying this mega project.

2.4.3 The Redaction at Work in the Narratives of the Book of Samuel

Samuel in the book of Samuel has a profile very akin to that of Moses in the book of Numbers, the Moses of Aaron. His children are reported to go astray as those of Aaron, but he does not appear as a dynast, having been called by God as Moses is in the book of Exodus. He is less ambivalent than Eli, who seems to correspond directly to Aaron, but he seems to share the ambivalence of the Aaron-Moses. He actively enthrones Saul, which will eventually lead to catastrophe. However, the primary question is the fate of the Ark, and thus consequently of the "book." The Ark is nominally "recovered," or better, it achieves its own recovery, but the "book of the law" is "discovered" towards the end of the book of Kings "hidden" in the temple. More than the Philistines, it is kingship and temple that bring about a total eclipse of the book. One can see in this a literary figuration reflecting the point of view of the redactional group, that their opponents have sequestered the God of the law in the temple; this is clearly the position of the book of Ezekiel and the book of Jeremiah. The "capture" by the Philistines of the Ark is only a prefiguration of the latter development. The sons of Eli, Hophni and Phinehas, join together with the people in viewing the Ark as a magic wand at their service (1 Sam 4:2–5), prefiguring the perception of the temple by the priests and prophets opposing Jeremiah (cf. Jer 7:1–15; 28:1–17). The result is the same one envisaged by Ezekiel and Jeremiah (1 Sam 4:10–18). On hearing the report thereof, the wife of Phinehas, while giving birth, names her newborn son Ichabod and expires (1 Sam 4:19–22). The name means "where is the glory," explained in the text as "The glory has departed from Israel." This is precisely what is stated and related pictorially in the book of Ezekiel regarding the fall of the temple and Jerusalem (Ezek 9–11). This time we have a judge, Eli, whose "reign" ends in catastrophe. We are no longer in the book of Judges. The sons of the next judge, Samuel, will not fare any better (1 Sam 8:1–5). In the book of Judges, the narratives highlighted the soteriological action of God while his penal action as judge is reduced in the main to a stereotyped phrase. In Samuel and Kings, the narratives detail His penal action, while the leadership, the judges and then kings, are no longer soteriological figures but perpetrators of that which leads to the fall of the people. There are few exceptions, Samuel and David being the most prominent, but even they are concurrently saviors and source of the problem. The message that we see repeated in the book of the Latter Prophets, to the effect that the leaders are culpable, is portrayed here in narrative form. The coordinates determining the narrative in the book of

Samuel are most clear in the case of Saul: he is both judge and savior, and yet the paradigmatic rejected leader by the deity.

A basic literary turning point is often overlooked as being simply a passing note; it is 1 Sam 9:9: "(Formerly in Israel, anyone who went to inquire of God would say, 'Come, let us go to the seer'; for the one who is now called a prophet was formerly called a seer.)" (NRSV). Even now, most people would, on hearing the word "prophet," bring to mind the image of a seer. The default conception of a prophet in people's minds is that of a seer, unless otherwise educated. This phrase in 1Sam 9:9 inaugurates the redactional group's pedagogy on the matter. Let us not forget that we are in the book of the Former Prophets, and that the redactors are working up to the second prophetic tetrateuch, the book of the Latter Prophets, much as the Pentateuch worked up to the book of "Words, *děbārîm*," Deuteronomy. Dynasties, annals, lists of names, as well as oracles, will have to be replaced with the "words" of the deity, directly accessible, without mediation, to everyone; this was the "mystery" action announced by Isa 40–55, and the guiding purpose of this redactional school in the production of the mega work. The pedagogical mind of the redactors is overleaping the remainder of the book of Samuel and the book of Kings and preparing for the book of the Latter Prophets, constructed with its cornerstone and keystone being Isa 40–55. Immediately after 1 Sam 9, in chapter 10, we have reports about the prophetic groups and people wondering whether Saul also is among the prophets! David is also reported in their midst. We are already being told that Saul will not be among them, that David will be among them, but, more importantly, that whether kings or prophets, it is the deity that is and will be at work through His "Words."

In what follows in the book of Samuel are the peripeteias of Saul and David contesting the throne and then the sons of David contesting each other and David for the throne. Try as one may, there is no way that anyone can write an aretology for

David. David functions like the apostles in the narratives of the gospels: they are recruited as paradigmatic learners. The reader must learn through their foibles. The only interpretive perspective that holds together the heteroclite narratives is the phrase in Isa 55:3, "Incline your ear, and come to me; listen, so that you may live. I will make with you an everlasting covenant, my steadfast, sure love for David." (NRSV). The story is about God's "steadfast, sure love" in spite of all our doings and their consequences. This is the essence of the "Book of Consolation," this is the pedagogy. The character traits that differentiate between Saul and David are not between good and bad, they are traits that make the one an unruly student, with an erratic temper, unwilling to be reproved and disciplined, and the other an attentive student, with a mild equanimous temper, open to being reproved and disciplined: one not ready to play second fiddle to the deity, while the other aware that the deity alone calls the shots. The remark about Michal, Saul's daughter, in 2 Sam 6:16, tells it all: "Now as the ark of Yahweh entered the City of David, Michal daughter of Saul was watching from the window and when she saw King David leaping and whirling round before Yahweh, the sight of him filled her with contempt." (NRSV). We must remember that both Isa 40–55 and the mega work are written in a situation of total devastation, interpreted by the writer and redactors as divine punishment. The message of consolation is that the deity's commitment is not a function of our actions, it is a function of His will. This is buttressed by the narrative elements that underline the deity's concern for the "little man," and his rejection of the haughty. "He" is not put off by total desolation. The "cutting off" of David's dynasty, while indicating God's judgement, underlines that the "principal actor" through whom the narrative finds continuation is the God of Abraham.

One very pronounced literary tool used is to be found in the names of the two major characters accompanying the David narrative: Jonathan and Nathan. These are basically the same name meaning "Yah gives/gave." "Jonathan" opens the way for David to survive Saul's plotting against him. In literary terms, Jonathan is God maintaining David's path open, Jonathan's "great love" for David is none other than the "steadfast, sure love" of God. The "prophet," Nathan, brings God's judging word and lesson to David, reminding him that "God, Yah, has given," that is "Jonathan."

The name of David's victim, Uriah the Hittite, is also very indicative of the "moral of the story/lesson." The Hebrew verbal root *htt* means "to be shattered/dismayed."[33] A good example of its use is in Isa 7:8, "Within sixty-five years Ephraim will be shattered, no longer a people." (NRSV). The man is from a broken, shattered ethnic group. The Hittites had been a powerful force in Asia Minor and northern Mesopotamia in the second millennium B.C., but by the second half of the first millennium they had faded from the stage of power politics. The name "Uriah" means "Yah is my light." His faithfulness and correctness is underlined in the narrative. His wife's name, Bathsheba, means "daughter of the oath," the reference being to the oath given by God to Abraham. The word brings to mind Beer-Sheba and the Abraham cycle in that region. Suffice to remember Gen 22:19:

> "By myself I have sworn, says the Lord: Because you have done this, and have not withheld your son, your only son, I will indeed bless you, and I will make your offspring as numerous as the stars of heaven and as the sand that is on the seashore. And your offspring shall possess the gate of their enemies, and by your offspring shall all the nations of the earth gain blessing for themselves, because you have obeyed my voice." So Abraham returned to his young men, and they arose and went together to Beer-sheba; and Abraham lived at Beer-sheba. (Gen 22:16–19 NRSV).

David in what he does to Uriah breaks the premise underlying the covenant (2 Sam 11–12). The David motif crashes the Abraham motif. Uriah in this narrative corresponds to the

---

[33] Cf. BDB, 369.

servant-*rāhām* and to the projected addressees of the servant-*rāhām*; after all, the task of the servant in Isa 40–55 was to be a "light to the nations." This pericope brings to a head the predicament as faced by the writer/redactors: total devastation, the covenant broken, dismay, and chaos. This is the situation addressed by Isa 40–55 and which is being worked out in this narrative. Beyond this point remains only the book of consolation. In the narrative, even as the failings of the kingship are yet to be elaborated, the continuation of the literary narrative mimics the message: God is still continuing the interlocution, when human beings can only be gripped by silence.

At the beginning of this section, it was pointed out that the book of Samuel seems to parallel in the first prophetic tetrateuch the book of Numbers in the Pentateuch. The demand for a king in the first half (1 Sam) together with the malfeasance of Saul vis-a-vis David, regarded as an insurrection against Yahweh, corresponds to the mutiny of the people with Miriam and Aaron and the counterpoising of Joshua and Caleb to them in the first half of the book of Numbers; the escapades of David in the second half of the book (2 Sam), basically in the region of the Calebites centered in Hebron, would seem to correspond to the ascendancy of Joshua and Caleb in the second half of the book of Numbers. Further, as was pointed out above, the story about the capture of the Ark and the "Glory" departing from Jacob parallels the portrayal of the book of Ezekiel of the fall of the temple in Jerusalem and the Glory departing Jerusalem. A further parallel between the third book of the first prophetic tetrateuch and the third book of the second prophetic tetrateuch, the book of Ezekiel, is found in the name of the title character in each of the two books. Since Ezekiel is seen here as prior to the mega work, it is the name Samuel which must be seen as adapted to parallel that of Ezekiel. The parallelism is only in the second part of the composite names. Both use the term "El" in the composite name rather than Yah or Yahweh. "El" is a common Semitic designation for "god."

After the "circle/enclosure is broken," both the people and their goods are in the "wilderness" of the peoples/nations (as coined in the book of Ezekiel, Ezek 20:35, probably by DH). Both the messages of Ezekiel and Samuel have to deal with this situation. The conjecture put forward above is that the redactional group was hosted by the Calebites in the south, between Hebron and Beer-Sheba. "Calebites" was a designation applied to a group of north-western Arab tribes. At times in history it would be used as a collective term for all the north-western tribes. These tribes controlled a trade route stretching from central Africa, Ethiopia, to north of the Black Sea. It is possible to conjecture that through this trade route, the message of the Joshua redactional group was seen spreading along this route to the "nations." It would have been an early "gentile mission" success seen endangered by actions such as David's with Uriah or earlier Levi and Simeon's in Shechem, provoking, as we saw above, Jacob's anger. Bathsheba's father is named as Eliam, often rendered as "El/God is my kinsman." This could be taken as an indication that Bathsheba, the wife of Uriah then David, was from one of these groups, establishing alliances and kinship with David and Jacob, and that consequently Solomon would have been a child of this "mixed marriage," explaining much of what we will read about him in the book of Kings, as well as what we read about Moses in the book of Exodus and his Midianite-Kenite father-in-law.

2.4.4 The Redaction at Work in the Narratives of the Book of Kings

The book of Kings seems to be the inverse of the book of Deuteronomy. It revolves around dynasties and purported annals. It is parallel to it, however, in that it resumes and brings to a climax the message of the first prophetic tetrateuch, much as Deuteronomy resumes and brings the message of the Pentateuch in its most climactic and condensed form. They both end with Jacob outside the land of promise looking prospectively to it.

The monotony of the listing of the sins of Jacob against the backdrop of kingly "annals" and stereotyped dynastic succession is interrupted at times with the furtive appearance of prophets. The one big exception to this flow is the Elijah–Elisha narrative cycle. Positioned centrally in this book, it thrones as the social message counterpointing the evils of kingship foretold already in Deuteronomy (Deut 17:14–20) and the book of Samuel (1 Sam 8), and described before all in Isa 40–55 and the Joseph story in Genesis. What initially appears to be the basic motif, the temple, proves to be the basic foil, predetermining the catastrophic ending. The central Elijah–Elisha cycle functions in the literary pedagogy as the pivot catapulting the temple passage at the beginning to the catastrophic end, underlining, particularly in the dispute between Ahab and Elijah over Naboth's vineyard, the inevitability of the ultimate collapse. The issue is on one hand, "who is king in Israel?"; on the other hand, it is about the difference in nature of the two proposed contestants, seen as intrinsic to the difference between Baal and Yahweh and narrated as the difference between the purviews of Elijah and Ahab. The name of Naboth the Jezreelite means literally "a shoot planted by God," otherwise put, "any/every person." In the first chapter of the book of Genesis, we are told that God created Adam in his image and likeness. In the ancient world, this applied only to the king. We are told in the Naboth pericope that this applies to any person. For Yahweh, there is no difference between the "king," Ahab, and the "commoner," Naboth. When this is postulated otherwise, it is Yahweh's kingship that is put into question. The nondescript and anonymous servant of Isaiah 40–55 is the interpretational horizon of this point of view, inasmuch as the said text confounds this servant with God's self-presentation. Just as the David motif in the book of Samuel crashes against the Abraham motif, in the book of Kings it is kingship as such that crashes against the Abraham motif, paradigmatically, iconically in the Naboth narrative. It is noteworthy that both Elijah and Elisha seem to reside on the periphery of Jacob's tribes and exercise their charge both inside and outside Israel and Judah, much as has been conjectured here to be the situation of the redactional group this presentation is concerned with. Centrally in the book of Kings, Elijah and Elisha control and preside over the story/history of Judah and Israel, much as the redactional group conceives its work. It is also noteworthy that Elisha, the disciple of Elijah, carries in his name one of the two central concerns of this school: God will save, present in the first name of Joshua, Hoshea, meaning God has saved; the other concern being that God will hear the plaint of the needy and judge, present in the name Joshua itself. This second concern is reflected in the work of Elijah and Elisha. On the fundament of the judging work of Elijah (my God is Yah), the judging/saving work of Elisha commences.

Just before the final end, we are told that the book of the law was found hidden in the temple. The alternative to kingship and temple is introduced just in time before the lights go out. It refers the reader to the Pentateuch, to the mega work as the alternative to the catastrophic kingship. I understand the mention of the "Book of the Law" as an inner-textual reference to the work in progress, to the program announced in Isa 40–55. The reference to the charge to write down the words of the deity will be repeated in the books of all the three major "latter" prophets, Isaiah, Jeremiah, and Ezekiel.

One last remark on the book of Kings; a very important parenthesis is opened at the beginning of the Solomon narrative, when the young king was still "good king Solomon." This takes place before the construction of the temple. Solomon's "wisdom" is praised by the deity as being the trait which would qualify him for kingship (1 Kgs 3:4–28). In the following, Solomon will be portrayed as progressively becoming bereft of all that is presented in wisdom literature as elements of wisdom. Again, as in the case of David, it is not a person that is being endorsed, it is a paradigm. This will be expanded in the final section of this presentation on the third part of Scripture.

But as we see throughout the Law and the Prophets, the alternative to the folly of temple and kingship is seen on one hand in the parable of Abraham of Isa 40–55, and on the other hand in the deliberations of Qoheleth. Throughout the narratives about human foibles, whether of Jacob in the book of Genesis, or David in the book of kings, or the various characters that are encountered, for better or worse, we see the appreciation for cunning, wit, and repartee, characteristic for wisdom literature in general and for Ecclesiates in particular. What is most interesting in the narrative about Solomon's wisdom is that wisdom and jurisprudence are joined together, and cunning comes to be at the service of justice.

2.5 Redactional Elements Specific to Individual Books of the Second Prophetic Tetrateuch, the Latter Prophets

2.5.1 Redactional Work in the Book of Isaiah

The core of the book of Isaiah is Isa 40–55. It has no literary historical framework or mention of authorship. This has been postulated here as the blueprint initiating the production of what we know as Scripture. Isaiah 56–66 is an expansion of Isa 40–55, equally timeless, equality with no literary rubrics. The chapters 56–66 have been postulated here as the work of the first generation of disciples of Isa 40–55. Together the two sections correspond in their location in the book of the Latter Prophets to the location of the Joseph narrative in the book of Genesis and the Pentateuch. Isaiah chapters 1–39 presuppose at least the ongoing literary production of this school. They are to be seen as the latest part of the book and, as such, the production of the second generation of disciples. We have pointed out several of their characteristics in the course of this presentation and need not repeat here. It is they who gave a name to the book and the work of the founder, derived from the text of Isa 40–55. The prophet is given the name Isaiah, meaning "Yah will save." The book is given literary "historical" rubrics placing it in the compositional framework of the book of the Prophets. No attempt is made to correlate between this framework and the internal situation reflected in the text of Isa 40–55. The fictive historical framework is oblivious and indifferent to the fact that it antedates "Cyrus" by some two centuries. It sets up the argument within the context of the Latter Prophets that is referenced and pointed to in the book of Jeremiah: if repentance is shown as in the time of King Hezekiah, perhaps the actual final catastrophe could have been averted. The literary work is skillfully carried out; the issue is not historical plausibility but pedagogical highlighting of the teaching of Isa 40–55. In this, it functions like chapters 56–66. Chapters 56–66 highlight and amplify the prospective second half of Isa 40–55, whereas chapters 1–39 highlight and amplify the retrospective first half of Isa 40–55. The school highlights the same alternating sequence of judgement and salvation, and the same "universalist" outlook. The charge to write down is repeated and contextualized. The use of personal names to spell out programs is a favorite tool. Isaiah chapters 1–39 are perhaps the best self-portrait of what I have called here the "Joshua scribal school." They give us insight into its literary concept and tools, how it worked out and deliberated the text of Isa 40–55, and how it carried out its discipleship.

The redactors may have used elements in chs. 1–39 that go back to the "master" of the school. The song of the vineyard in Isa 5:1–7 comes to mind as a possibility. It is a concise poetic unit, and it is followed by a diatribe encapsulating the point of view that has been traced above as determinative for the governing redactional work across the various books and units. Perhaps it was a lecture by the master of the school on redactional work. It is difficult to say, because the interwoven final work is seamless and yet reflects the final stage of production. It is interesting to note that there is an uncannily analogous passage in Eccl 2:1–13 to the song of the vineyard and the diatribe following it:

Chapter 3

> I said to myself, "Come now, I will make a test of pleasure; enjoy yourself." But again, this also was vanity. I said of laughter, "It is mad," and of pleasure, "What use is it?" I searched with my mind how to cheer my body with wine -- my mind still guiding me with wisdom -- and how to lay hold on folly, until I might see what was good for mortals to do under heaven during the few days of their life. I made great works; I built houses and planted vineyards for myself; I made myself gardens and parks, and planted in them all kinds of fruit trees. I made myself pools from which to water the forest of growing trees. I bought male and female slaves, and had slaves who were born in my house; I also had great possessions of herds and flocks, more than any who had been before me in Jerusalem. I also gathered for myself silver and gold and the treasure of kings and of the provinces; I got singers, both men and women, and delights of the flesh, and many concubines. So I became great and surpassed all who were before me in Jerusalem; also my wisdom remained with me. Whatever my eyes desired I did not keep from them; I kept my heart from no pleasure, for my heart found pleasure in all my toil, and this was my reward for all my toil. Then I considered all that my hands had done and the toil I had spent in doing it, and again, all was vanity and a chasing after wind, and there was nothing to be gained under the sun. So I turned to consider wisdom and madness and folly; for what can the one do who comes after the king? Then I saw that wisdom excels folly as light excels darkness. (NRSV).

It is possible that a brilliant student reading this passage was inspired to compose the song of the vineyard. The passage quoted from Ecclesiastes seems to be the primary source: the deliberations of a high court official pondering life and its meaning. It reflects the guiding concept governing the redactional work of DH in what appears to be a "raw" formulation. It is at the same time a "perfect" resume of Isa 1–39, where diatribe and wisdom alternate in masterly variations on Isa 40–55 and Ecclesiastes.

In the series of variations, it is characteristic that motifs recur more than once. One such recurring theme reflects the concern of pedagogues and writers: Is anyone listening? Is anyone hearing? In Isa 42:18-23 we hear:

> Listen, you that are deaf; and you that are blind, look up and see! Who is blind but my servant, or deaf like my messenger whom I send? Who is blind like my dedicated one, or blind like the servant of the Lord? He sees many things, but does not observe them; his ears are open, but he does not hear. The Lord was pleased, for the sake of his righteousness, to magnify his teaching and make it glorious. But this is a people robbed and plundered, all of them are trapped in holes and hidden in prisons; they have become a prey with no one to rescue, a spoil with no one to say, 'Restore!' Who among you will give heed to this, who will attend and listen for the time to come? (NRSV).

This is echoed in Isa 6:8-12 in the early part of chs.1-39:

> Then I heard the voice of the Lord saying, "Whom shall I send, and who will go for us?" And I said, "Here am I; send me!" And he said, "Go and say to this people: 'Keep listening, but do not comprehend; keep looking, but do not understand.' Make the mind of this people dull, and stop their ears, and shut their eyes, so that they may not look with their eyes, and listen with their ears, and comprehend with their minds, and turn and be healed." Then I said, "How long, O Lord?" And he said: "Until cities lie waste without inhabitant, and houses without people, and the land is utterly desolate; until the Lord sends everyone far away, and vast is the emptiness in the midst of the land. . . ." (NRSV).

And we find the motif echoed again in Isa 30:8-13 in the latter part of chs. 1-39:

> Go now, write it before them on a tablet, and inscribe it in a book, so that it may be for the time to come as a witness forever. For they are a rebellious people, faithless children, children who will not hear the instruction of the Lord; who say to the seers, "Do not see"; and to the prophets, "Do not prophesy to us what is right; speak to us smooth things, prophesy illusions, leave the way, turn aside from the path, let us hear no more about the Holy One of Israel." Therefore thus says the Holy One of Israel: Because you reject this word, and put your trust in oppression and deceit, and rely on them; therefore this iniquity shall become for you like

a break in a high wall, bulging out, and about to collapse, whose crash comes suddenly, in an instant; (NRSV).

Compare these now also with Eccl 5:1.

If the thesis being presented here is true, the book of Isaiah includes both the blueprint for the mega work and a masterful paradigm of its application. It is a tour de force by the disciples, exemplary of the work of the school. One could easily read the book of Isaiah and acquire a broad view of Scripture. The Lucan double work for one seems to take this book as a basis for its work and as practically synonymous with Scripture. The Dead Sea Scrolls reflect the popularity and widespread use of this scroll among the various factions.

2.5.2 Redactional Work in the Book of Jeremiah

The book of Jeremiah functions as the main literary tool against the temple party. It is parallel to the portrayal of Moses in the book of Exodus and of the Pentateuch as a whole.[34] It is the counterweight to the misappropriation of the book of Ezekiel by the Zadokite party.[35] The rubrics used as a framework for the book pick up on the Abiathar opposition to Solomon and Zadok in the book of Kings, 1 Kgs 1–2. Abiathar is seen as descended from the priests at Shiloh, 1 Kgs 2:26–27, who remained after the family of Eli was condemned and the Arc was transferred to Jerusalem. He is said to come from Anathoth, a town given as a portion to the sons of Aaron, Josh 21:18. If we explain the name Abiathar as a literary name contextual to the drama, then it seems to mean "my father remains/survives." He is a survival from the house of Eli and the priests at Shiloh; he also survives the ban by Solomon. Jeremiah is linked to Abiathar by being mentioned as coming from Anathoth, Jer 1:1, and by his invocation of Shiloh as

---

34 Cf. Cf. Paul Nadim Tarazi, "The Book of Jeremiah and the Pentateuchal Torah," in *Sacred Text and Interpretation: Perspectives in Orthodox Biblical Studies* (ed. Theodore G. Stylianopoulos; Brookline, Mass.: Holy Cross Orthodox Press, 2006).
35 Ibid.

having priority over Jerusalem, Jer 7:12. Anathoth is mentioned in Isa 10:30 in a pun on its name: "answer her Anathoth." Anathoth is seen in this verse as derived from the triliteral *'nh* (to answer/be afflicted). Anathoth is read by Isa 10:30 as a paradigm of affliction, as meaning "affliction." Anathoth, Shiloh, and the implicit reference to the house of Eli are used in the book of Jeremiah as a sign of God's judgement that will be directed against Jerusalem, the temple, and Judah. Just as God "threw away" the first abode of the Ark, so will he do to Jerusalem. The name of Jeremiah carries the double meaning inherent in the task assigned to him: "'Now I have put my words in your mouth. See, today I appoint you over nations and over kingdoms, to pluck up and to pull down, to destroy and to overthrow, to build and to plant.'" (Jer 1:9b–10 NRSV). The name of Jeremiah can be construed from the triliteral root *rmh* (to cast away, or the triliteral root *rwm* (to exalt/be exalted). The name would mean "Yah threw away/discarded" and "Yah will exalt/be exalted." The tasks assigned to him encompass four of destruction and two for rebuilding. We hear in Isa 40–55 that Jacob has received double punishment; this is reflected in this count. The prophet is portrayed as the suffering servant of Isa 40–55, whose own townspeople seek to kill:

> But I was like a gentle lamb led to the slaughter. And I did not know it was against me that they devised schemes, saying, "Let us destroy the tree with its fruit, let us cut him off from the land of the living, so that his name will no longer be remembered!" But you, O Lord of hosts, who judge righteously, who try the heart and the mind, let me see your retribution upon them, for to you I have committed my cause. Therefore thus says the Lord concerning the people of Anathoth, who seek your life, and say, "You shall not prophesy in the name of the Lord, or you will die by our hand –" (Jer 11:19–21 NRSV).

Within these coordinates, the book of Jeremiah is used as a ramrod against the temple party; his searing diatribes are backed by his credentials, as representative of those who had been the first recipients of God's wrath. Abiathar had accompanied the Ark with Zadok, he had stood with David against his enemies, but had singularly opposed from the beginning the accession of Solomon to the throne against Zadok. This is how he is presented in the book of Kings. By proxy of Jeremiah, he now faces down the Zadokite temple party.

Another redactional element employed in the book of Jeremiah is represented by the so-called "confessions," cf. 11:18–12:6; 15:10–21; 17:12–18; 18:18–23; 20:7–18. The "personal" reflections are deftly employed to engage the reader in the argument similarly to the psalms "of David." They function as a liturgical and dramatic element in the pedagogy. Also, passages are "borrowed" from the book of Kings, as is done in the first part of the book of Isaiah (chs. 1–39) in order to impart an official tone to the framework. It is noteworthy that this is not done with the book of Ezekiel; being the bone of contention and prior to the work of the redactional school the leeway for editing and redacting will have been to some extent limited. We have seen, however, that a resume of the Pentateuchal narrative and DH has been inserted in Ezek 20, as well as other insertions/glosses.

The radical language used in the book of Jeremiah becomes occasion for presenting the future as a total break with the past, as a "new covenant" (Jer 31:31). Restoration is said to be in the distant future, after seventy years, Jer 25:11–12; 29:10. The number seventy is seven multiplied by ten, that is, the sacred number seven raised to the power ten. The resulting number is the number of the nations. The Jubilee year in the Holiness Code was an exponential number: seven times seven, raising the sacral number to a higher plane of sacrality. The number seventy, however, is an expansion on the same plane. Just before the second invocation of the seventy-year period in Jer 29:10, in the letter of Jeremiah to the exiles, the prophet tells the exiles in 29:4–7:

> Thus says the Lord of hosts, the God of Israel, to all the exiles whom I have sent into exile from Jerusalem to Babylon: Build houses and live in them; plant gardens and eat what they produce. Take wives and have sons and daughters; take wives for your sons, and give your daughters in marriage, that they may bear sons and daughters; multiply there, and do not decrease. But seek the welfare of the city where I have sent you into exile, and pray to the Lord on its behalf, for in its welfare you will find your welfare. (NRSV).

It is in the welfare of the nations that the future for the exiles and Jerusalem resides. The sacred realm must encompass the gentiles; hence the enlargement of the sacred number of the precinct of Jerusalem and Judah to the number seventy in order to encompass the nations. While the sacrality of the Jubilee year contrasts the higher plane of God's time as against that of Jerusalem, the number seventy enlarges on the same plane of sacrality the compass of the sacred precinct to include the nations. The "apocalyptic discourse" in the Gospel of Luke, ch. 21, offers an apt term for such a period: "the times of the gentiles," Luke 21:24. In an analogous situation of the destruction of Jerusalem and Judaea, the Lukan redactor coins this term instead of using a number. The number seventy is a literary term, not a temporal specification, expanding the ambit of God's salutary action.

The current Hebrew version of the book is most likely a second edition, the extant LXX Greek reflecting more probably the original Hebrew text and arrangement, but more on this below in the fourth chapter. After the further collapse, the book of Jeremiah became itself the bone of contention and the banner head of the school for the various opposing factions, with some breaking away and espousing the former opponent. While the book of Isaiah was in a sense more distant from contemporary events in terms of being a framework for the presentation of the work of the master and the school, and thus placed in more distant literary historical coordinates belying the actual circumstance, the book of Jeremiah, being the polemical spearhead, engaged contemporary events and the opponents to a greater extent, in spite of being presented similarly with dissimulated coordinates. One further literary element employed to engage the readers is the epistolary element. This too would have an impact and repercussions on "intertestamental" literature. As the proverbial "second punch," Jeremiah shares with the book of Exodus in the Pentateuch and the book of Judges in the first prophetic tetrateuch this status in the second prophetic tetrateuch, and as such leaves an iconic impression in the mind of the reader as representative of the whole tome.

2.5.3 Redactional work with regard to the Book of Ezekiel

Basically, the redaction of this book is outside the scope of the current presentation, as it is postulated as prior to the work of the redactional school in question. Its placement in the second prophetic tetrateuch, if ascribed to the work of this school, would certainly have to be considered. There is no reason to contest the sequence and collection of the books we call the Pentateuch. Beyond the question of sources, the actual finished product would be difficult to understand except as an intentional redactional compilation. This can be said unequivocally with regard to the first prophetic tetrateuch. As we have them, the redaction of the individual books would be difficult to understand outside the compilation. With the Latter Prophets, it becomes much more difficult to be categorical. Still the interrelations and synoptic view between Isaiah, Jeremiah and DH indicate clearly a redactional design. Also, the book of the twelve smaller prophets has all the indications of being an intentionally redacted unit within the scope of the mega project. Without the literary fiction of the book of Kings, the individual smaller prophets would to a great extent become incomprehensible other than for the fable of Jonah. However, the book of Ezekiel is a different matter. It does show evidence of redactional activity in the sense of the redactional school we have been discussing. Its primordial interest for both this school and the opponents means that its compositional elements have been assimilated into the larger work rather than vice versa. Its singularity shows in the passages where it differs from the rubrics and codes in the Pentateuch and the division of land in DH. The schematic style of the land division diverges from the style of DH, and its idiosyncratic presentation of the eschatological temple, if original, does not seem to have found an echo in DH nor reflects the style of DH. It is a very powerful work with very powerful imagery. The teaching has been assimilated almost in its entirety by DH, but much less the imagery. Can we justify seeing it as intentionally incorporated into what has been called here the second prophetic tetrateuch?

External evidence is not very helpful, because the books were initially kept as individual scrolls. The lack of external contestation of its sequence in the book of the Latter Prophets in spite of the fact that at times its canonical status has been contested is practically all we can say. What has been conjectured here about its having been a bone of contention between the redactional group and its opponents is buttressed by the fact that its canonical status and transmission within the tetrateuch seems to have offered it a protected seat of transmission and canonical status in spite of its idiosyncrasies and the contestation of its canonical status. Its incorporation into the book of the Latter Prophets has functioned as a stabilizing force in its transmission. The acrimony between the book of Jeremiah and the temple party together with what we know about the Zadokite attempt to centralize the cult in its own hands seems to militate in favor of this conjecture. The highest respect shown the teachings of the book by the school of Isa 40–55 and the assimilation of its main tenets and ideas remains the most powerful argument for our conjecture. If it did indeed incorporate it into the third seat of the second prophetic tetrateuch, then it would have been cast as parallel to the book of Numbers in the Pentateuch, as a testimony to the "wilderness" journey and the contestations that are recounted in the book of Numbers. The Aaron and Aaron-Moses figures in Numbers would have reflected the contestations that were going on, among others, with regard to the book of Ezekiel. The uncertainty about the "original" shape of the book makes it very difficult to be more precise. What we can say is that the shape of the book as it stands and has been transmitted and received is the one that has the imprint of the school of Isa 40–55, of DH. Ezekiel is made now to correspond to the exiles, from whom, Jeremiah said, would come the future salvation. The only other comment we can make is that the symbolic use of numbers by this school means that a book of the prophets, symbolizing the four gates of the temple, and, as envisaged by Ezekiel, watering the whole earth, cannot be but fourfold!

2.5.4 Redactional Work in the Book of the Twelve Prophets

The sequence of the collection has not been stable in transmission. The sequence of the Hebrew text differs from that of the LXX. Partisan collections such as those of the Dead Sea Scrolls offer differing sequences. There is no reason not to accept the Hebrew sequence in the Jewish tradition as original. It is the one taken as the basis for the discussion here. The first element of redaction that is relevant is the number of the collection. It is clearly deliberate: the book of Malachi is an oracle detached from the series of oracles in the book of Zechariah in order to complete the number. There is every reason to consider this as pertaining to the original redaction of the book. The "words" are delivered to the twelve tribes of Jacob and thence to the whole world. This same view is reflected in the NT. The twelve apostles, representative of all the tribes of Jacob, not individually but symbolically, receive the teaching, and then deliver it to the whole world.

But beyond the number, the book of the Twelve Prophets is a recapitulation of the whole book of the Prophets, of the two tetrateuchs together, and represents the viewpoint of DH. The first book in the Hebrew order is the book of Hosea. The English translations want us to think it is another name, but the Hebrew is the same as in the name of Joshua son of Nun, rendered in English as Hoshea. The name means "God has saved/may God save," and emphatically thereby repeats the message of the book of Joshua. The prophet Hosea directs his harangue against Samaria/Ephraim and against Jacob. If we disregard the historical dissimulation of the framework and the dissimulation by translations in English, what we have, in literary terms, is: Hoshea-Joshua, the representative of Ephraim in Num 13:8, addresses the judging words of the deity against Ephraim and against Jacob reminiscent of the reports about him (Jacob) in Genesis.[36] We are returned not only to the first book of the book of the Prophets, we are returned to the first book of the Pentateuch. The emphasis on Jacob is in direct continuation of the first half of Isa 40–55. The use of names for progeny as programmatic names is in continuation of Isa 1–39. The identity of the redacting party leaves no room for doubt. The message only confirms what the method tells us. A total break is announced; instead of convocation a dismissal is announced. The redactors manage to put in a short book an epitome of the teaching in the books discussed so far in all its facets; even the polemic style of Ezekiel is emulated.

The second book in sequence is Joel, which means "he began." The continuation of the phrase is in the title of the third book, Amos, which means "carrying a burden." Taking the names of these three books we would have the phrase: "He saved and then began carrying (our) burden." This is basically the charge against Jacob by Isa 40–55 and by DH. The final three books are an unconsummated return to the land, with the view prospectively in the second half of Zechariah and Malachi directed towards God's intervention, similar to Isa 56–66.

The message of the twelve books repeats the message of the Latter Prophets. Indeed they could have constituted chapters of

---

36 Cf. chapter 1, section 3.2.

one book with the usual pattern: God's saving action presented as grounds for indictment, and then a shift to future judgement and saving action. At the end of the very stern indictment in the book of Amos of Samaria and of Judah, we end with a short note on "raising up the fallen hut of David." This is usually seen as a "later" addition. In fact it reflects the point of view of DH based on Isa 55:3, expressing God's everlasting steadfast love for David; the motif that God's commitment bridges over the break caused by the sins of Jacob and David. This in fact is the epitome of the "book of consolation," Isa 40–55.

Are there indications in the text that can help in establishing that the sequence in the Hebrew bible was intended by the redactors? The Septuagint characteristically groups the books thematically, and this has led to the thematic grouping of the books of the OT in the Christian churches. These compilations all too often distort the original paradigmatic and pedagogical redactional flow and deform elements and characteristics of the redaction. I suggested an interpretation above of the sequence of the first and last triads of books in the book of the Twelve Prophets following the sequence of the Hebrew bible. The Septuagint, intent on thematic grouping, places the book of Micah third in the sequence, moving the book of Joel to fourth position. Indeed, the book of Micah belongs temporally and materially with the books of Hosea and Amos. As suggested above, this would break up the possibly intended acrostic sequence in the names of the first three prophets in the Hebrew transmission. Are there internal syntactical elements that would also be distorted if one were to follow the Septuagint sequence?

Taking this question up at the place where we reached above, namely the book of Amos, we find that this indeed is the case. There is an inner-textual fundamental link between the book of Amos and the book immediately following in the Hebrew bible, Obadiah, which illustrates the statement made above that the twelve books could be seen as chapters of one book. In the book of Amos, we find in the seventh chapter a unique indictment of "the high places of Isaac," unique for the whole of the Pentateuch and the book of the Prophets. Jacob is always the object of indictment in the literature that we have reviewed, never Isaac, except in Amos 7:9! Hans Walter Wolff postulates that this passage, Amos 7:9–17, was added by the school of Amos, residing in the south, to address northern pilgrims, adepts of a postulated Isaac shrine in the south, in Beer-sheba, when these came on their pilgrimage. Wolff says:

> The reference to the high places of "Isaac" probably indicates that this oracle was addressed to those on pilgrimage to Beer-sheba from the northern kingdom who claimed Isaac as their eponymous ancestor. The use of "Isaac" as a designation for the inhabitants of the northern kingdom . . . may well indicate the work of Amos' school.[37]

Wolff makes a very incisive literary analysis. However, he reads Amos and the postulated "Amos school" as historical quantities. The reading I make is a pedagogical paradigmatic one. The passage Amos 7:9–17 is certainly redactional, but so is the material overall in the book as transmitted. The situation is a dissimulated one. The redaction is by what I have called the "Joshua school," possibly staggered over a short period of time. The name "Amos" is found only in Amos 1:1; 7:8, 10, 11, 12, 14; 8:2 in our literature (that is, other than in the introductory line, only in this passage and the bordering verses). As pointed out above, the "name" comes from the verb meaning "to carry a load," cf. Isa 46:1, 3. The name in the context of the book of Amos can be understood as a midrash on Isa 46:1, 3. The name in this context has as its pendant the name of the prophet's opponent, Amaziah (mentioned only in this passage in 7:10, 12, 14). The name means "Yah is strong." As a pendant to Amos, "to carry a load/bear a burden," it is a caricature in response to the name Amos. It sounds like: "Yah is up to the task." The

---

[37] Hans Walter Wolff, *Joel and Amos* (ed. S. Dean McBride, Jr.; trans. Waldemar Janzen, S. Dean McBride, Jr., and Charles A. Muenchow; Hermeneia; Philadelphia: Fortress, 1977), 301–302. Cf. also p. 110.

couple Amos–Amaziah parallels the couple Jeremiah–Hananiah. In the book of the Twelve, Amos is a stand-in for Jeremiah. His message is one of doom, even more severe than Jeremiah's. The doom will spill over Jacob and reach Isaac, the father of Jacob and Esau/Edom. Not only Jacob goes under, so does Esau/Edom! Without Amos 7:9–17, we would have neither the pun on the name Amos nor the extent of the climactic nature of his message. The whole of the book of Amos is encapsulated in Amos 7:9–17. This feeds directly into the immediately following book of Obadiah, which is the punishment and fall of Edom. The sequence Amos–Obadiah is intertextual before relating to the names of the books. The climactic buildup in the book of Amos spills over into the book of Obadiah through Amos 7:9–17!

Chapter 8 of the book of Amos recapitulates the central thematic thread of the Joseph narrative, which constitutes also the climactic motif of Isa 40–55 and the book of Deuteronomy. In Amos 8:11–13 we hear:

> The time is surely coming, says the Lord God, when I will send a famine on the land; not a famine of bread, or a thirst for water, but of hearing the words of the Lord. They shall wander from sea to sea, and from north to east; they shall run to and fro, seeking the word of the Lord, but they shall not find it. In that day the beautiful young women and the young men shall faint for thirst. (NRSV).

This is the conclusion that was drawn in this presentation concerning the figurative use of the motif of bread in the Joseph narrative.

Amos 9:7 goes on to highlight the mono-anthropic view of the deity that is such a central aspect of Isa 40–55 and the Joshua school, thus rounding up, together with the invocation of God's steadfastness to the "hut" of David (9:11–15), the full and climactic midrash on Isa 40–55 and the lesson of the first triad. At the same time, this functions as a send-off to the lesson of the book of Jonah and the second triad.

The book of Amos is the third book in the sequence of the twelve that this investigation has adopted as a working hypothesis. In conjunction with the formula used as a climactic refrain in the structuring of the first section of the book of Amos this should be a foreboding of greater ill. Indeed we hear in Amos 1:3, 6, 9, 11, 13; 2:1, 4, 6 the following: "Thus says the Lord: For three transgressions of . . ., and for four, I will not revoke the punishment;" (NRSV). What might the fourth book hold for us? In fact, we first "stumble" on an expanded condemnation and punishment of Edom as was intimated in Amos 1:11–12 on the fourth step of the climactic ladder. What might lie in wait for Jacob?

Let us go back now to the sequence of the names of the books. Obadiah introduces the second triad of books in the book of the Twelve. The name Obadiah is from the same root as the word "servant." The name "Obadiah" is practically equivalent to "servant/worshipper of Yahweh." The servant in Isa 40–55 initiates the salvation of Jacob, indeed, he carries "the burden" of Jacob's sins. As Jacob would expect, the salvation would start by knocking down Esau/Edom. It is at this point that we encounter the genius of the Joshua school face to face. In the Hebrew bible, the book of Obadiah is followed by the book of Jonah. Just as Jacob would think he had finally gotten what he wanted, the condemnation and destruction of Edom, he actually gets the lesson of Jonah (Edom was being offered to Jacob as a paradigm, just as in Jonah Assyria is offered as a paradigm). Jonah means "dove." The acrostic phrase made up of the names of the books of the second triad would read as: "The servant/worshipper of Yah, a dove (announcing): who is like God?"

The book of Jonah among the twelve is a special case. It is not a prophetic book in the sense of bearing God's word through the prophet. It is a pedagogical prophetic novella or fable. It expresses precisely God's commitment to humankind over the break caused by the sins of Jacob and Adam. The book of Jonah invokes anachronistically the Assyrians as a paradigm rather than David or Jacob. It is a lesson addressed to Jacob, in the person of the "student" prophet Jonah, so as to understand God's position towards His entire creation, and to prospective students of the mega work to understand that "Jacob" and "David" in the texts stand paradigmatically for all human beings. It is a model lesson for the school of Isa 40–55. This small novella conveys in the concise form of a fable the basic universalistic message inherent in Isa 40–55. It is an excellent example of how occasional rubrics in the work of this school are merely a thin see-through shell for paradigmatic pedagogy. This is the way that has been proposed here for reading the Law and the Prophets.[38]

The lesson is the central lesson of this school: God's pedagogy/judgement is an essential aspect of his salutary "steadfast sure love." The judgement of Edom in the first book of the second triad is only a prelude to the judgement of Judah and Israel in the third book of the second triad, the book of Micah. Sandwiched between the judgement of Edom and the judgement of Judah and Samaria/Israel is the fable/lesson of Jonah! This triad mirrors the climactic oracles of the book of Amos (cf. Amos 1:1–3:1, where the judgement of the nations surrounding Israel are a climactic prelude to the judgement of Israel), but, as a triad, explains in lesson form the nature of God's judgement (that is, in view to salvation of humankind). The name of Micah (the name is a short form of Michael, "Who is like God,") functions as an exclamation at the end of this lesson (Mic 7:18).[39] The weight of this exclamation is reflected in that the central fourth chapter of Micah begins (Mic 4:1–3) with a recapitulation of Isa 2:2–4 describing the perspective of eschatological reconciliation defining the book of Isaiah as a

---

38 Cf. Paul Nadim Tarazi, *Decoding Genesis 1–11* (St Paul, Minn: OCABS Press, 2020). Tarazi expansively analyzes the book of Jonah as encapsulating the teaching of the creation narratives and the Noah narrative in the book of Genesis, as well as the books of Ezekiel and Isaiah.
39 Ibid., pp. 269–270.

whole.⁴⁰ This is immediately preceded in Mic 3:12 with a cross reference taken up in the book of Jeremiah 26:18 invoking the total judgement and destruction of Zion. This "antecedent" oracle functions in the literary sequence of the book of the Latter Prophets, conversely to the portrayed "historical" sequence, as a recapitulation of the message of Jeremiah invoking it (a "literary warp" version of "back to the future")! Thus at the center of the book of Micah we have an emphatic restatement of the lesson of the second triad and the book of the Latter Prophets: judgement as a requisite prelude and sine qua non facet of God's everlasting love in view of the salvation of Jacob and the nations. The elaborate literary architecture of the book of the Latter Prophets becomes here fully manifest. The climactic buildup thus far in the Twelve is, in fact, masterful pedagogy. That the book of Jonah in this sequence comes as the fifth book in the sequence of the Twelve seems to reflect the mindset of the redactional school of Isa 40–55: the fable of Jonah for them reflects the teaching of the Pentateuch, concisely as a fable.⁴¹ To parody the NT phrase, the book of Jonah is for this school the "whole of the Law and the Prophets."

The third triad begins with the book of Nahum. If the reading here is correct, this is a direct reference to Isa 40–55. The name Nahum comes from the verbal root meaning "to comfort." This refers to the opening phrase of Isa 40–55. The "servant Obadiah," the title head of the lesson of the second triad, announces (as a dove "Jonah") the work of consolation in the third triad. The great enemy, Nineveh, is now punished. Following the lesson of the second triad, this can now be understood figuratively. Jonah had been sent to Nineveh, and, contrary to his wishes, it had been saved. Its judgement now is to be understood in the context of the lesson of the second triad. The judgement of Edom had been a ploy to trap Jacob into the

---

40 Ibid., pp. 268–270.
41 Ibid., cf. pp. 235–277. After analyzing the impact of the book of Jonah on the OT writings in the indicated sections, Tarazi goes on to discuss its impact on the NT writings.

lesson. The student disciple should have matured here to understand the lesson. The first book of the third triad is the seventh book of the twelve. This is the number of the temple. For our group, Isa 40–55 is the opposite pole to the temple, the school of Joshua the ambulant *debir* (the Holy of Holies). The second book of the third triad, Habakkuk, asks the disciples to await on the watchtower the coming salvation. After all, they can already sense the "fragrance" of its coming, they can practically feel its "embrace." These are the two meanings inherent in the name "Habakkuk." They also are provided with a psalm to chant (Habakkuk ch. 3) as they expectantly hold watch. The name of the third book of the third triad, Zephaniah, spells out the source of salvation for the "daughter of Zion." The name "Zephaniah" means "Yahweh's/God's treasury." We have seen this already in Isa 40–55 and in the "Egyptian" name of Joseph (cf. chapter 2, section 3.1). The acrostic constituted by the names of the books of the third triad would be the phrase: "the bringer of comfort, the all-embracing fragrance (from/of) Yah's treasury."

After the "servant" in the second triad brings the "lesson" of salvation, and the third triad brings news of the approaching salvation (from God's treasury), the fourth triad, completing the four gates of the prophets, tells us to await, in our earthly and earthen situation, God's spirit and salvation, taking the form of an eschatological Elijah preparing the way in the book of Malachi. The book of the Prophets has cross-referenced itself in its entirety in the book of the twelve. The name Haggai means "my (of God) pilgrimage (feast)." Zechariah means "God/Yah remembers." The coming salvation is modelled on the Exodus from Egypt. In the book of Exodus, God remembers his people and their travail and leads them out (by way of His messenger, "Malachi") on a pilgrimage to feast Him on Sinai, His mount (cf. Exod 3:1–18). The approaching salvation is a new Passover. However, it is also modelled on Isa 56–66; it will encompass all the nations (Zechariah ch. 14). Thus the four acrostics of the book of the twelve constitute a (full) resume of Isa 40–66.

2.6 Excursus: The Two Spellings of the Root and Name of Isaac

The name Isaac and its verbal root have been referenced above on several occasions. However, one problem regarding the spelling of the root was left to be elucidated. The reason is that this presentation has repeatedly highlighted this verb and contrasted it with the attributes coherent with the servant-*rāhām* figure and Joseph as the *rāhām*, and consequently with the narrative defining the deity as opposed to the narratives of Jacob and Adam. The question runs across all the books under consideration, both the book of the Law and the book of the Prophets. It spills over to the books of the third part of the canon as well, still to be discussed in chapter 4. In all this literature we encounter two spellings for the same word. The root from which the verbal action and name of Isaac is derived is alternately spelled with *ṣādê* or with *śîn*; thus we have either *ṣāḥaq* or *śāḥaq* for the verb, and *yiṣḥaq* or *yiśḥaq* for the name Isaac. They seem to have the same verbal forms and the same meanings. It should be remembered that in our literature the name Isaac is used only for the "patriarch" son of Abraham and father of Jacob and Esau. The difference seems to be due to regional or temporal variation. For those reading any of the translations, including the Septuagint or other ancient versions, this fact remains imperceptible. In Arabic, this root is written uniformly with *sīn*, which corresponds to Hebrew *śîn*. What can we say about the variation in the Hebrew text? An initial rule of thumb that can be stated is that in the Pentateuch the form for both the verb and the name is uniformly written with *ṣādê*; in DH and in the other books, the form with *ṣādê* is used for the name Isaac, while the verbal forms are written with *śîn*. It would seem that the redactors of the Pentateuch had one spelling, the one with *ṣādê*. The redactors of the other books were wont to use the form with *śîn*, except when referring to the name of Isaac, in which case they followed the spelling in the Pentateuch. To this rule of thumb, however, we seem to have five exceptions. In two cases outside the Pentateuch, we have the verbal form written with ṣādê, Judg 16:25 and Ezek 23:32. In three cases, all three outside the Pentateuch, we find the name Isaac written with śîn, Ps 105:9; Jer 33:26; and Amos 7:9, 16. Let us consider them individually:

- The most intriguing of these five cases is Judg 16:25. Reference was made above to this in chapter 2, section 2.3.3 footnote 20 and in the current chapter three, section 2.4.2 footnote 31. In judges 16:25 the *pi'el* verbal form of this root is used twice, once with śîn and once with ṣādê. Then in 16:27 the *qal* verbal form is used with śîn. The normal usage for the redactor here seems to be the root with śîn. The singular use with ṣādê for the second instance in v. 25 appears to be an intentional reference to Isaac. It was mentioned in section 2.4.2 above that Samson seems to be a stand-in for Judah and David. The lowest point to which the fortunes of Samson had sunk in v. 25, his total humiliation, recalled for the redactors the "Isaac verbal action" and consequently the name of Isaac was brought to mind and invoked through the use of the ṣādê verbal form.

- The use of the verbal form with ṣādê in Ezek 23:32 appears initially to be the older usage that we find reflected in the Pentateuchal redaction. Gustav Hölscher in his literary analysis of the book of Ezekiel ascribes this passage, Ezek 23:31–34, to an initial redactor who expanded the text of Ezekiel with a variation on Ezekiel's motif.[42] If this is so, then this would be the redactor/redactors of the Pentateuch, for which this was the "normal" spelling. This is the only

---

42 Gustav Hölscher, Hesekiel: Der Dichter und das Buch, 123.

use of this root (verb or noun) in either spelling in the book of Ezekiel.

- The use of the name Isaac with *śîn* in Ps 105:9 reflects the opposite trend. I would ascribe this psalm to the "Johanan school" (cf. chapter 4, section 2.1, below regarding this designation). It is a one-dimensional psalm, singing the praises of God's actions in favor of Jacob against their enemies. The phrase "the sworn promise to Isaac" (NRSV) repeats the same phrase of 1 Chr 16:16. The Chronicler meticulously maintains the spelling of Isaac with *ṣādê*, not so the Johanan school. They give themselves a freer hand to deal with previous scripture as can be seen in their edition of the book of Jeremiah. The invocation of "the sworn promise/oath to Isaac" sounds almost like an arraignment to deliver. Thus, I see this as a reflection of a later usage, distinct from that of the Pentateuch and the Joshua school.

- The use of the name Isaac with *śîn* in Jer 33:26 is manifestly to be ascribed to the Johanan school (as defined in chapter 4, section 2.1, below). The entire passage, Jer 33:14–26, is not in the Septuagint at all, not even transposed. It is one of the additions by the Johanan school to the book of Jeremiah and reflects the nationalistic character of the Maccabean school and its attempt to co-articulate the dynastic claim with the priestly function. They practically "automate" the action of God on behalf of David and Judah.[43] This is most pointed in vv. 20–22. (The exclusion condition cited here as

---

[43] Cf. chapter 4, section 1.2.1, below.

impossible is actually a possible condition in Josh 10:12–14).⁴⁴

- As for the use of the name Isaac with *śîn* in Amos 7:9 and 16, it would seem to reflect an Edomite pronunciation. It could very well be that the *śîn* pronunciation for the verbal root we encounter in DH is a southern "Arabic" and Edomite one. The second generation Joshua school, hosted by the Calebites, would have adopted the southern Calebite pronunciation except for the name Isaac, for which it maintained the spelling of the Pentateuch. This underscores the predicament we are faced with regarding the unexpected spelling in Amos 7:9 and 16. Wolff's referral of this passage to a later school of Amos in Beersheba would thus not solve the problem for this presentation. As explained above on the book of Amos, I see this redaction as intrinsic to the book of the Twelve and consequently to DH. I would suggest that the usage in Amos 7:9 and 16 is due to what was proposed above in section 2.5.4, that is, that this passage is written in view of the judgement in the book of Obadiah against Edom and hence is assimilated to the usage in Edom. It does not refer to the Patriarch Isaac as such, but to Edom/Esau, that is, to the "Isaac" representative of Edom.

---

44 Cf. section 2.4.2 above in the current chapter 3, footnote 29.

Chapter 4
The Third Part of the Canon and Epilogue

Prolegomena

The redaction critical review of the books of the Law and the Prophets that was announced in the upper heading of this presentation has now been completed. There is, however, the nagging suspicion that perhaps the work of the redactional school that has been delineated encompasses also the third part of Scripture, of the Tanakh, the Ketubim, otherwise known as the Psalter and Wisdom books. It is the point of view of the present writer that it indeed did. There is a proviso, however, that the present collection is not the one that was in purview of the redactional school under consideration. The "original" collection is seen here to have comprised six books: Psalms; Job; Wisdom; Ruth; Canticles; and Ecclesiastes.

As for the other books in the collection, I see them as pertaining to two other distinct and different redactional schools. The first of the two can be given different designations. One simple designation can be termed as the Maccabean school, or the Johanan school, referencing thus the patronym of the Maccabean school and at the same time the opponent of the prophet Jeremiah. Another designation can be taken from the later Maccabean tradition and a name used often in the intertestamental period: the Jonathan school, or the Greek translation thereof, the Theodotion school; this last name is associated with the Greek translation of the book of Daniel that conforms to the Hebrew text as distinct from the LXX translation. I credit this school with the book of Daniel, Esther, and the book of Lamentations. The second of the two is the Chronicler, responsible for the book of Chronicles, Ezra, and Nehemiah.

In the following, I will first review the redaction of the six books I believe are within the scope of the redactional work of the school at issue in this monograph. Then I will deal briefly with why I find that the last mentioned six books are not encompassed within the scope of what I have called the school of Isa 40–55, or the Joshua school.

1. The School of Isa 40–55 and the Third Part of the Canon

Some references have been made above in chapter 3 to points of convergence between the Pentateuch and the books of the Prophets and the books of Ruth and Ecclesiastes. Here I will review the six books I envisage as part of the intentional redactional canon of the school of Isa 40–55, indeed as part of its conception of its mega work. I will present the arguments for this, as well as propose the function of the third part of the canon within the redactional framework of this school. The charge and work of the master of this school are seen as primordial to this part of Scripture, and it is proposed that he was very active in its production.

1.1 The Function and Framework of the Third Part of the Canon

The central concern in Isa 40–55 was directed to delineating the will of the deity. The parable of Abraham was the basic hermeneutical tool proposed. The figure providing the basic carrier beam for this was the servant-*rāḥām*. The backdrop for this tool was the definition of God's posture as "steadfast, everlasting love" for David. Central to the deliberation of the author was the context: a total return to chaos through the actions of Jacob, standing paradigmatically for all humankind. David, as a focal point for the definition of God's posture, was also paradigmatic for all humans; precisely in his brokenness and culpability his paradigm would counterpoint God's said posture within the extant contemporary situation of human produced chaos and brutishness. The program he/He envisaged in response was the mega work revealing God's mind and posture, addressing Adam and Eve's children with words of consolation, words of reason and wisdom, words that call to account in a void of accountability and reason, words that convene and call to order!

He (the author/redactor) may have been born in exile in a Hellenistic court to someone taken hostage, or been taken himself as hostage as a child and grew to a high position in the court. He could observe much, deliberate much, but do little. He could observe human folly, perceptive of its futility and vanity, empathetic with its suffering. Actionism was not an option he had at hand, and his observation of the potentates of his time could only confirm the brutishness, futility and vanity of their actions. He could give advice, address those who would listen, and thus all his élan and talent in rhetoric and letters was channeled to the production of a body of literature and the teaching of disciples: this was the charge presented in Isa 40–55 as God's program. In the preceding phrasing I have purposely conflated a reading of both Ecclesiastes and Isa 40–55. In Ecclesiastes we are given a view of the "priming" of the mind of this master, on which was painted the canvas of the mega work. It is this priming which is the unifying and identifying factor characterizing this body of literature, unseen yet binding the painting to the canvas and surreptitiously invading the sinews of the mind of the readers, preparing it diachronically as a receptacle for the addressed words.

In analytical terms, what is this third part of Scripture? Schematically, the shape of "Adam" who would coincide with the will of the deity in order to "fit" the entry port to God's garden was already given in the profile of the servant-*rāhām*. In Isa 40–55 there was a deliberation in the text as to the profile. Jacob is considered and rejected, but repeatedly there appears in the first half of Isa 40–55 an ambivalence and a stated questioning of who would/could fill the position. This is emphatically resolved in the second part. In the Pentateuch, consequently, only the "scape"-goat thrones at the center in the book of Leviticus. The two prophetic tetrateuchs are only the ports of this throne room. There is one will of the deity, one occupant. Thus there is no "central" book in the two tetrateuchs. There remains one central question though: what is the profile of the broken human being that is needed for restoration? This is the central deliberative question of the third part of the canon. The human condition in its extreme fallen secular reality, the reality of the culpable Adam and Eve, of the culpable Jacob, of the culpable David must be addressed in the multifaceted range of life experiences. The question is how to bridge the chasm between the demanded servant-*rāḥām* and the actual available Adam and Jacob; for our master rhetorician the question is: how to educate disciples. The pedagogical task demands a constitutive third part of the curriculum; otherwise the school will not stand. The organization of this curriculum seems, broadly speaking, to conform to the more fixed scheme of the Pentateuch. The first part lays the groundwork (Genesis), the second is the initial proposal (Exodus), the third is the central pivot (Leviticus) that, when applied to the first two, transforms the postulates and lifts them to a new plane in the fifth part. The fourth part (Numbers) is the give and take that follows on the statement of the central part before the change of plane is applied in the final part (Deuteronomy). Essentially it is a three-day pilgrimage, a *ḥag*, whereby the starting point/situation of the pilgrimage must cross a divide to reach the aspired point/situation of the third day. In the fivefold version, this is expanded to a five part pilgrimage, effectively two three day spans sharing the focal central day. The point to remember is that the final point corresponds to the initial point "transformed," that is, on a new plane with transformed coordinates. In the fifth year of your study curriculum, you should not be on the level of the first year.

This schematic framework is obviously a conjectured framework in analogy to the hitherto observed organization of the Pentateuch, which gives us the clearest indication of the organizational mind of the redactors, as well as to DH, which is clearly a unified work and gives us a second perspective on the organizational pattern in the mind of this redactional school. The third part of the canon seems to be a loose grouping of diverse writings. Two of the books, Proverbs and Canticles need not have been produced by this school and can simply be borrowings. The book of Psalms follows closely in its present form DH. The book of Job, in terms of form, need not be original, and there are analogies formally to it in ancient libraries; but the content covers the range of issues met with in the books of the Law and the Prophets. Its concerns and redaction cover the exact same grounds as these. The discussions, in the form that we have them show every sign of being the product of the Joshua redactional school. Ruth, as we shall see below, is, in the main body of the text, most probably the work of the master of the school himself (or of the first generation of disciples). It is quintessential of the teaching of the school. As for Ecclesiastes, it is the position of the present writer that it is the profile of the master of this school in his own formulation and in the closing witness of the disciples to him. The difficulty is in defining the collection as having intentionally the sequence and progression that was conjectured above. The first argument for this is what has just been said: it is in analogy to the redactional work method deciphered in the works hitherto reviewed that this schematic framework has been proposed. Further, the stability of the sequence of the books in the tradition of the Hebrew bible speaks for the originality of the sequence. The books added, as we shall see, were simply added at the end of the proposed canon. The vast differences in the Septuagint and in other Hebrew traditions, such as the Dead Sea Scrolls, show that this need not have been the case. The Hebrew bible in the Jewish tradition was a "defensively" secured text against the vagaries of embellishments and incursions widely and variously introduced into the text. The present proposal takes the fixed nature of the sequence in the

Hebrew bible as a working hypothesis and, in analogy to the redactional design that has been delineated for the other parts of the canon, tries to decipher the pattern displayed by this sequence in terms of the material that is manifestly the work of this school. The result of applying this working hypothesis is what was proposed above. A haphazard collection of heteroclite works seems very improbable.

1.2 A Brief Review of the Individual Books

In the following, we will take a look at the individual books of the third part of the canon in function of the redactional work of the school of Isa 40–55.

1.2.1 The Book of Psalms

In as much as the task is the "education" of David paradigmatically as to the mind of the deity, the first book on the curriculum is the book of the Psalms of David. The predicament as viewed by David is spelled out in terms of the full spectrum of human experience, and David is allowed to voice the full measure of his plaint to the deity. Group dynamics cannot function more effectively. This is an expression of the stark reality of the addressed human being as the prospective disciple. Learn to articulate yourself; or allow yourself to be guided to articulate yourself! Spell it out! This is interspersed with the recitation of the preliminary lessons being drilled. The epitome of the lessons must be seen in psalm 51 (Hebrew numbering). The rubric indicates: "A Psalm of David, when the prophet Nathan came to him, after he had gone in to Bathsheba." (Ps 51:1 NRSV). This is the culminating break point in the book of Samuel for God with David. Following a brief resume of the preaching of the prophets, the key phrase for the psalm and the book as a whole is: "For you have no delight in sacrifice; if I were to give a burnt offering, you would not be pleased. The sacrifice acceptable to God is a broken spirit; a broken and contrite heart, O God, you will not despise." (Ps 51:16–17 NRSV).

Chapter 4

The psalms would seem to follow in general the sequence of DH with the psalms of the Torah coming towards the end, much as the book of the Law is discovered under Josiah towards the end of the book of Kings. The sequence and numbering of the psalter has undergone alteration, and very possibly the rubrics, but for a book used in liturgical services, the basic inventory and sequence seem to have remained basically well-preserved. They remain a "perfect match" with DH and the book of the Prophets.

At this point I will make a radical break with what I have just said. The preceding paragraph is introduced and concluded with the qualification "would seem/seem." This leaves open the possibility that, in reality, the situation might be different. The book of Psalms is traditionally and critically presented as divided into five parts, each part demarked by a concluding formulary benediction (cf. Ps 41:13; 72:18–20; 89:52; 106:48; 150:1–6). On previous occasions I also have espoused this point of view. At the present time, I find that this might be a faulty perception in terms of the redactional intent of the school of Joshua. In the following I will present an alternate approach.

I have indicated above that in the work of the Joshua school, as perceived and presented here, the book of Psalms is essentially the plaint of David, paradigmatic for all human beings. This would seem to fit the first three "books," Ps 1–89. Indeed, in the organization, headings, and rubrics we find a sharp divide between these three books and the following two sections. Mitchell Dahood[1] has demonstrated the antiquity of the genre and its phraseology in analogy of and on the basis of the finds of Ugarit. The present work is concerned not with the genre and phraseology as such, but with the redactional formal criteria and intertextual indications of circumstance and

---

1 Mitchell Dahood, *Psalms* (3 vols.; AB 16–17A; Garden City, N.Y.: Doubleday, 1965–1970).

purpose. This is why in the following analysis, the rubrics and redactional organization are of primary concern.

One fundamental point of demarcation between the two parts indicated is the use and frequency of the word *selâ* in the Hebrew text. This word has confounded interpreters and translators throughout the ages. It is sometimes translated as "pause," other times variously or not at all. We find it repeatedly used in the part encompassing Ps 1–89, some 67 times, as well as three times in the psalm in the book of Habakkuk ch. 3. In the remaining psalms in the psalter we reencounter it again only three times in Ps 140 and once in Ps 143. It would appear that the redactors of the part of the psalter encompassing Ps 90–150 were as confounded by the term as all subsequent interpreters; they could not do anything with it. This contrasts with its use in Habakkuk, which this presentation ascribes to the redactional work of the Joshua school. Its use can be traced to Isa 57:14 and 62:10 and the verbal root *sll*. This root means "to lift up, open a way, exalt, heap up." In Isa 57:14 we hear: "It shall be said, 'Build up, build up, prepare the way, remove every obstruction from my people's way.'" (NRSV); in Isa 62:10 we hear: "Go through, go through the gates, prepare the way for the people; build up, build up the highway, clear it of stones, lift up an ensign over the peoples." (NRSV). In both verses there is an emphatic double use of the verb, "build up, build up"; in the second verse the root is used a third time as a noun, translated in the NRSV as "highway." Considering that this verbal root is only used eight other times in Scripture, only three of them analogous to the use in Isaiah (cf. Ps 68:5; Prov 4:8; 15:19), we are justified in qualifying it as an important verbal root in Isa 56–66, functioning as a means to call forth adepts to prepare the way for God's action. Thus we can identify the first generation of the disciples of Isa 40–55, as postulated in this presentation, as the likely redactional group for the use of *selâ* in the psalter. The word would be equivalent to a liturgical "arise," "look upwards to the Lord," "exalt the Lord." This liturgical use of the verb is indicated by its use in Ps 68:5. We hear in Ps

68:5: "Sing to God, sing praises to his name; lift up a song to him who rides upon the clouds — his name is the Lord — be exultant before him." (NRSV). The two words rendered here as "sing" are actually from the verbal root from which we have two designations used repeatedly for the psalms, *mizmôr* and *šîr*. The NRSV renders here the verb from the root *sll* as "lift up a song." In v. 33 of this psalm, the same verbal sequence of *šîr* and *zmr* is followed by the term in question, *selâ*.

Another point of demarcation between the two parts of the book of psalms is the near absence of rubrics in the second part, whereas the first part has a plethora of initial rubrics. The rubrics of the first part reflect DH, again pointing to the redactional work of the Joshua school. What can be said about the redaction of the second part? If, as is being conjectured here, the second part reflects a very high-handed reworking of a previous collection, evidenced by the savaging of the acrostic sequence in Pss 9 and 10,[2] which, in the Septuagint, are a single psalm, then the extraordinary exceedingly regimented structuring of the second part (particularly of book five) becomes a telltale indication of a deliberate new edition. There is an ambivalent approach to the mega opus of the Joshua school. There is disregard for DH in the rubrics on the one hand, and on the other hand there appears to be an attempt to emulate the structure described above for the Pentateuch, the fivefold book. The first psalm of the second half, Ps 90, is ascribed to Moses. This is a singular ascription. It stands at the beginning of what is identified as the fourth book, possibly intended as parallel to the book of Numbers, the wandering in the desert. We find the name of Moses mentioned in the text of four psalms in this fourth book comprising Ps 90–106. These are: 99:6; 103:7; 105:26; 106:16, 23, 32; this is in addition to the title of Ps 90. Psalm 103 is ascribed to David, possibly taken

---

2 Cf. the literary analysis by the orientalist Justus Olshausen, *Die Psalmen erklärt* (Kurzgefasstes exegetisches Handbuch zum Alten Testament; Leipzig: S. Hirzel, 1853), 55–68. Interesting also is his analysis of Ps 110, which he locates in Maccabean times, pp. 420–425.

from the previous collection. Other than these mentions of Moses, there is only one other mention of Moses in the book of Psalms, Ps 77:21. The "Moses" fourth book "introduces" the fifth book, Ps 107–150. This would be expected to correspond to Deuteronomy. In fact, it is a Torah and liturgical temple worship part interspersed with kingly passages. Moses (as the fourth book) thus introduces the temple and kingship in the fifth part, contrary to Deuteronomy, DH, and Isa 40–55. Both books four and five have psalms ascribed to David; in this they are similar to the first part. There is one psalm of Solomon, Ps 127. In book 2 in part 1 there is also a psalm of Solomon, Ps 72. However, Ps 72 is actually a psalm of David for the king's son Solomon, closing book 2 and supposedly the psalms of David. It is concerned with God guiding the king to have the right judgement to rule in justice. Book 3, Ps 73–89, still in the first part, has the emphasis in the rubrics on the wise men in Solomon's court. Thus, it follows the David part with the part highlighting the wisdom aspect of Solomon. In contrast, Ps 127 highlights Solomon in connection with the establishment of the temple (It is the central psalm in the psalms of ascent). In addition to trying to emulate the fivefold structure of the Pentateuch but with a contrary approach to kingship and temple, the second part, particularly in book five, is imbued with a structural construction that is foreign to the redactional work of the Joshua school. Following the initial psalm in book five and three psalms referencing David, climaxing with the kingly psalm 110, there follow two acrostic psalms, 111 and 112, followed by the hallel psalms 113–118, introducing the extensive and elaborate acrostic Torah psalm 119. This is followed by the songs of ascent, Ps 120–134, then the Alleluia psalm, 135, the so-called "great hallel" (though it does not employ the root *hll*) psalm 136, the nostalgic psalm 137, psalms of David 138–145, and then the third hallel, Ps 146–150. The technical use of the *pi'el* imperative of the root *hll* (Alleluia) as a structural element is found only in the second part of the psalter;[3] it is used in the psalms leading up to book five, closing Pss 104 and 105 and initiating Ps 106, and then across book five. This book (five) is a carefully constructed liturgical climactic closing of the psalter.

The character of this structure in part two reflects on one hand the interests of the chronicler, with David introducing the temple worship, but, on the other hand, more so the Maccabean point of view. This is highlighted by several psalms. Psalm 105 was already mentioned in chapter 3, section 2.6, as displaying Maccabean characteristics. This can be said also of Ps 135 and 136. Indeed, Ps 136 parallels the song of the three young men in the furnace in the book of Daniel in the Septuagint, Dan (LXX) 3:52–90. The immediately following Ps 137 (By the rivers of Babylon) is a very popular and populistic psalm, reflecting in its appeal the populist appeal of the Maccabean movement and literature. But above all, psalm 110 betrays the Maccabean point of view. Christian readers, accustomed to the NT invocation of this psalm, will be scandalized by the following analysis. Taken on its own, this psalm lays claim to the office of the priest-king that developed in the Maccabean movement following the initial Maccabean period. God is held to an "automated" oath. The invocation of Melchizedek, read without the NT in mind, is a foundational Sadducean claim. We meet with Melchizedek for the first time in Gen 14:18. He is in the unsavory company of the king of Sodom. He is uncannily similar to King Adoni-zedek, whom we met in ch. 10 of the book of Joshua. This king-priest (Melchizedek) goes out to meet Abram. Abram had not yet been renamed Abraham. He very possibly at this stage is a stand-in for Ezekiel. The scene is very possibly the reception by the priestly dynasty of Jerusalem of the book of Ezekiel. As long as

---

3 There is sporadic use of derivatives of the root *hll* in part 1 (both verbal and nominal). The derivatives of this root are severally used in Ps 22 in part one, including once the *pi'el* imperative (with Yah replaced by the attached pronoun), but their employment in this psalm is not a technical structural usage, nor a refrain. A particularly emphatic use of the nominal form is found in v. 4.

Ezekiel was outside, at arm's length, and the book seemed to them to give legitimation to their dynasty, the (Maccabean) priest-kings were happy to receive the book. At the time of Adoni-zedek, the Joshua troop was gaining among the populace in the towns and villages. Especially alarming was their gain among the Gibeonites in ch. 9 of Joshua (cf. Josh 10:1). Adoni-zedek, representing the same Jerusalem dynasty, organizes a treacherous attack against the Joshua troop. This was no longer a distant Ezekiel offering an opportune occasion for them to legitimate their priest-king dynasty. Psalm 110 reflects the most dubious facets of the Maccabean movement when read within the coordinates of the OT rather than the NT. I suggest that the Maccabean, Johanan school (cf. section 2.1 below), is responsible for the edition of the book of Psalms as we have it. This possibly occurred before the breach developed between them and the antecedents of the Chronicler school. It is very likely they who gave the book the fivefold structure, mimicking the Pentateuch.[4]

---

[4] The analysis here is based on a comparison with the redactional concerns of the Joshua school delineated thus far. The studies of Hermann Gunkel, *Die Psalmen* (4th ed.; HKAT II-2; Göttingen: Vandenhoeck & Ruprecht, 1926); Sigmund Mowinckel, *Psalmenstudien* (vols. I–VI; Kristiania, 1921–1924); and Mitchel Dahood, *Psalms*, have contributed immensely to our knowledge of the Near Eastern background of the psalms as regards their form and genre (Gunkel), their usage in cult (Mowinckel), and their philological background and formulary usage in neighboring cultures and cognate languages (Dahood). These studies allow us to approach the psalter through comparative formal criteria without reconstructing a historical model. They offer access through comparative religious and philological data that functions diachronically as synchronic. However, when one overlooks the extreme polemical nature of biblical literature vis-à-vis their milieu as regards the socio-religious practices, one risks creating a phantom history and construct of temple, cult, and politics that replicates the description of the religious practices and polity that this literature vituperates against. This can lead to using these studies in a manner analogous to archeological artifacts, spinning around them stories sidetracking the actual address of this literature. Most if not all critical scholars agree on placing the redaction of biblical literature, at the earliest, in post-exilic times. Before the works of Gunkel, Mowickel, and Dahood, many critics in the nineteenth century postulated Ps 110 as belonging in Maccabean times based on literary analysis and the data available at that time. I will mention as examples in addition to Olshausen, referred

to above, two further exegetes: Ferdinand Hitzig, *Die Psalmen* (2nd ed. in two vols.; Leipzig: C. F. Winter's, Vol. 1 1863, Vol. 2 1865), Vol. 2, 317–324; Bernhard Duhm, *Die Psalmen* (2nd ed.; KHC XIV; Tübingen: J. C. B. Mohr, 1922), 398–400. These studies did not restrict themselves to literary analysis but tried to specify the exact historical circumstances; thus Hitzig connected Ps 110 with Jonathan, as Olshausen also tended to, and Duhm with Simon of the Maccabean dynasty. The problem is that when not applying critical study to Scripture, critics often take non-scriptural witnesses at face value. Thus the books of Maccabees and Josephus are given credence as "historical" stories, a status that secular historians would not credit the writings of Thucydides with. That these are as tendentious as other contemporary "histories," Judaic, Hellenistic, or Roman, seems to be overlooked. The critique of these approaches by the historian Hugo Willrich, *Urkundenfälschung in der hellenistisch-jüdischen Literatur* (Göttingen: Vandenhoeck & Ruprecht, 1924) remains very much to the point. The books of Maccabees, each on its own, presents a "wished for" view of events. The "imaginary" of the Joshua school stands in confrontation with their "wished for" view. Josephus is a contemporary of the author of the Lucan double-work. His koine style seems to be a co-variant of koine Greek with and of the same nature as the Lucan style. His writings intended to protect the various Jewish groups, survivals of the Jewish war, against extreme Roman hostility. He was not writing a "disinterested" historical work any more than the Lucan author was. In fact, all writing of any epoch employs literary dissimulation variously. The present work seeks to decipher the redactional characteristics of the writings at issue. The actual situation was one of flux between and within different conflicting groups. The differentiated review of early Christian literature by Walter Bauer, *Orthodoxy and Heresy in Earliest Christianity* (eds. Robert A. Kraft & Gerhard Krodel; translated by a team from the Philadelphia Seminar on Christian Origins from the second German edition edited by Georg Strecker; Philadelphia: Fortress, 1971) follows a pertinent methodology in the study of a fragmented field that is equally applicable to earlier intertestamental writings and otherwise to analogous fragmented situations. Intertextual and inter-redactional comparison provides the basis for the conclusions suggested here. The differing redactional traits are ascribed to "schools" or "scribal schools." The attempts by scholars to ascribe the psalter to a monolithic temple hierarchy in charge of or responsible for its transmission is belied by the witness of at least the Joshua school of itself as being outside and against monolithic entities based on power, as well as what is known about the repeated breaks in continuity of any such institution except for the briefest interregnum during the short-lived Maccabean ascendency. The "phantom" of such a monolithic entity ends up sidetracking the "imaginary" identified in this presentation as constituting the sinews of the literature at hand and the project of its redactors to provide this literature as its own unique means of transmission. The basic reason for differentiating at least two redactional inputs and describing the psalter as reflecting two opposing points of view can be summed up as follows: The Joshua school postulates a break following its presentation of David and regards the dynastic line, the temple, and the temple priesthood as a direct trajectory to total collapse. For this school, David flows/feeds into the wisdom of Solomon (in the third part of the canon), not Solomon; for the other two schools to be dealt with in section 2 below, David flows/feeds into the temple and temple priesthood, and for

It is difficult to ascertain the shape of the Psalter before this Maccabean edition. This is because they must have taken out "Davidic" psalms from the first three books and incorporated them into the fourth and fifth books. As was said above, it was a very heavy-handed reworking of the book. I would conjecture the following for the Joshua school psalter. It would have consisted of the first three books. There is no reason to assume a fivefold structure. Genesis has a threefold structure, as does the book of Isaiah, respectively the first books of the Pentateuch and the book of the Latter Prophets. I suggest further below a fivefold structuring of the third part of the canon by them in analogy to the Pentateuch in six books/lessons. (A preliminary intimation of this was indicated in section 1.1 above). Their psalter may have been more in number than the 89 psalms in the current three first books before the Maccabean edition removed some psalms to use in books four and five. Psalm 51, described above as the epitome of the Joshuan psalter, would possibly have been the "central" psalm. They may have utilized a "proto-psalter" encompassing the first two books, indicated in Ps 72:20 with regard to Ps 72 as constituting the last of the psalms of David. For them the psalms of David lead on to the wisdom of Solomon, not to the temple. Psalms 73–83 are reckoned to Asaph (meaning the one who gathers/convenes). A psalm of David, Ps 86, is sandwiched between psalms of/for the sons of Korah, Ps 84, 85, 87, 88. The prayer of David in Ps 86 appears to be the lesson for the sons of Korah. Psalm 88 is reckoned to Heman, and the closing psalm of the book, psalm 89, is reckoned to Ethan. Ethan and Heman are mentioned as paragons of wisdom in 1 Kgs 4:31, providing a measure for the surpassing wisdom of Solomon. In terms of content, Ps 89 would be a perfect sendoff to the book of Job. In stark terms,

---

the early Johanan school also into kingship, be it as priest-kingship as we find in the later Sadducean party, in total contradiction to the position of Deuteronomy, DH, Jeremiah, and Isaiah 40–66. This presentation highlights redactional design as opposed to automated, haphazard, or institutional transmission. Paul D. Hanson in *The Dawn of Apocalyptic*, referred to in chapter 1 above, makes clear that we are dealing sociologically with literature produced by disenfranchised insurgent groups.

God is reported as having broken the unbreakable covenant with David. The explicitness and the style of counterpoint are characteristic of the Joshuan edition of the third part of the canon. The psalm poses the question that initiates the discussion in the book of Job.

1.2.2 The Book of Job

After the orientation in the book of Psalms, the book of Job brings us into the classroom. We might as well be with Plato participating in dialogues with Socrates. We are given here a first-hand view of the training the master of the school gave to the trainees who would carry out the redacting process. We have front-row seats to see the deliberations that went on inside the classroom with the students and outside the classroom with the opponents in view of the production of the mega work. What is justice? How does the deity deal with the unjust? What about the just? Is there any sense to its (the deity's) dealings? Is anyone just? The underlying situation, we must remember, is one of total collapse. Where is God's justice? Is it whimsical? What about culpability? The burning question is: what does one have to do to become "restore-able," what is the attitude required? The deity seems to have lined up with the enemy. This is what we find in Isa 40–55, where Cyrus is God's anointed, and where God declares responsibility for the double punishment. This is what we find in the book of Jeremiah, where the Babylonian king is declared to be God's servant. God and the trickster/destroyer are the same! All the other partisan groups have their point of view regarding what is required. The priestly group requires adherence to the cult; the militant group demands exact application of justice as retribution; in the midst of total desolation, everyone looks around desperately for the exact rubrics to be followed in order to appease the deity or deities. Our master sits back with Husserlian "epoché" and lets his students debate their views and those of opponents, perhaps intervening and withdrawing all the while. What is clear is that he made sure that all points of view on the matter would be exhausted and articulated. The questions and responses pertain to the widest possible human compass of experiences; the texts which display to the fullest these deliberations are the texts of the mega work of this school.

The name Job, in Hebrew *iyôb*, is of the form of a verbal attribute indicating in northwestern Semitic that someone or something is amenable/of the type that displays the verbal trait, somewhat analogous to the English suffix "-able."[5] In Arabic, the triliteral *'wb* means "to return." If we accept this derivation from Arabic, (after all we are supposed to be in Edom according to the rubrics of the book), then it would mean "a person of the type that returns/is amenable to return or is restore-able." The ancient name of the month of August in the Levant, when the first rain of the new season is expected to fall, is called *āb*, "he returned", meaning Baal, the god of rain. The form and vocalization we have here is rather in the passive and likely intended as a diminutive. (To give an example of this derivational form in Arabic: the Arabic name and adjective 'ayyāš, having the same verbal attribute form and derived from the root *'āš/'yš*, to live, means "of the type that lives long, is prone to be perdurable." An alternate vocalization of selfsame is "'ayyūš," which can be construed as a diminutive of the same or as a regional variant.) The other derivation that is commonly proposed from the Hebrew word for enemy, *ōyēb*, I do not find convincing; it is foreign to the presumed cultural context as well as to the literary context. That Job wonders whether he is the enemy of God would hardly be convincing if that were predetermined in his appellation. It would destroy the hypothesis propelling the debate and preempt the sudden surprise ending, flattening the thread of the discussion. Certainly there is a pun on the name involved in the discussion,

---

5 Though I often dispute the Masoretic pointing of the Hebrew text, in this case I follow it. The name Job, as the reference to it in the book of Ezekiel indicates, seems to have been an extra-biblical literary or popular folkloric figure. One can expect it to have been a diachronically fixed "quantity." Moreover, its prominence in the book of Job makes it a fixture in the mind of the reader/listener.

but only that, a pun. The mention of Job in the triad of ancient righteous individuals in Ezek 14:14–20 also militates against such a derivation. The carryover perception of the figure as paradigmatic of patient faithfulness in adverse circumstances is sharply contested in the biblical version by the perspective of the master of the Joshua school.

The real denouement is certainly in God's severe reproach to Job. It is the view of the master of the school, and the view expressed throughout the mega work, both implicitly and explicitly. It is introduced by a tutor, a reader intruding unexpectedly, much as the arrival of a king is ceremoniously announced by a courtesan, but it is effective only when delivered by the deity. The passage that most explicitly spells out this position is the one central to the first part of Isa 40–55, the part indicting Jacob. Let us listen:

> I form light and create darkness, I make weal and create woe; I the Lord do all these things. Shower, O heavens, from above, and let the skies rain down righteousness; let the earth open, that salvation may spring up, and let it cause righteousness to sprout up also; I the Lord have created it. Woe to you who strive with your Maker, earthen vessels with the potter! Does the clay say to the one who fashions it, "What are you making"? or "Your work has no handles"? Woe to anyone who says to a father, "What are you begetting?" or to a woman, "With what are you in labor?" Thus says the Lord, the Holy One of Israel, and its Maker: Will you question me about my children, or command me concerning the work of my hands? I made the earth, and created humankind upon it; it was my hands that stretched out the heavens, and I commanded all their host. (Isa 45:7–12 NRSV).

The false denouement which restores Job's wealth is equivalent to a demotion and retirement. Wealth and fortune in this school is not looked upon favorably as we saw earlier regarding the untransformed Ephraim. It is a dismissal not a resolution; it releases the thread of the debate, the tension necessary for the hypothesis proposed for debate in the classroom, and turns off the lights. It functions like the dismissal of Isaac in the book of

Genesis; the hypothetical task is removed from his shoulders and the resolution is commuted to another lesson. Lesson two is done.

1.2.3 The Book of Proverbs

The third lesson gives us a glimpse of the throne room. This was not available in the two prophetic tetrateuchs. We are back to the throne room but this time from a different perspective than in Leviticus. We were already told in the narrative about Solomon that wisdom opens up a port of entry to the throne room (1 Kgs 3:5–12, 28). Wisdom joins the "scapegoat" in the literary throne room; the throne of God is established on wisdom. The disciples of this master have learnt well the third lesson. As was pointed out, Isaiah chs 1–39 alternate masterfully between diatribe and wisdom.

The contents of the book are not particular to this school. They are widely found in ancient literature; the collections were usually produced by high court officials, clerks, who through their experience provided for continuity and stability of governance As such they would be used as manuals to educate young trainees and acolytes. Their central position here reflects the perspective of the master of the school. He sees his work in terms of human space and the human condition at large. He is not hemmed in by tribal space; his call to the tribes is a call to rejoin in their perspective the wider human perspective of the creator God. His "realism" in viewing the human condition undergirds the whole composition of what has been referred to here as the mega work. The redactional work in this case is reduced to the incorporation and framing of the book within the mega work.

The last passage in the book of Proverbs is an alphabetic poem in praise of the "capable wife" (Prov 31:10–31). This feeds directly to the book of Ruth in the Hebrew bible.

1.2.4 The Book of Ruth

This book parallels the Holiness Code. It has elements of vocabulary and style that place it among the candidates of texts to be ascribed to the master of the school, to the author of Isa 40–55, or at least to the very first generation of disciples. This it has in common also with the Holiness Code.[6] It is the fourth lesson, centrally placed and functioning as a continuation of the final chapter of the book of Proverbs. It is in narrative form, a novella. It is so distinctive of the school of Isa 40–55, functioning as a compilation of the issues of contention between the school and its opponents, that it is given the prime central position. It thus elaborates the central proposition of the school defining it against its opponents. The issue is best expressed in the name of Ruth's father-in-law, Elimelech, God is King. *Nomen est omen*, and in this case the name is the lesson. This is central as we saw to Isa 40–55. Both Ruth, the foreign Moabite woman, and the devout Judean Boaz, in the course of this story, honor by their actions the "name" of this man and perpetuate it, that is, honor the central tenet of Isa 40–55 and the Pentateuch and thus further its perpetuation. This alone would have been enough as a fourth lesson, but other elements in the story augment considerably its impact. The first is that the foreign woman by accepting the God of Abraham, of the Torah, is equivalent to the devout Judean who does the same. This reflects the position of Isa 40–66. The name "Boaz" is the same as the name of one of the two columns in front of the temple, 1 Kgs 7:21, as set up by Solomon. It is the second half of the phrase constituted by the names of the two columns. It is thus an invocation of the phrase: "He (God) will establish it with strength." Here we are at the center of the polemic against the temple party. The

---

6 One such element, in particular, deserves to be mentioned. The verb, *gā'al* (to redeem) is a central theme in all three compositions and thematically and quantitatively distinctively characteristic of them. God's function as redeemer (*gō'ēl*) is thus highlighted in Isa 40–55 and the Holiness Code. In Ruth, Boaz is prevailed upon paradigmatically to exercise this role in obedience to perpetuate the name and heritage of Elimelech, "God is King."

actions of Boaz together with those of Ruth are what function as the two columns in front of the temple. The scandal for the temple party has reached its climax. However, there is one more escalation in the provocation. The name "Ruth" has the three letters of the Hebrew and Arabic triliteral root *rwh/rwy*. This means to have one's thirst fully satiated or in the causative form "to water abundantly." We have it in this causative usage in Isa 55:10–11, "For as the rain and the snow come down from heaven, and do not return there until they have watered the earth, making it bring forth and sprout, giving seed to the sower and bread to the eater, so shall my word be that goes out from my mouth; it shall not return to me empty, but it shall accomplish that which I purpose, and succeed in the thing for which I sent it." (NRSV). We also have the derived adjective in Isa 58:11, "The Lord will guide you continually, and satisfy your needs in parched places, and make your bones strong; and you shall be like a watered garden, like a spring of water, whose waters never fail." (NRSV). Our author or redactors are telling us that she, the foreign Moabite woman, is central to the work of the God of Abraham, to the work that their school is dedicated to. Her name is a feminine form. She has been watered by the God of Abraham, and consequently has watered the land.[7] Finally, for the final infamy for the opposing group, she is postulated as the great-grandmother of David.

This concise gem is a group defining text. It joins all the tenets of the school of Isa 40–55 and delimits it vis-à-vis its opponents. The group is an "open-sourced" community (after all, it is spilling its heart out to publish the mega opus), stands for exogamy, for inclusion, is addressed to all, rejects the apartness of the temple group, and invests itself in the open spaces and ambulant worship. It has no problem with residing in "liminal" spaces, between Jacob and the nations. As was mentioned at the

---

[7] All too often, a derivation from the triliteral *rʿh* is proposed and it is translated as "female companion," *rěʿût*. The problem is that the name, as found in the text, does not have the consonant *ʿayin* required by this derivation.

beginning of this section, it seems to be watered (informed) by Jubilee time.

1.2.5 The Book of Canticles

The fifth lesson takes us back to the wilderness journey. The luxuriant "set" and exuberant language should not deceive us. After reaching the pinnacle of the mountain of God, figuratively, we are sent back to parched lands and left to search for a fata morgana, a mirage of a luxuriant garden, of the ultimate satiation of desires. Most interpretations choose to see a figurative or mystical depiction of divine love; I must break rank with this. What we have here depicted is teenage concupiscence for yet another lesson. The master of this school might appear to live in the clouds, in imaginary time, but he is a realist through and through, and brutally so. We are just one lesson away from the ultimate lesson, the book of Ecclesiastes. What is the comment of Qoheleth on what we have in this book? Although I have already quoted it at length above, let us read it again:

> I said to myself, "Come now, I will make a test of pleasure; enjoy yourself." But again, this also was vanity. I said of laughter, "It is mad," and of pleasure, "What use is it?" I searched with my mind how to cheer my body with wine — my mind still guiding me with wisdom — and how to lay hold on folly, until I might see what was good for mortals to do under heaven during the few days of their life. I made great works; I built houses and planted vineyards for myself; I made myself gardens and parks, and planted in them all kinds of fruit trees. I made myself pools from which to water the forest of growing trees. I bought male and female slaves, and had slaves who were born in my house; I also had great possessions of herds and flocks, more than any who had been before me in Jerusalem. I also gathered for myself silver and gold and the treasure of kings and of the provinces; I got singers, both men and women, and delights of the flesh, and many concubines. So I became great and surpassed all who were before me in Jerusalem; also my wisdom remained with me. Whatever my eyes desired I did not keep from them; I kept my heart from

no pleasure, for my heart found pleasure in all my toil, and this was my reward for all my toil. Then I considered all that my hands had done and the toil I had spent in doing it, and again, all was vanity and a chasing after wind, and there was nothing to be gained under the sun. So I turned to consider wisdom and madness and folly; for what can the one do who comes after the king? Then I saw that wisdom excels folly as light excels darkness. (Eccl 2:1–13 NRSV).

This is how Qoheleth views it. It is a lesson in the futility of chasing desires, and a prod to seek wisdom; training by trial and error in preparation for the master course, the final lesson. Again, he is a hands-on realist. He is a wizard of articulation of thoughts in concrete images. His pedagogical skills are unequalled. In stark realistic language he translates us into imaginary time. He employs graphic realism to transpose the students' mind so as to teach them to read the hypertext of daily experiences, to gain "in-sight" into the workings of the world and their own perception of it. This is the function of the wandering in the wilderness in the book of Numbers. The fifth lesson is a wandering in the wilderness of one's own desires. The school need not have had any hand in its redaction. Its framing within the "curriculum" of the third part of the canon is what makes it impart this lesson. It is an advanced part of the curriculum. It has bewildered generations of readers and interpreters precisely because of its position in the canon. Sometimes it helps to take a sneak look at the following chapter to understand the current one.

1.2.6 The Book of Ecclesiastes

This is the master lesson, the crowning lesson. We have six days of creation and a six lesson curriculum although organized in five portions. No reading of Scripture is possible, no correct reading, without this lesson of the master of the school. The first triad of this part of the canon transported us from the plaint of David to the Wisdom of Solomon crossing the "wilderness" of Job. The second triad transports us from the "Wisdom" of

Ruth, Sharing the central seat with the Wisdom of Solomon, and propels us to the totally different plane of Ecclesiastes, crossing the wilderness of desires, of the book of Canticles. In the second triad an abstraction level is introduced that departs from the hitherto literary construct. The book of Ruth functions as a gentle lock system, abstracting from the previous literary construct but shifting the register of the readers' mindset. When we are received at the destination in Ecclesiastes, we are immediately confronted with a new figure, a new "son of David," we had not encountered him before . . . or possibly he was the "ghost figure" guiding us hitherto on our journey, Qoheleth. After the "Solomonic" temptations of the book of Canticles, we are faced with a "son of David" who is the complete antithesis of Solomon. The whole complex of issues associated with Solomon: kingship, temple, excess is jettisoned; only Wisdom remains.

Qoheleth in Hebrew is derived from *qāhāl*, official assembly of the people, differing from *'ēdāh*, which refers to the hieratic, worshipping assembly. In this, *qāhāl* corresponds to the secular use of the word εκκλησια in Greek to refer to the political assembly of the city. Qoheleth is the person who calls to assembly, who congregates. It is a feminine form. This is the expected form when the congregating message is primordial to the constitution of the assembly. In Arabic this is still so. A proponent of a particular message or teaching is called *al-dāʿiyāh*, a feminine form. The person is confounded with the assembly he/she has congregated through his/her preaching. This could be a convener of a particular interpretation or school of Islam, or a proponent/leader of a particular "heresy." Less of an analogy to this linguistic usage but nevertheless analogous to it is the name of the book Ecclesiastes in Arabic. It is the same word used for "university." The "university" is seen as convening the various branches of knowledge and thus takes the feminine form. The convener, confounded with the assembly by virtue of the convening message, regardless of whether masculine, feminine, (or neuter), takes the feminine form.

In Isa 40–55 there is no reference to the author, and this literary fiction is continued in Isa 56–66. The first section of the book of Isaiah, chs. 1–39, simply abstracts from the key word "salvation" of Isa 40–55 to give a name to the "prophet" and the book. The hitherto not only anonymous but totally recessive author/writer remains a "ghost" figure. For the first time here in Ecclesiastes we are formally introduced to him in his "secular" thought rather than in his capacity as "ghost writer" for the deity. "Qoheleth" can only be understood as convener through the work announced in Isa 40–55, the production of a body of writings revealing the mind of the deity. The book Ecclesiastes itself would hardly be occasion for this very official title.

The expansive thought of this composition is the twin of the expansive mind behind the Law and the Prophets. The detachedly engaged mind with uncanny realism and applied amazingly creative imagination is the same. The cadenced writing, the joining of the prosaic and the poetic is the same. An individual who can dabble with legal and cultic matters and engage those involved with them but more easily brackets or leapfrogs over them for a serene view of the essential, this is who was encountered in the writings we have reviewed and whom we encounter here in the most condensed form, analogous to the condensation we saw in Isa 40–55. The mind of the master of the school is unmistakable here.

I will venture here to propose that this work was conceived as the "plaint" of the servant-*rāhām*, in contrast to the plaints of David we saw in the first book of this part of the canon. Let us listen to the words of the servant in the second song of the servant:

> And he said to me, "You are my servant, Israel, in whom I will be glorified." But I said, "I have labored in vain, I have spent my strength for nothing and vanity; yet surely my cause is with the Lord, and my reward with my God." And now the Lord says, who formed me in the womb to be his servant, to bring Jacob back to him, and that Israel might be gathered to him, for I am

honored in the sight of the Lord, and my God has become my strength — he says, "It is too light a thing that you should be my servant to raise up the tribes of Jacob and to restore the survivors of Israel; I will give you as a light to the nations, that my salvation may reach to the end of the earth." (Isa 49:3–6 NRSV).

However, in this book we not only have the visage and testament of the master of the school, we have also the signature of the disciples convening to pay homage to the master. Let us read the closing passage of this book, the epilogue of the disciples:

> Vanity of vanities, says the Teacher; all is vanity. Besides being wise, the Teacher also taught the people knowledge, weighing and studying and arranging many proverbs. The Teacher sought to find pleasing words, and he wrote words of truth plainly. The sayings of the wise are like goads, and like nails firmly fixed are the collected sayings that are given by one shepherd. Of anything beyond these, my child, beware. Of making many books there is no end, and much study is a weariness of the flesh. The end of the matter; all has been heard. Fear God, and keep his commandments; for that is the whole duty of everyone. For God will bring every deed into judgment, including every secret thing, whether good or evil. (Eccl 12:8–14 NRSV).

This passage sums up the work of the school of Isa 40–55. The word translated as "teacher" in this passage by the NRSV is Qoheleth. We have here a resume of the mega work and the mind of the master behind it. His engagement and wisdom is remembered, no less his detached view of his work, and his attention to style and plain speech in the service of pedagogy. The body of writings announced in Isa 40–55 prospectively is here referred to retrospectively and posthumously. The work is done; the testament of the master and the testament of the disciples to the master are now scripture.

2. The Other Redactional Schools: Subsequent Additions and Editions

I will limit the discussion here to the redactions that have found entry into the Hebrew bible. The wider literature associated with the Greek bible and more recently with the Dead Sea Scrolls is outside the scope of this book. Some reference will occasionally be made, but this presentation addresses the question of the redaction of the Hebrew bible canon and the schools involved in it, not intertestamental literature as such nor specifically the so-called deuterocanonical books or the anagignoskomena. The intention is to delineate the redactional role of Isa 40–55.

2.1 The Johanan School: A Derivative of the Maccabean Movement

I take the name of the school from the name of the father of Mattathias, the father of the Maccabee brothers and instigator of the Maccabean revolt. But more pointedly, I take it from the name of the opponent of the prophet Jeremiah that we meet with in the narrative "historical" passages of the book of Jeremiah and in the book of Kings. He is introduced in 2 Kgs 25:23 and Jer 40:8 as Johanan son of Kareah. Kareah means bald; spelled with the same triliteral as the name Korah, but differently vocalized. Korah leads the revolt in Num 16 against Moses. Johanan is among the group mustered to approach the newly installed Gedaliah. The group includes Ishmael son of Nethaniah with whom the other members of the group seem to have an ambivalent relationship. When Ishmael kills Gedaliah, the others fear Babylonian retribution and approach Jeremiah to intercede with his God for them. When Jeremiah returns with a severe condemnation of them, they reject his response and flee to Egypt abducting him and forcing him with them to Egypt. The name Johanan is also cognate with the name Hananiah, the name of the principal representative of the pro-temple party against Jeremiah. The verbal root *ḥnn* means to be compassionate/kindly disposed to. It is the opposite of a military martial attribute, more fitting for a mother's disposition to her child. This makes the term perfect for euphemistic use as a nickname for a militiaman. The temple party insisted that the kindly disposition of the deity towards the temple would protect it. The militants readily adopted this nickname as a gruesome contrast to their disposition. In Exodus 34:6, the God of Moses pointedly takes on the intensive form of the adjective after the incident of the golden calf; it is an ominous threat in the context! This Johanan thus comes with dubious connections through the connotations associated with his and his father's name. He qualifies as the spearhead against Jeremiah just as Korah was the prime instigator of the insurrection against Moses. What then is the reason for this introduction about him and his name? It is because this name accompanies us from the OT through the intertestamental literature and then meets us in the NT in the "Graecized" name John. It is a peculiar literary name that traces for us an oblique line from the Old to the New Testament. One could write an introduction to Scripture and call it "The education of John." Most figures and fixtures in Scripture seem to be unchanging quantities, except for Johanan/John. It seems to be the fixture that undergoes the greatest change in entropy, from its first appearance in the OT to the last of its swings in the NT. It is to be associated initially with the hot-headed nationalist militants, but it progressively changes. One could construe the Joshua school as an address to this group, a judging and pedagogical address, trying to break the fragile alliance of this group with the temple party and swing it to the perspective of Isa 40–55. This is a caricature, of course, of the severe altercation we see between the two groups in the book of Jeremiah, but in the end effect, this is what was effected with respect to at least one splitter of this group further on in time.

The first step in this odyssey is the one that is the object of our discussion here. It centers on the book of Daniel. It was mentioned above that the books to be ascribed to this redaction are the books of Lamentations, Esther, and Daniel. The first two are not helpful for delineating the contours of this redactional school. It is the book of Daniel that gives us the venue to become acquainted with its workings. The fact that Esther in particular and Lamentations share most (in the case of Esther) or some (in the case of Lamentations) of its other characteristics makes us group them under its aegis.

The name of the main character, Daniel, means God's judgement. The book is written as a lesson about divine judgement against itself, the same judgement that was spoken against it by Jeremiah in Jer 42:7-22, and which was angrily rejected by it, Jer 43:1-5. We can assume that after the initial desolation, there followed the further devastation prophesied by Jeremiah. It is at that time that this redactional school must have been convened. Reading the name of its students, we can immediately understand the reason for the convocation. The three young companions of Daniel, that is, those under judgement, are Hananiah, Mishael, and Azariah. Hananiah and Azariah are the names of the primary opponents of Jeremiah. Between them sits Mishael. We meet a Mishael in the book of Leviticus. It is the name of one of the two nephews of Aaron and Moses who are called to pick up the remains of the two disobedient sons of Aaron and take them and bury them outside the camp. They function as the caretakers after the horrendous divine judgement. This hint suffices. But why do we assume that this book represents a change of mind? This is because the book of Daniel is obsessed with the oracle of the book of Jeremiah regarding the time of restoration.[8] It persists in trying to provide exegetical suggestions that would make it "accurate." That the judgement against it by Jeremiah came into realization means for it that the restoration foreseen by

---

8 Cf. chapter 3, section 2.5.2 above. Compare what is said there regarding the seventy-year period in the book of Jeremiah (until restoration) and the discussion of this period in ch. 9 of the book of Daniel; cf. also Dan 8:14; 12:11-12.

Jeremiah would also be realized. Enough for the circumstantial conjecture about the school!

What about the content and characteristics of the composition? One thing we can say is that it is still bound in its thinking to the time when "prophets were called seers." It still has an oracular understanding of the prophetic calling assimilating it to that of the seer. Another characteristic is obviously its emphasis on dietary stipulations. Its lessons are essentially still tied to ritual casuistic. Its conception of the deity is still one that expects the function of the deity to be to help against the other nations rather than an address to the members of the group and secondarily to the other nations. This is a group of ethnic militants still. The harrowing devastation that has come upon them has made inroads into their mind. They have begun to appreciate the value of the suffering of the just leader as we hear in Dan 9:25-27. However, the framework of their world view has not changed. The world outside is still inimical. In the Joshua school it is the inside that is inimical, and the human mind as such is inimical to the will of the deity. The universalistic, monotheistic scriptural approach of Isa 40-55 has yet to dawn. The book alternates between Hebrew and Aramaic. It is codified; it is not intended to be accessible to everyone as in the canon of the Joshua school. One must be an insider to gain full access. All these characteristics we find also in the book of Esther. The Hebrew edition of these two books is populistic, nationalistic in its appeal. For the Greek editions, "theological" additions had to be provided before they could be addressed to Greek speakers. We are extremely distant from the redactional pedagogical purview of the Joshua school. The book of Lamentations also is particularistic in its primary appeal. It does not achieve the common human appeal of the plaints of David. Characteristic for this school is Lam 3. They are aware that they have been punished and wonder when God will lift his ban. The last passage of the book, Lam 5:19-22, poignantly gives vent to this anguish. Although the book of Daniel is included in the Septuagint among the prophetic books, in the

Hebrew bible it is included among the books of the third part of the canon together with the books of Esther and Lamentations after Ecclesiastes.

We can attribute the current Hebrew edition of the book of Jeremiah to this school as well. The LXX version appears to represent the original Hebrew edition; however, we no longer have that edition. The change in sequence introduced in the Hebrew edition is indicative. In the LXX, the oracles against the nations, gathered in the chiastic center of the book, provide the backdrop for the concluding judgement against the temple party, the Hananiah and Johanan group. In other words, the judgement against the nations confirms the inevitability of the judgement against the temple group. In the Hebrew edition of this school, the judgement against themselves is placed ahead of the main body of oracles against the nations. They have accepted the judgement against themselves, but their reception of it makes them understand it as confirming the inevitability of the judgement against the nations. There is a switch of emphasis that is characteristic of this school. There is an attempt to learn, but the perception, the framework of the mindset has yet to change.[9]

The learning process will continue and is reflected in the Gospel of Mark. The sons of Zebedee together with the other disciples must be taught through the three announcements about the suffering and death of the Son of Man to understand Scripture; and yet directly after the third announcement the two Zebedee brothers approach Christ requesting that they sit on his right and left hand when he comes in glory and are answered that they do not know what they are asking for. The triumphalist mentality of the militant Johanan party still holds hard. At the beginning of the pedagogical journey to Jerusalem in the Gospel of Luke, John and James request to be allowed to

---

9 In section 1.2.1 above in this chapter, arguments were given for ascribing the redaction of the so-called fourth and fifth books of the book of psalms, Ps 90–150, as transmitted in the Hebrew bible, to an early stage in the development of this school.

bring fire down from heaven to consume the Samaritans because they would not receive Christ, but he rebukes the two of them. Initially, after all, they had been identified as the "sons of Zebedee." We meet Zabdi in the book of Joshua as having engendered by way of Carmi Achan. The meaning of Achan is to be derived from Arabic, where the root ʾkn refers to the folds of a fat belly. Achan is a fat cat, the child of the "froth" (Zabdi) of society who transgresses the command of the god of Joshua and lays his hand on goods under the ban, forbidden booty, thereby thwarting the work of God through Joshua and bringing God's curse on all. He becomes a paradigm for God's judging condemnation in the book of Joshua. In Mark 3:17, Christ nicknames them "Boanerges," which in Aramaic is best translated as "sons of (divine) wrath"; the Greek translation given in Mark, "sons of thunder," is effectively equivalent, "thunder" being a figure for divine wrath.

The conversion of the Benjaminite Paul and that of the two sons of Zebedee to the Pauline gospel are effectively the conversion and adhesion to the Joshua school, to Isa 40–55 and Jeremiah, of the two former arch-opponents of that school. It had overwhelmed the mind of the previous opponents. The conversion is regarded as a divine act that, according to Luke, required the direct intervention of God in Pentecost to consummate. The two apostles who were on their way to Emmaus in Luke 24 are intercepted by the risen Christ and he "opens their eyes" to "understand Scripture." They do not go on to Emmaus. Emmaus in 1 Macc 3–4 is the rallying point for the Maccabean revolt. The title "apostle" in the New Testament is probably a takeover from this school. They conceived of themselves as officers of a state vis-à-vis other states, dispatching and receiving envoys to negotiate with other powers (cf. 1 Macc passim). The word apostle in Greek means envoy, an empowered delegate to another entity. The term "New Testament" comes from the book of Jeremiah, but it may have come into the usage of the NT by way of this school adopting the book of Jeremiah and attempting to adapt it to its world view. However we look at it, the work of Isa 40–55 functioned as a formidable attractor through the successive adverse developments, exerting a gravitational pull on the mind of the Johanan school and its adherents, splintering them, challenging them, pulling them away from the temple party, and finally winning over the mind of at least two paragons of that school.

2.2 *The School of the Chronicler*

This redactional school is responsible for the book of Chronicles and the books of Ezra and Nehemiah. Its characteristics and concerns are well-defined and distinct from those of the other two schools. The book of Chronicles provides an alternate version to the events related in the books of Samuel and Kings. The introduction takes us back to Adam and bridges the span with genealogical listings. In contradistinction to the Pentateuch, there is no counterpointing of two narratives, one of the deity and one of Adam. The listings are an important organizational element here. There is an all-consuming concentration on the temple and its rubrics. David is central as is the temple. Prophetic criticism is irrelevant here. It is a book for adherents of the Herodian temple and its rubrics. With the fall of the temple its relevance fades. Its mindset is that of establishing an enclosure, a hieratic enclosure, both ritually and in terms of genealogical trees. This becomes particularly clear in its edition of the books of Ezra and Nehemiah, of which there are many differing and conflicting editions in the intertestamental literature. Its edition is concerned with establishing the physical and ritual wall around the new community. There is a total rejection of marriage with foreign women. The publishing of a variant version of the events depicted in Samuel and Kings already indicates a polemical or at least critical view of the work of DH. The position against marriage with foreign women stands diametrically opposite to what we have in the book of Ruth, as well as what we find in the narratives about Moses in the Pentateuch. It is a school clearly not happy or at ease with the work of the Joshua school.

At the same time that the Herodian temple was being built, the temple enclosure of Baalbek was also being built. It was the major construction by the Romans to consolidate its hold on the Levant. The complex of Baalbek was of superlative magnitude. Four centuries after the construction had started it had not been completed by the time the emperor Theodosius stopped its construction together with the closing of pagan worship in the empire. The Baalbek complex brought together the Roman Jupiter (with the largest temple in magnitude in the complex) with the Hellenistic Bacchus (Dionysus). For the native population it was identified with Baal worship. Its names Baalbek and Heliopolis indicate its overwhelming importance for the Romans. Under the aegis of Jupiter, all the religiosity of the region, whether Baalist or Hellenistic, would be directed to and subservient to the cult of Jupiter Capitolinus, to Rome. In Jerusalem and Judea this would not work. Herod, the ally and servant of Roman emperors, provided a solution. A temple would be built without offending Judaic sensibilities and under his aegis as a proxy of Rome. His allegiance to Rome would provide surety for Rome that it would channel the allegiance of the people to Rome. The work of the Isa 40–55 school was an uncomfortable presence for this to work. It was very critical of all the components of such a state "ideology." The work of the Chronicler seems to have been intended to provide a "scriptural interface" for this state ideology; one that would smooth out the wrinkles, or presumably thought it would. Since it would provide subservience to Rome, it sought an enclosure in terms of ritual rubrics and closed family connections to protect the enclosure. Thus a privileged class could protect its special interests and wealth, as we see with the Sadducees, the Tobias, and the Herodians, apparently in conflict with each other but in reality complicit in sharing the benefits of this setup. This resulted in a reappearance of the same ills attacked in the canon of the Joshua school. The Johanan school, representing a faction of militant nationals, was hardly amenable to be at ease with this arrangement. Popular displeasure only increased. The Johanan group was popular. Attempts to remove its works were opposed by the populace, especially since the books of Esther and Lamentations were associated with popular feasts. With the end of the construction of the Herodian temple and the stop of the influx of funds going into its construction, the resulting economic straits joined with religious discontent to bring about the "Judean" revolt against the Romans. The Herodian temple had failed in its intended aims, which were flawed from the very beginning. The response from Rome came swiftly and brutally. The temple was no more. The work of the Chronicler became anachronistic. Still the books were added at the end of the Hebrew canon. The Septuagint assimilated them into its divisions, placing the books of Chronicles among the "historical books." In the Hebrew bible, however, both the work of the Johanan school and that of the Chronicler were simply added at the end of the third part of the canon, attached after the opus of what I have called the Joshua school of Isa 40–55.

If anything, the works of these two later redactions highlight the unity and distinctness of the Joshua school. They show how difficult it is to replicate the work of the disciples of Isa 40–55. They help us to see in relief the cohesiveness of the initial canon, the intentionality and distinctiveness of its production. At least this is what this presentation has sought to delineate.

3. Epilogue: Summation of the Thesis and Method

This has been a journey through Scripture to trace the redactional intent that can be deciphered in the collection of this material in the form that we have received it. It follows a redactional critical method based on a literary critical approach. The historical circumstances that are discerned or conjectured are those of the redactional circumstances that can be inferred from the texts, they are not about the "events"

Chapter 4   277

described in the narrative; these are seen as pedagogical lessons, parables to inculcate the teaching. The characters and figures are seen as paradigms and types. The characters and elements of the narrative are regarded as narrative pedagogical components to be understood contextually as elements of the parable/paradigm. Their reality resides in the lesson they deliver. The lessons are "real" lessons, written and redacted by "real" people, addressed in "real" circumstances, to "real" people. The reality is established by way of the literary fiction. This is what literature is. It dissimulates reality in order to intensify and "condense" its reality through the addressed word/narrative. The time and circumstances of the redaction are the real time, not the dramatic or theatrical time of the stories/narratives. The narratives translate the teaching. They cannot be translated "back" as though they were "real" time. Shakespeare's Julius Caesar is not translatable back to the first century B.C. and Italy, it is in Elizabethan England. It takes place in the very real Globe Theater, not in Rome. Whoever might have been the writer of the play, it still will be a "Shakespearean play," defined intrinsically by its material. That there was a "real" Julius Caesar is irrelevant to the play; the play is about Shakespeare's Julius Caesar not the "real" Caesar. Its significance is in relation to the time and addressees of Elizabethan England. It is no more or less "real" than "A Midsummer Night's Dream," and both are certainly more "real" than the vagaries of the "historical" Julius Caesar. The historical Henry the Fifth was a catastrophic failure as a leader. Shakespeare's "unreal" Henry the Fifth has gripped the imagination of countless generations through the narrative skill and iambic pentameter of its writer. If we were to place the same iambic pentameter of the prologue on a set constructed with a fortune no king could dream of, it would fall apart into thin dust, it would be bereft of the very sinews of the imagination it was composed to address in the Globe Theater. The rules for transferring from one medium to another are more exacting than the rules of translation in descriptive geometry.

The effort has been made here to present a proposal that provides a framework for understanding Scripture as literature. So many historicizing frameworks through history have been superposed on Scripture that through the projected "realism" the teaching has become unrecognizable. This began with the efforts of Helena, Emperor Constantine's mother, to "reconstruct" the Palestinian setting and the "efforts" of disingenuous opportunists to make money out of it, and has ended up being a huge tourist business buttressed by supposedly learned "scientific" archeologists. Already at the outset of this "trade," Gregory of Nyssa's indignation and tirade against its inappropriateness was unequivocal (PG 46:1009–1016); for an English version cf. *On Pilgrimages* (NPNF[2] 5:382–383).

Martin Noth's extensive work on literary criticism was monumental in lifting Scriptural studies from historicistic approaches, and from the fragmentation of source analysis. His polemic against the circular argumentation of biblical archeology faced off with one of the most stultifying impediments in modern times to the understanding of biblical literature. But it was the monumental work in redaction criticism of Willi Marxsen that finally refocused the study on the texts themselves and reopened a vehicle for them to come to word again.

This study employs redaction criticism to access the texts. In order to do so, analysis of pericopes and passages alternate with analysis of the framework of selfsame. However, the heavy burden of accumulated historicistic readings required that an alternate framework for understanding and reading these texts should be presented. This is by its very nature conjectural; but it is necessary so that the reader can have available an alternate fallback topology to place the material in mentally when the "historical" framework dissipates. This redactional framework is a decisive factor in determining the intent of any passage. It has been neglected for too long; thus the work done here, however much conjectural, is a challenge to broach this question in biblical studies and intended to provoke it. It is nonsense to assume that a body of literature gathers itself together; or that the heavens channel its collocation across centuries; or that writings "happen" to congregate because an ethnic group happens to be extant and "happens" to archive texts that it cannot quite comprehend. Some groups may do this, but the texts are not haphazard phenomena. A collector might imagine so, but not a literate person. The amazing thing is that the classification of these texts as "divine" in origin has nourished these approaches, especially by dynasts and investment minded people. The incarnate reality of these texts was denied, and a will-o'-the-wisp so-called "historical" reality replaced the flesh of this body of literature. The mind that was convened by it was dismissed under the pretense that it was "other-worldly." As we saw, this contradicts the basic posture of Deuteronomy. It is this murderous void that this work wishes to arraign; to re-convoke the minds that have been dismissed in order to facilitate the excesses of dynasts; to allow the "words," the *děbārîm*, to convoke again. This has been the task that Professor Paul Nadim Tarazi has devoted his pedagogical life to: it is the intention of this presentation to be an homage to his work. To what extent this work is indebted to him has already been explained in the first part/chapter; I can only refer back to it and say that it applies equally to the finished work.

3.1 Some more exegetical pointers

This work is not an exegesis of the texts it reviews and comments. It is a redaction critical study attempting to decipher the hand of the redactor or redactors who produced the texts in the form that we have received them. In this sense it is a study of the perceived scaffolding that was in the mind of the redactor(s) when working out this body of literature. In the process an attempt was made to delineate this scaffolding in order to offer the reader an alternate framework for locating these texts and accessing their topology. The thesis presented here challenges all the carryover approaches to these scriptures that have been presented over the centuries: the allegorical, the fundamentalist, the imperial, the spiritual, the source-critical, the historicistic, the archeological, the mystical, . . . In doing so, there was a need to provide an alternate proposal, an alternate framework derived from the redactional artifice located within the texts themselves. Thus, in analogy to the Arden Shakespeare, they must be read as marginal notes to the texts, giving insight as to the linguistic usages of the writer/redactors and the circumstances of their work. It references the texts and refers the reader back to them. It is not an exegesis of the narratives as such. It provides a mental scaffolding within which to read the texts so as not to approach them as though they were hanging in the air, as it were, in a void. It is a proposed scaffolding, highly conjectural by the very nature of the endeavor. It wishes to refocus the view of the reader on the compositional elements of the texts. It cannot be read without the texts themselves. It presupposes affinity with the texts and the narratives, and often presupposes a certain affinity with critical studies. A running exegetical commentary in hand, such as Paul Nadim Tarazi's Chrysostom Bible commentary series would be highly useful when reading this presentation. The connecting narrative thread when reading the proposed framework analysis remains in the running text of the analyzed books, again as in the case of the Arden Shakespeare series with respect to the Shakespearean corpus. In particular, it proposes a redactional framework in lieu of the allegorical, the "spiritual," or the historicistic "text doubles" that have become rampant.

3.1.1 Ethnicity has no place in Exegesis

To apply ethnic or geographical categories to the exegesis of the texts belies their own expressed aspiration to be "*kath-olikos*," addressed and applicable to all. It also belies the claim to intellectual integrity and neutrality that is afloat everywhere, while reality is more akin to a sea of sinking ships.

More specifically, to use terms such as "eastern tradition" and "western tradition," and try to adjudicate between them and partition roles cannot but betray that we are still talking about private enclosures and not about an open arena; we are talking about our ego or, better, our superego, and not about the texts. When we do this, we bring to naught the convocation intended by the texts. This is particularly the case with regard to the texts of the Isa 40–55 school. They aspire to convoke a heteroclite group. This is expressly formulated in Exod 12:37–38 describing the group of people in the Exodus from Egypt: "The Israelites journeyed from Rameses to Succoth, about six hundred thousand men on foot, besides children. A mixed crowd also went up with them, and livestock in great numbers, both flocks and herds" (NRSV). This is echoed in a very emphatic statement against group hubris in 1 Cor 1:26–29:

> Consider your own call, brothers and sisters: not many of you were wise by human standards, not many were powerful, not many were of noble birth. But God chose what is foolish in the world to shame the wise; God chose what is weak in the world to shame the strong; God chose what is low and despised in the world, things that are not, to reduce to nothing things that are, so that no one might boast in the presence of God. (NRSV).

The cultural topology and *Sitz im Leben* are important to identify and understand texts that are the focus of study; they are inappropriate to apply to our exegetical effort, unless our exegetical effort itself was to be the focus of the study. The texts cannot be reduced in our mind to the nebulously conceived production of an ethnic or confessional group (let alone a geographical determinant). Our exegetical effort cannot be reduced to a hazily defined ethnic entity, making of the group somehow the amorphous author of texts, unless a clearly defined redactional or exegetical school effort can be defined. We make sport of culture and intellectual pursuit when we do so. It is minds, however much indebted to a group or culture, that produce texts. It is minds, however much indebted to a group or culture, that are applied to study and interpret texts. However much texts are culturally biased, they are a production of minds addressing other minds. The master and redactors of the Joshua school delineated here have made their choice: their work is addressed "abroad." They rejected enclosures, closed reserves, ethnic bias; their vision was of the human being as human being. This defined their monotheism: it was not only the will of the one God, but the will of the one God regarding the human being, the one and the same human being. The expansive mind and approach of the writer of Isa 40–55 and master of the redactional school discussed here made it impossible for all the bulwarks and enclosures that were set up throughout history to succeed in containing the resultant work and harnessing it for particular interests. It was intentionally an open source approach and remains irreversibly so.[10]

3.1.2 Functionality and Artifice in Literature

Function and artifice stand in a reciprocal relationship in literature. This exposition has insisted on deciphering the methods and the elements of the word craft in texts before a conclusion is drawn as to function. The texts are seen as crafted works not as compiled ideas or images. Before judging a text to be figurative, one must ascertain that this is the intention of the author, decipher the elements which point in this direction, and determine what the function of using figurative language in the specific text is. Allegorical interpretation that effectively substitutes one text for another is not exegesis. This applies to "spiritual" interpretation and to "mystical" interpretation. Before they can become valid as exegesis they have to be

---

10 In the first publication of chapter 1 of this presentation in the Tarazi Festschrift, the editor misunderstood the first sentence of the author and reformulated it in terms of Eastern and Western churches. The republication in JOCABS restored the author's original formulation. This presentation is challenging all carryover approaches to the OT regardless of their provenance.

validated by the contextual functional elements of composition; otherwise one would be substituting one text for another. The "flesh" of a text constitutes its reality; to bypass it is to effectively dismiss the text and deny the addressee participation in its reality. This is often conjectural, but the more coordinates there are that intersect on a point, the more probable the conjecture. When the conjecture "relaxes" the text and makes its elements more articulate and converging, the more probable it becomes.

3.1.3 Redactional framework and Exegesis

When, as in the case of this presentation, a redactional intent is deciphered that spans several works, this can provide cross-referencing that helps in the exegesis of an obscure passage through cross references with another work within the same redactional effort. This is also the case with modern novelists who write say a trilogy of distinct novels that share elements of composition. The series may display a movement from one part to another, it may introduce contrast, or it may provide for character development. This too must be deduced from the elements of the composition, often in the interaction between the mind of the author and that of the interpreter. Differing interpretations may come to stand; their congruence is a function of their engagement with the mind and craft of the author.

3.1.4 Names in Literature as Applied to Biblical Literature

Names in literature are factors in the narrative. When a common overarching redactional effort is discernable, cross-referencing can be an important factor for the interpretation. In the present work this has been regularly applied. When the same events or synchronic events reappear with the same or similar themes and motifs but are staged as diachronically distinct, in time and circumstance, similar or identical names can be a recurrent theme in the overarching redactional framework. They provide cues for the reader/listener to understand and interact with the text. Composite names can indicate different characteristics for the same figure and help in understanding the role played in a specific narrative. Names indicating family relationships are often simply a listing of character traits of a figure involved and change for the same figure as the hypothesis of the narrative changes.

I have repeatedly reproached translations in the course of the current presentation for changing names for extra-textual reasons. For example, they dissimulate the identity of the name of Joshua as Hoshea and the prophet of the same name as Hosea. The texts have exactly the same name. If there is an overarching redaction as proposed by the present author, this hides the intended cross-referencing. If not, why change the name if the interest is in an extra-textual person or reality? It should be remembered that vocalization in Hebrew and in Semitic languages in general is secondary. The basic import is borne by the root consonants.

Another problem occurs when the opposite phenomenon is in play: differing rendition of the same or similar name in the original text is "corrected" by the translator. In fact, different renditions of the same name in literature are, more often than not, an important indicator of the flow of a narrative and the figure of speech intended. Too often, translators are obsessed with "fixing" names as though they were maintaining the integrity of an entry in an official registry.

Still another problem arises when the language of the text proves unhelpful in understanding the meaning of a name. In such cases going to cognate languages can be very important. However, going to cognate languages before one has, in our case, exhausted the Hebrew options leads to false conclusions. This is usually related to the process of historicistic reading of the text. The reality is seen in events external to the text rather than contextual. The result often is that Babylonian or even Assyrian associations are brought into play on the basis of an

Chapter 4

anachronistic historicistic reading. When Hebrew fails us, the nearest cognate languages are Aramaic and northwestern Arabic. In this presentation Arabic has been heavily relied on, because it has been conjectured that this setting hosted most of the texts during the Hellenistic period. The return on this hypothesis has proven to be very fruitful.

In the following, I will illustrate with two examples some of the propositions I have just explained; they are taken from the book of Daniel and the NT (examples from the opus of the Joshuan school have been dealt with at length above in the course of the main exposition):

The first example is from the book of Daniel. Above I have spoken about the Hebrew names of the three youths with Daniel. In the narrative, we are told that they were given names by the Babylonians. Interpreters immediately assume the names to be Babylonian and tell us that they are obscure. According to what I have just expanded upon, we should first look for a contextual Hebrew derivation before looking further afield. The name given to Daniel is a variation on the name of Belshazzar, the Babylonian dynast; it is Belteshazzar. The insertion of one Hebrew letter makes it a satirical name. The name Belshazzar it seems means "Bel protect the king," this is fine in Babylonian. But what does the name given to Daniel mean? I propose that the introduced ṭêt stands euphonically for tāw and makes of the first syllable the equivalent of *biltî* (without). The resulting name becomes the phrase "without protection of the king." Daniel will tell Belshazzar in the course of the narrative that God will cut him down and give his throne to the Medes. As for Hananiah, he is named Shadrach. I propose that this is from Hebrew. It is the composite of two Hebrew words (*šad* and *rak*) that make for the meaning "tender breast." The blustering Hananiah against Jeremiah becomes "tender breast" (a very early version of Tenderfoot!) under the Babylonians. Not only is it a put down, the characteristics would be appropriate to a woman in Hebrew; it is a scathingly sarcastic putdown and returns the euphemistically used root to its original topos. Similarly with the other two names. They are comic putdowns. The combination of sounds is intended for its comic effect and/or comic variation from the actual names. This is part and parcel of the narrative and the lesson, and in end effect political satirical theater. The name of Mishael (not to be confused with Michael) can be translated as "who is asking?", a morbid name for the "grim reaper." The "Babylonian" name is in fact a Hebrew pun on the name that can be rendered as a response: "and who are you?" The grim reaper is himself being called to account. The caretaker is being told: Mr. Caretaker, this time it is your time! As to Azariah, meaning "Yah is my help," he becomes "the servant of his own gleam/starlight" (from *nōgah* with the attached third person singular possessive pronoun), that is, a conceited, self-centered slave of his own ego.

The second example is cross-testamental and involves the names Miriam, Mariam, and Maria. These are often presented as though they were the same name. In fact each plays a different and distinct role in their respective narratives. Miriam is in the Hebrew OT. She is the sister of Aaron. Her name means the bitter sea/waters. The name refers to Jerusalem and the bitter harvest it brings to the deity. Maria and Mariam are in the Greek of the NT. Both are used. Each gospel has a different usage and they apply to more than one community depending on the phrase, the book, and the concomitant names. They always refer to a community or group in Jerusalem/Judea. Luke uses both Maria and Mariam varying according to the context. The context I wish to address is the pericope of Mary and Martha in Luke 10. In this pericope, Luke uses Mariam not Maria. The reason is very simple: Mariam here is juxtaposed to Martha. It is a parable about two communities: the Mariam community and the Martha community. What do the names mean in this parable? Although this is a Greek text, the two names are elementary Aramaic. We know the name of Martha from the early Christian prayer we find in the NT: Maranatha, to be parsed according to the context either as "maran-atha" (Our Lord has come) or "marana-tha" (Come Lord). The two communities juxtaposed in Luke 10 are on one hand the Pauline community and on the other hand the non-Pauline communities (for example the James community or the Petrine community). The credo of the Pauline community is *"mar yam,"* the Lord has gone to sea, (that is he has gone to the gentiles). The credo of the other communities is *"mar tha"* (Lord come), meaning "we are still waiting, where are you?" Martha is gently reprimanded that she is busy with too many things, and the required is one. After all, while waiting in Jerusalem and Judea, she is busy with questions of ritual and cult. People often cannot understand the simplest of parables because they cannot "read" names in a narrative, not even one as simple as a parable! The connotation of each of the names Miriam, Mariam, and Maria is totally different depending on the context. They are not all simply "Mary."

3.2 In Conclusion: Resume of the Thesis

The thesis was presented above that the redactor of Isa 40–55 consciously initiated the project of the Torah and the Prophets. The structure of Isa 40–55 was analyzed as being a two part structure. In Isa 40–49 we have the presentation of the problem, the sins of Adam and Jacob. In Isa 50–55 we have the solution presented as the parable of Abraham and Sarah. God, through the *rahām,* will bring about a solution out of the bowels of Sarah (representing Jacob), which will be addressed to the progeny of Sarah and consequently to all Adam. This two part/track structure continues in the story of Joseph in the book of Genesis with the crystallization of two opposing concepts of increase (of Joseph). The one is the *Rahām*-Servant-Joseph, the other is the Jacob-Ephraim-and-Manasseh (wealth and progeny) -Joseph. The two tracks are picked up on in the book of Exodus, and in Exod 33 we have the divorce into two encampments, one of God and one of Jacob. That of God is characterized by the Joshua-Moses. The connection between the Servant-Joseph and the servant of Moses Joshua is established through the term *'ărôn*. This functions in the Pentateuch as the container for the remains of Joseph, and otherwise exclusively for the Ark of the Covenant, containing the tablets of the ten commandments representative of the law given to Moses. The literary connection, established through this ceremonial word, places the *Rahām*-Servant-Joseph in the camp of the tent of the tabernacle/of meeting, and through him the father of the *rahām*, Abraham. Consequently, through this literary gimmick the domain of Abraham, of Joseph and of Joshua is subsumed to that of God's part/tent/track. This is expressed by another literary gimmick. All three will not have a *tôlēdôt*, a historical domain circumscribing the story of their actions, ascribed to them. Jacob, Adam, and all other progeny of Adam will have *tôlēdôt* ascribed to them in the Pentateuch. They all reside in the encampment of Jacob, figuratively, claiming a domain other than the domain of God. This includes both the Joseph of Jacob, Ephraim and Manasseh, as well as the Moses as interpreted not by Joshua but by the priestly line, the Aaron-Moses.

This redactional structure defined as such, applies to the structure of the Torah and the Prophets. The Law and the entry into the land, in the second part of the Pentateuch, that is throughout the book of Numbers and at the end of the book of Deuteronomy, is delegated to Joshua in the company of Caleb. All other attempts to access the land or the law are rejected. Aaron and Miriam fail, and together with them their presentation of Moses fails. The Moses of Aaron may not enter the land. Only the Moses as written by Joshua according to the command of Moses will access the land.

The two tracks become manifestly so in the book of the Prophets. These become two books. The book of the Former Prophets is the history of the sins of Jacob under the judgment of God, leading to the utter destruction of Jacob/Judah. This reflects the teaching of Isa 40–49, and what is described therein as the "former things." At the commencement of the book of the Former Prophets Joshua, judge and savior, provides the land and the law[11], at no effort or cost to Jacob, which will subsequently be squandered by Jacob/Judah. He leaves for them a stone and the remains of Joseph at Shechem as a sign for them. God will address those assembled at Shechem from his abode in Shiloh. This continues until the sin of Jacob overtakes events, requisitioning the kingship, and setting up a temple. The way to doom is inexorably set. The covenant to Abraham is now expressed as the everlasting love of God for David, which will try to find a way to resurrect the fallen hut of David. The *tôlēdôt* of Adam and Jacob in the Pentateuch find continuation in the dynasties of the various houses. They end up with the totally broken covenant with Jacob.

The book of the Latter Prophets is the track of God's words addressed to Jacob and Adam. This corresponds to the "new things," promised in Isa 40–49, and presented in Isa 50–55. The noun *yĕšû'â* (salvation) is used in the second part of the composition (50–55), in 51:6, 8; 52:7, 10, and in preparation for it in 49:6, 8, to describe the situation concomitant with the work of the servant. The verbal action of salvation, *yš'*, is used only in the first part (40–49). It describes the action incumbent on God as King. In this monograph the appellation "Second Isaiah" has not been used. Isaiah 40–55 is proposed as the original core of the book of Isaiah. Both Isa 56–66 and Isa 1–39 are seen as subsequent to Isa 40–55. In Isaiah 56–66 we continue, as in Isa 40–55, not to have the name Isaiah employed for the redactor. He remains, like the servant and his God, nameless and faceless, manifest through his words. But Isa 1–39 picks up on the action of God as defined in Isa 40–55, and employs the appellation Isaiah "God will save" as a proper noun, designating the prophet proclaiming both the fall and the future salvation of Jerusalem/the barren Zion. This will be reiterated in the book of the Twelve Prophets, the fourth book of the Latter Prophets.

---

11 At the end of the book of the Former Prophets the Law will reappear and announce the end. It had been "buried" rather than utilized in the temple!

The first book therein will be named the book of Hosea (God save/God has saved), the alternate name of Joshua son of Nun. In other words, the book of the Latter Prophets commences with the announcement of judgment and salvation leading up to Isa 40–55 and the work of the anonymous redactor. The encapsulation of Isa 40–55 within the book of Isaiah, the book of the salvation of God, makes it the cornerstone of the whole composition, the stone of stumbling and the cornerstone of Isa 8:14; 28:16. Thus we have in the mega double work a redactional compositional line leading from Abraham to Joseph, to Joshua/Hoshea through Isaiah to Isa 40–55 and the *Rahām*-Servant (Positioned, together with Isa 56–66, in the parallel position within the first book of the Latter Prophets to that of the position of the Joseph cycle in the first book of the Pentateuch). This is the Servant-Joseph line of the covenant of salvation which cannot be broken (Isa 55:13). What functions to connect the points on this line are the words of scripture, not a human succession (whether construed in terms of procreation or in terms of continuity of seat/throne). This scripture defines God's domain, God's track. The redactor of Isa 40–55 plans for this body of writings such that it would function to address instruction to would-be wayfarers of the desecrated *Rahām*-Servant from outside any human enclosure, any sanctimonious attempt to set up a sacred consecrated closed circle. The book of the Law presented from outside the enclosure, from the tent where Joshua abides, will challenge even the presentation made of itself from within the enclosure by a would-be "Aaronide," as we see in the cycle of Elisha (whose name is cognate with that of Joshua/Hoshea). The books of the Law and the Prophets are a diptych, with both leaves/tablets interweaving and counterpointing the two tracks, seen from the judging view of the God of the *Rahām*-Servant.

As already mentioned, this scriptural project seems to have been envisaged with the aim to providing a scriptural matrix for the "correct" reception of the book of Ezekiel. This last seems to have been requisitioned by the priestly dynasty, claiming descent from Aaron, and providing the stone temple as a receptacle for the book.[12] From its position within the book of Isaiah, Isaiah 40–55 introduces the corrected diptych of Jeremiah and Ezekiel. Jeremiah-Moses becomes the premise for the reception and the reading of the book of Ezekiel-Aaron. Ezekiel now corresponds to the exiles, from whom, Jeremiah said, would come the future salvation. The would be Zadokites within the enclosure are arraigned as out of line, in misrepresentation of Ezekiel, misappropriating the title.[13] The last book of the Latter Prophets recapitulates the lesson, with the prophet Hosea (standing in for Joshua/Hoshea) deriding Jacob and his so avidly coveted Ephraim.

3.3 Postscript

This reading of Scripture as the interplay of two tracks of thought has nowhere been dealt with as succinctly as in the hymn of the epistle addressed to the Philippians in the Pauline corpus (Phil 2:6–11). The servant is presented as having a mind unlike that of Adam/Jacob. Increase for him was decrease. He did not consider his being in the image of God, like Adam, something to be grabbed at (v. 6), but "emptied" himself taking on the image of a servant (v. 7). The expression εαυτον εκενωσεν "emptied himself" is the Greek rendition of *h'rh lmwt npšw* "he made himself naked to death" of Isa 53:12. The word αρπαγμος "something to be grabbed at," is the most apt rendition in Greek of the action/mindset associated with the name of Jacob, and subsequent to which he was given his name in Gen 25:26. The mind of the servant is posited as opposite to that of both Adam and Jacob. He does not have the mind of Adam/Jacob. The Pauline writer, faced with what for him was a misappropriation of the Law and the Prophets, had no other recourse other than to the same text of Isa 40–55, which has been postulated in this

---

12 Tarazi, "The Book of Jeremiah and the Pentateuchal Torah."
13 Ibid.

paper as the deliberate blueprint for the composition of this literature.

Select Bibliography

Collins, John J. *Daniel: A Commentary on the Book of Daniel*. Edited by Frank Moore Cross. Hermeneia: A Critical and Historical Commentary on the Bible. Philadelphia: Fortress, 1993.

Dahood, Mitchell. *Psalms*. 3 vols. Anchor Bible 16–17A. Garden City, N.Y.: Doubleday, 1965–1970.

Hanson, Paul D. *The Dawn of Apocalyptic: The Historical and Sociological Roots of Jewish Apocalyptic Eschatology*. Rev. ed. Philadelphia: Fortress, 1979.

Höffken, Peter. *Jesaya: Der Stand der Theologischen Diskussion*. Darmstadt: WBG, 2004.

Hölscher, Gustav. *Hesekiel: Der Dichter und das Buch*. Beihefte zur Zeitschrift für Alttestamentliche Wissenschaft 39. Giessen: Alfred Töpelmann, 1924.

Noth, Martin. *Exodus:: A Commentary*. Translated by J. S. Bowden. Old Testament Library. Philadelphia: Westminster, 1962.

———. *Leviticus: A Commentary*. Translated by J. E. Anderson. Revised second edition by the staff of SCM Press. Old Testament Library. London: SCM, 1977.

———. *Numbers: A Commentary*. Translated by James D. Martin. Old Testament Library. London: SCM, 1968.

Olshausen, Justus. *Die Psalmen erklärt*. Kurzgefasstes exegetisches Handbuch zum Alten Testament. Leipzig: S. Hirzel, 1853.

Rad, Gerhard von. *Genesis: A Commentary*. Translated by John H. Marks. Text revised by John Bowden on the basis of the ninth German edition. Old Testament Library. London: SCM, 1972.

———. *Deuteronomy: A Commentary*. Translated by Dorothea Barton. Old Testament Library. London: SCM, 1966.

Soggin, J. Alberto. *Joshua: A Commentary*. Translated by by R. A. Wilson. Old Testament Library. London: SCM, 1972.

Soggin, J. Alberto. *Judges: A Commentary*. Translated by by John Bowdon. Old Testament Library. London: SCM, 1981.

Tarazi, Paul Nadim. *Decoding Genesis 1–11*. St Paul, Minn.: OCABS Press, 2020.

———. *Ezekiel: A Commentary*. The Chrysostom Bible: A Commentary Series for Preaching and Teaching. St Paul, Minn.: OCABS Press, 2012.

———. *Genesis: A Commentary*. The Chrysostom Bible: A Commentary Series for Preaching and Teaching. St Paul, Minn.: OCABS Press, 2009.

———. *Isaiah: A Commentary*. The Chrysostom Bible: A Commentary Series for Preaching and Teaching. St Paul, Minn.: OCABS Press, 2013.

———. *Jeremiah: A Commentary*. The Chrysostom Bible: A Commentary Series for Preaching and Teaching. St Paul, Minn.: OCABS Press, 2013.

———. *Joshua: A Commentary*. The Chrysostom Bible: A Commentary Series for Preaching and Teaching. St Paul, Minn.: OCABS Press, 2013.

———. *Land and Covenant*. St Paul, Minn.: OCABS Press, 2009.

———. "The Book of Jeremiah and the Pentateuchal Torah." Pages 7–36 in *Sacred Text and Interpretation: Perspectives in Orthodox Biblical Studies*. Edited by Theodore G. Stylianopoulos. Brookline, Mass.: Holy Cross Orthodox Press, 2006.

———. *The Old Testament: An Introduction: Volume 1: Historical Traditions*. Rev. ed. Crestwood, N.Y.: St Vladimir's Seminary Press, 2003.

_____. *The Old Testament: An Introduction: Volume 2: Prophetic Traditions*. Crestwood, N.Y.: St Vladimir's Seminary Press, 1994.

_____. *The Old Testament: An Introduction: Volume 3: Psalms & Wisdom*. Crestwood, N.Y.: St Vladimir's Seminary Press, 1996.

_____. *The Rise of Scripture*. St Paul, Minn.: OCABS Press, 2017.

Weiser, Artur. *The Psalms: A Commentary*. Translated by Herbert Hartwell. Old Testament Library. London: SCM, 1962.

Westermann, Claus. *Genesis 12–36: A Commentary*. Translated by John J. Scullion. London: SPCK, 1985.

_____. *Genesis 37–50: A Commentary*. Translated by John J. Scullion. London: SPCK, 1987.

_____. *Isaiah 40–66: A Commentary*. Translated by David M. G. Stalker. Old Testament Library. London: SCM, 1969.

Wolff, Hans Walter. *Hosea: A Commentary on the Book of the Prophet Hosea*. Edited by Paul D. Hanson. Translated by Gary Stansell. Hermeneia: A Critical and Historical Commentary on the Bible. Philadelphia: Fortress, 1974.

_____. *Joel and Amos: A Commentary on the Books of the Prophets Joel and Amos*. Edited by S. Dean McBride, Jr. Translated by Waldemar Janzen, S. Dean Mcbride, Jr., and Charles A. Muenchow. Hermeneia: A Critical and Historical Commentary on the Bible. Philadelphia: Fortress, 1977.

About the Author

Iskandar Abou-Chaar was born and grew up in Beirut, Lebanon, except for two years as a child in fourth and fifth grades in Seattle, Wash., USA. He attended two semesters at the School of Engineering and Architecture at the American University in Beirut (AUB) in 1969-70. Following the second semester, the St. John of Damascus School of Theology was inaugurated in Balamand, Lebanon. He enrolled in the first class in that inaugural year, 1970, and was the class valedictorian of the first class to graduate in 1974. After graduation, he spent the length of an academic year learning about monastic life at the St. George Monastery in Deir-el-Harf, Lebanon. He then attended the semester of ecumenical studies at the Ecumenical Institute at the Chateau de Bossey near Geneva, Switzerland, in 1975-76. This was followed in spring 1976 with field work at a two-month ecumenical youth work camp in Kemminghausen in the Federal Republic of Germany. He then enrolled for four semesters at the Evangelical (Protestant) theological faculty at the University of Münster in Westphalia, Federal Republic of Germany, between 1976 and 1978, where he attended mainly biblical seminars and lectures at both the Protestant and Catholic faculties. Between 1978 and 1980 he completed the coursework requirements in graduate biblical studies at the theological faculty of the Aristotle University of Thessaloniki in Greece but did not write a dissertation.

Between 1984 and 1990 Abou-Chaar was a full-time instructor in biblical literature and languages (both NT and OT) at the St. John of Damascus School of Theology in Balamand. During that time he taught in succession nearly the full complement of courses offered in the subject of biblical studies and languages. During 1987-88 he acted as dean of the school. He was delegated to represent ATIME (The Association of Theological Institutes in the Middle East) at the inaugural meeting of what came to be known as WOCATI (World

Conference of Associations of Theological Institutions) in Yogyakarta, Indonesia.

In September 1990, he resigned from the St. John of Damascus School of Theology and withdrew from academic theological engagement. Between the end of 1990 and 2010, he was employed in a private business company. In his free time he did freelance research in biblical studies. Between 1993 and 1995, he gave coursework as a part-time visiting lecturer at the St. John of Damascus School of Theology. In 2010 he retired from his employment in the private business domain. Since then, he has continued his freelance research in biblical literature. He lives in Ras-Beirut (Beirut), Lebanon.

www.ingramcontent.com/pod-product-compliance
Lightning Source LLC
Chambersburg PA
CBHW071328190426
43193CB00041B/1000